AS A TEENAGER, CINDY MOON WAS BITTEN BY THE SAME SPIDER THAT BIT PETER PARKER, GIVING HER POWERS SIMILAR TO THOSE OF THE AMAZING SPIDER-MAN: POWERS OF ADHESION, A UNIQUE PRECOGNITIVE AWARENESS OF DANGER AND THE ABILITY TO WEAVE SPIDERWEBS FROM HER FINGERTIPS. SHE NOW SWINGS THROUGH THE SKIES OF NEW YORK CITY AS...

SILK

AFTER BEING FREED FROM THE BUNKER SHE CALLED HOME FOR A DECADE, CINDY MOON DISCOVERED HER FAMILY HAD GONE MISSING. SHE FOUND HER BROTHER ALBERT, WHO HAD STARTED RUNNING WITH A GANG CALLED THE **GOBLIN NATION** AND HAD NO RECOLLECTION OF THEIR PARENTS' WHEREABOUTS. NOW, WHEN SHE'S NOT BUSY LOOKING FOR THEM, YOU CAN FIND HER SWINGING THROUGH THE SKIES OF NEW YORK.

SINISTER

Writer **Robbie Thompson**

Artists **Stacey Lee** (#1 & "Breaking Bad"),
Tana Ford (#2–3, #6) &
Veronica Fish (#4–5)

Color Artist **Ian Herring**
Letterer **VC's Travis Lanham**
Cover Artist **Helen Chen**
Assistant Editor **Devin Lewis**
Editor **Nick Lowe**

Collection Editor: **Jennifer Grünwald**
Associate Editor: **Sarah Brunstad**
Associate Managing Editor: **Alex Starbuck**
Editor, Special Projects: **Mark D. Beazley**
VP, Production & Special Projects: **Jeff Youngquist**
SVP Print, Sales & Marketing: **David Gabriel**
Book Designer: **Adam Del Re**

Editor in Chief **Axel Alonso**
Chief Creative Officer **Joe Quesada**
Publisher **Dan Buckley**
Executive Producer **Alan Fine**

SILK VOL. 1: SINISTER. Contains material originally published in magazine form as SILK #1-6 and AMAZING SPIDER-MAN #1. First printing 2016. ISBN# 978-0-7851-9957-1. Published by MARVEL WORLDWIDE, INC., a subsidiary of MARVEL ENTERTAINMENT, LLC. OFFICE OF PUBLICATION: 135 West 50th Street, New York, NY 10020. **Printed in the U.S.A.** ALAN FINE, President, Marvel Entertainment; DAN BUCKLEY, President, TV, Publishing & Brand Management; JOE QUESADA, Chief Creative Officer; TOM BREVOORT, SVP of Publishing; DAVID BOGART, SVP of Business Affairs & Operations, Publishing & Partnership; C.B. CEBULSKI, VP of Brand Management & Development, Asia; DAVID GABRIEL, SVP of Sales & Marketing, Publishing; JEFF YOUNGQUIST, VP of Production & Special Projects; DAN CARR, Executive Director of Publishing Technology; ALEX MORALES, Director of Publishing Operations; SUSAN CRESPI, Production Manager; STAN LEE, Chairman Emeritus. For information regarding advertising in Marvel Comics or on Marvel.com, please contact Vit DeBellis, Integrated Sales Manager, at vdebellis@marvel.com. For Marvel subscription inquiries, please call 888-511-5480. **Manufactured between 3/25/2016 and 5/2/2016 by R.R. DONNELLEY, INC., SALEM, VA, USA.**

10 9 8 7 6 5 4 3 2 1

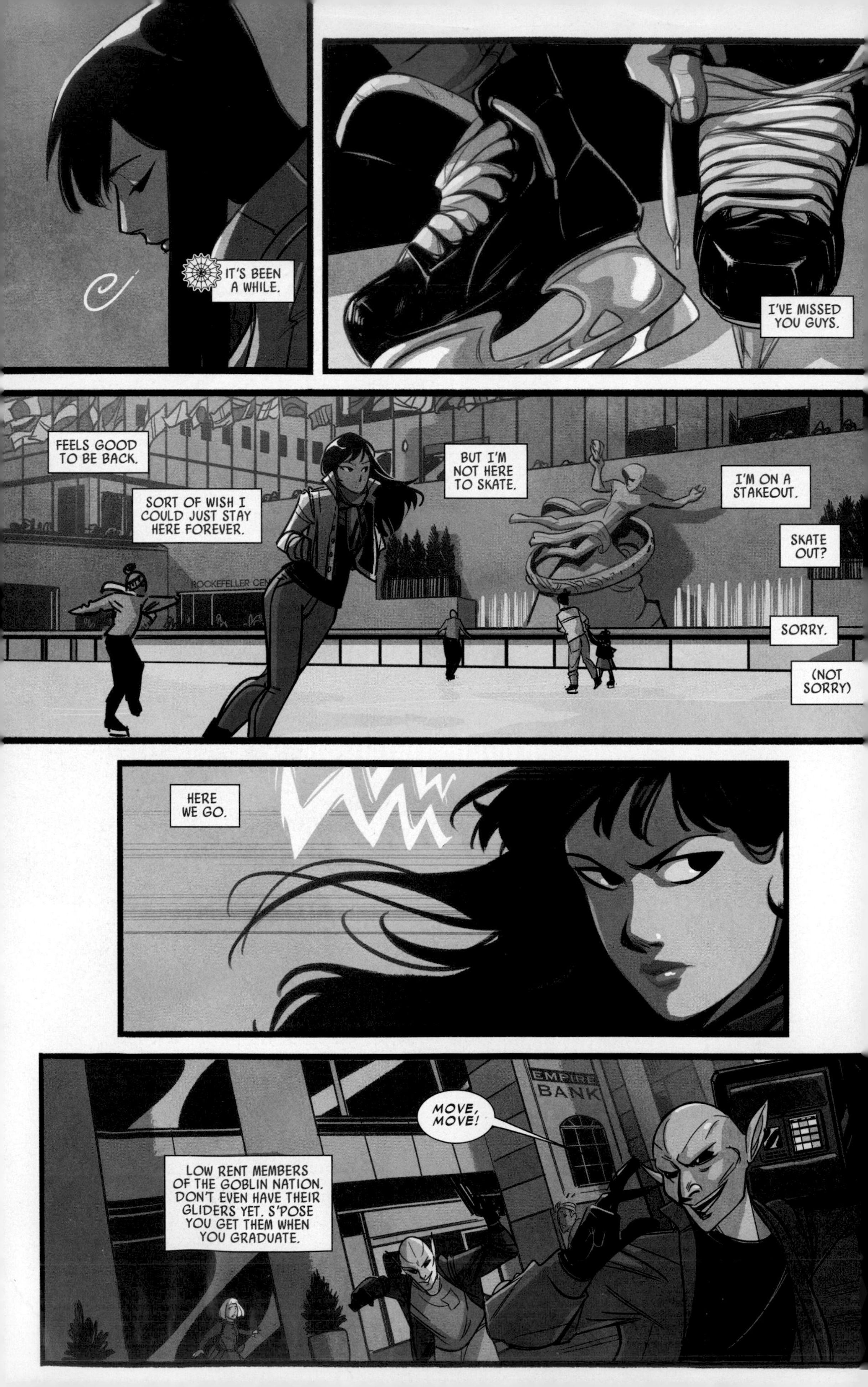
IT'S BEEN A WHILE.
I'VE MISSED YOU GUYS.
FEELS GOOD TO BE BACK.
SORT OF WISH I COULD JUST STAY HERE FOREVER.
BUT I'M NOT HERE TO SKATE.
I'M ON A STAKEOUT.
SKATE OUT?
SORRY.
(NOT SORRY)
ROCKEFELLER CEN
HERE WE GO.
LOW RENT MEMBERS OF THE GOBLIN NATION. DON'T EVEN HAVE THEIR GLIDERS YET. S'POSE YOU GET THEM WHEN YOU GRADUATE.
MOVE, MOVE!
EMPIRE BANK

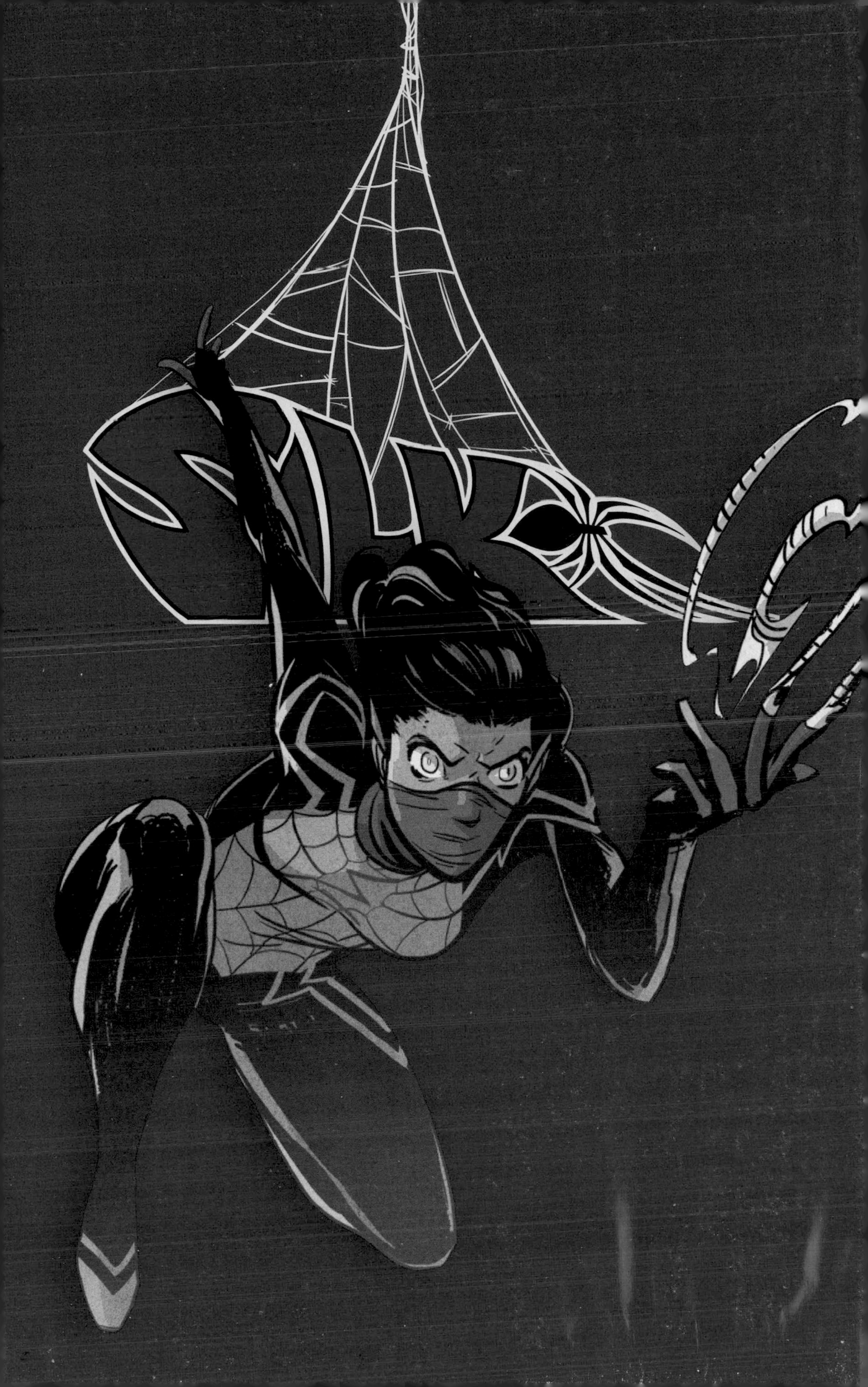

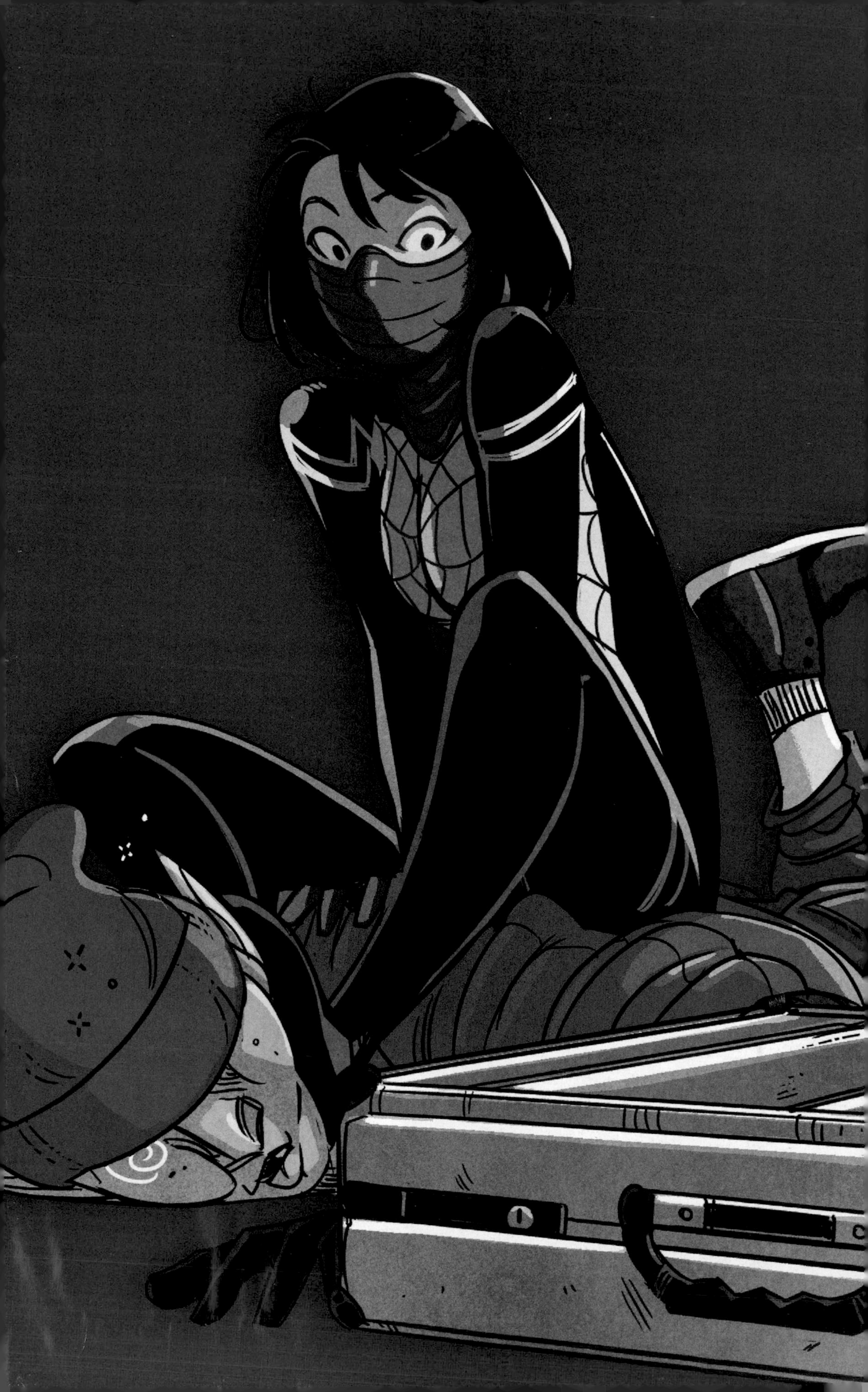

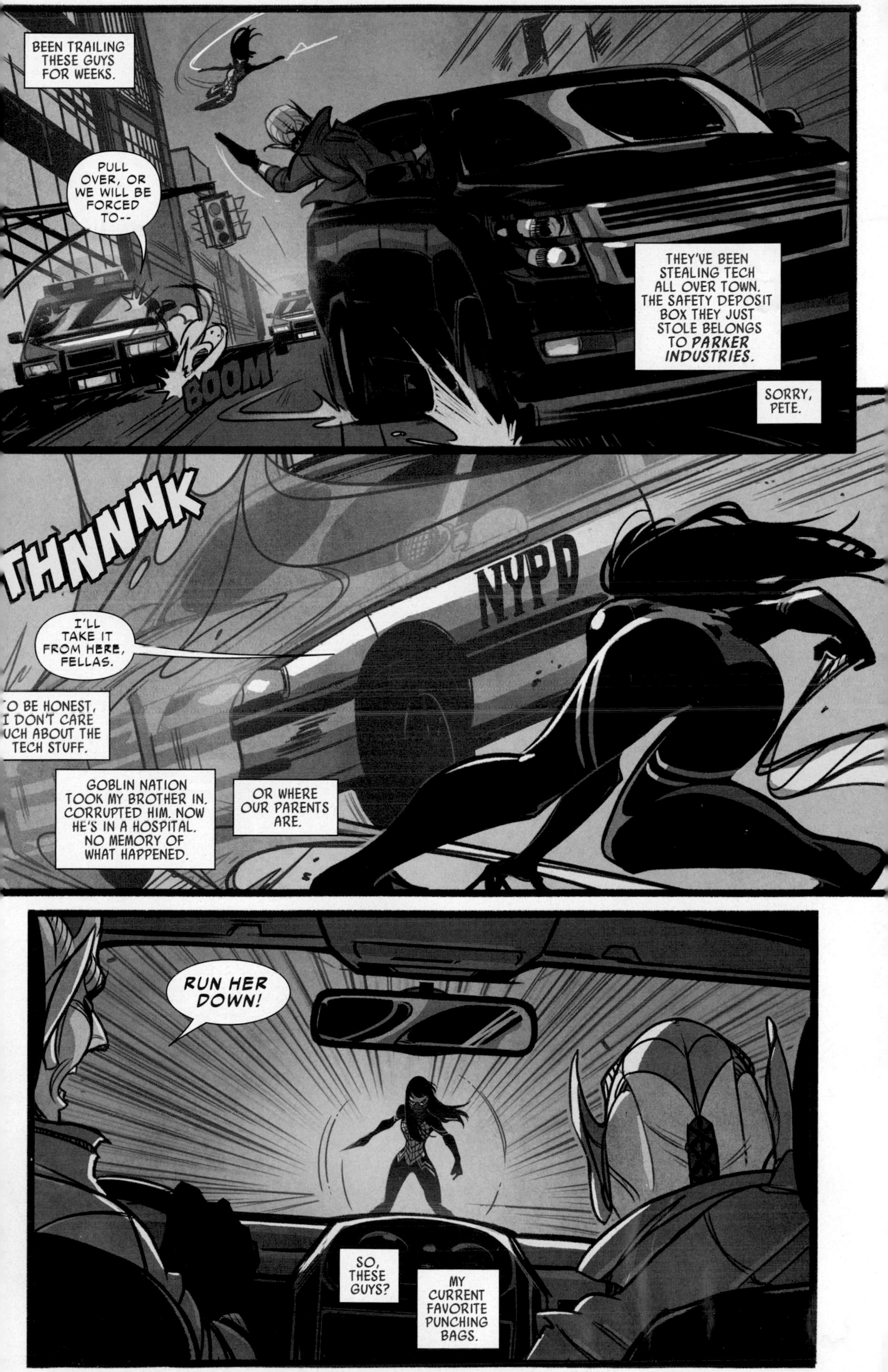
BEEN TRAILING THESE GUYS FOR WEEKS.
PULL OVER, OR WE WILL BE FORCED TO--
BOOM
THEY'VE BEEN STEALING TECH ALL OVER TOWN. THE SAFETY DEPOSIT BOX THEY JUST STOLE BELONGS TO PARKER INDUSTRIES.
SORRY, PETE.
THNNNK
NYPD
I'LL TAKE IT FROM HERE, FELLAS.
TO BE HONEST, I DON'T CARE MUCH ABOUT THE TECH STUFF.
GOBLIN NATION TOOK MY BROTHER IN. CORRUPTED HIM. NOW HE'S IN A HOSPITAL. NO MEMORY OF WHAT HAPPENED.
OR WHERE OUR PARENTS ARE.
RUN HER DOWN!
SO, THESE GUYS?
MY CURRENT FAVORITE PUNCHING BAGS.

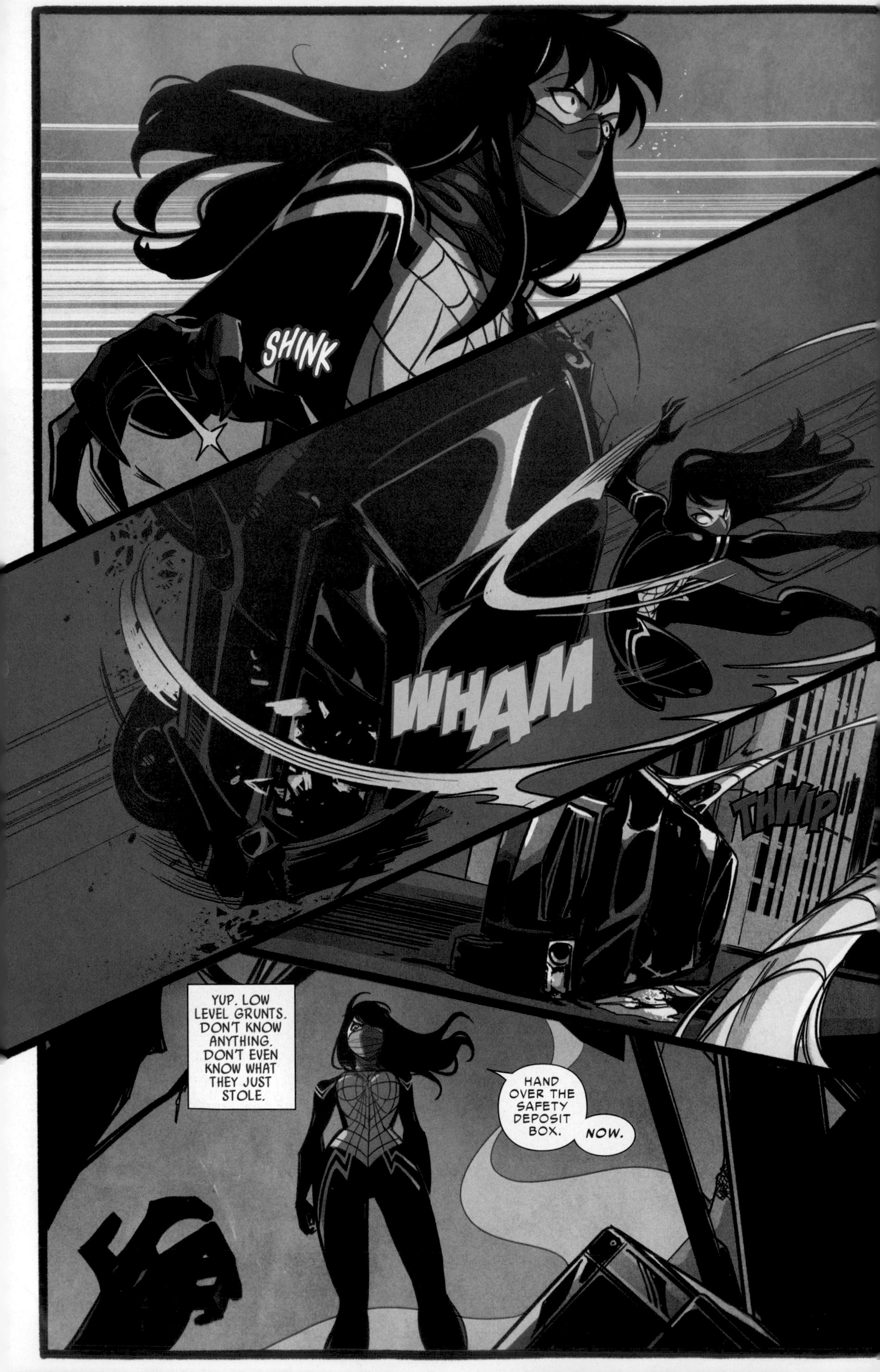

SHINK
WHAM
THWIP
YUP. LOW LEVEL GRUNTS. DON'T KNOW ANYTHING. DON'T EVEN KNOW WHAT THEY JUST STOLE.
HAND OVER THE SAFETY DEPOSIT BOX.
NOW.

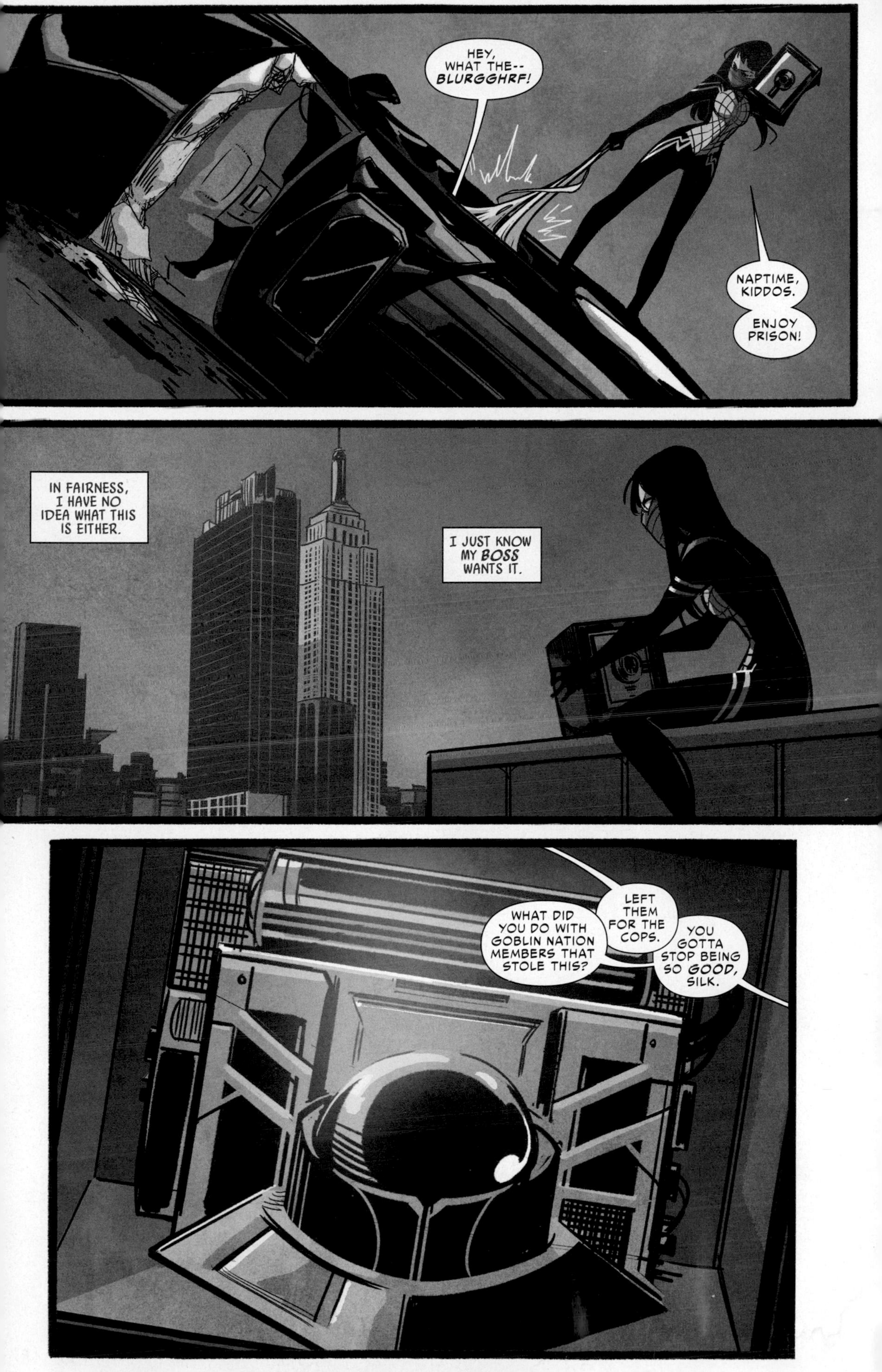
HEY, WHAT THE-- BLURGGHRF!
NAPTIME, KIDDOS.
ENJOY PRISON!
IN FAIRNESS, I HAVE NO IDEA WHAT THIS IS EITHER.
I JUST KNOW MY BOSS WANTS IT.
WHAT DID YOU DO WITH GOBLIN NATION MEMBERS THAT STOLE THIS?
LEFT THEM FOR THE COPS.
YOU GOTTA STOP BEING SO GOOD, SILK.

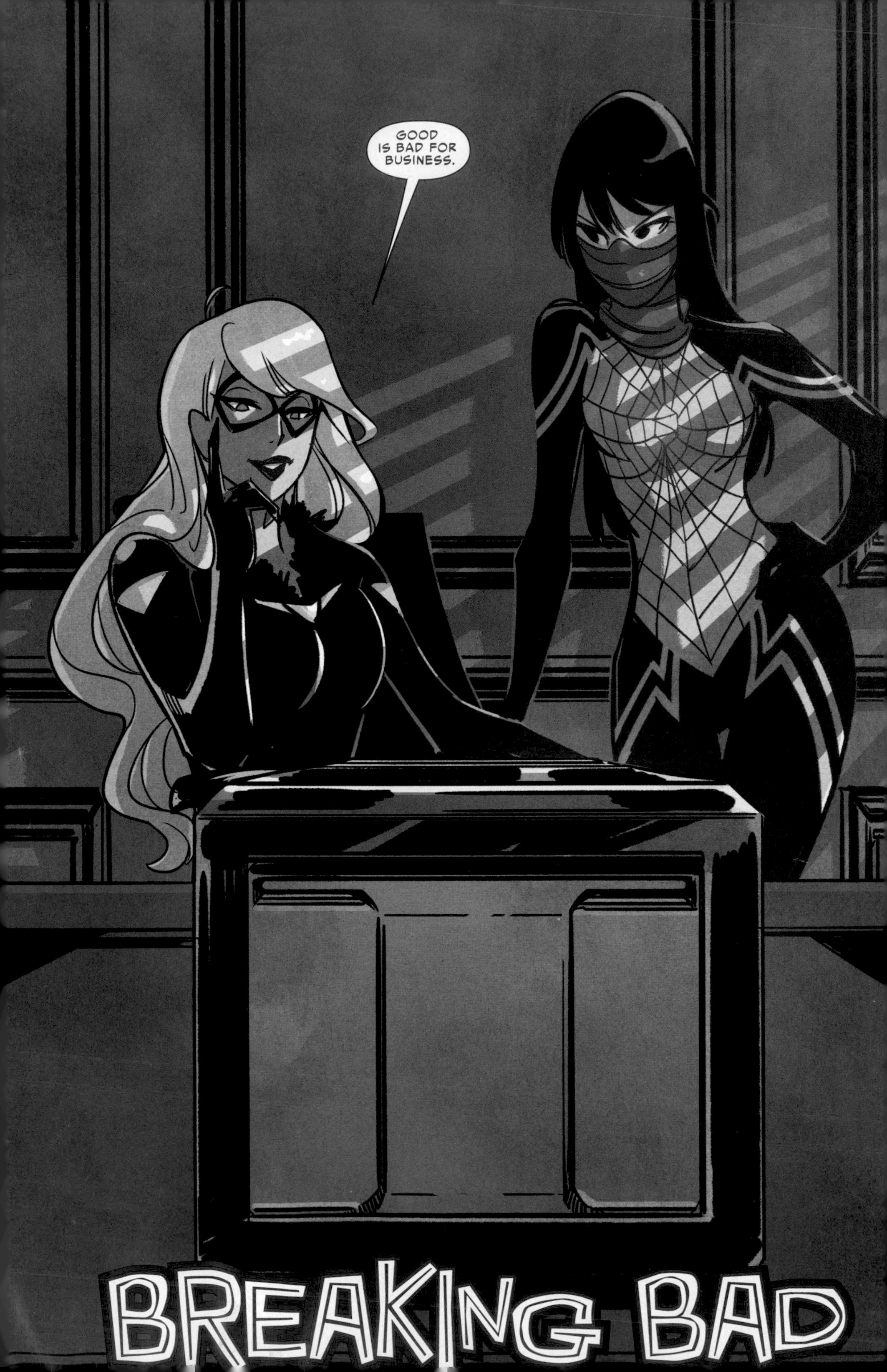
GOOD IS BAD FOR BUSINESS.
BREAKING BAD

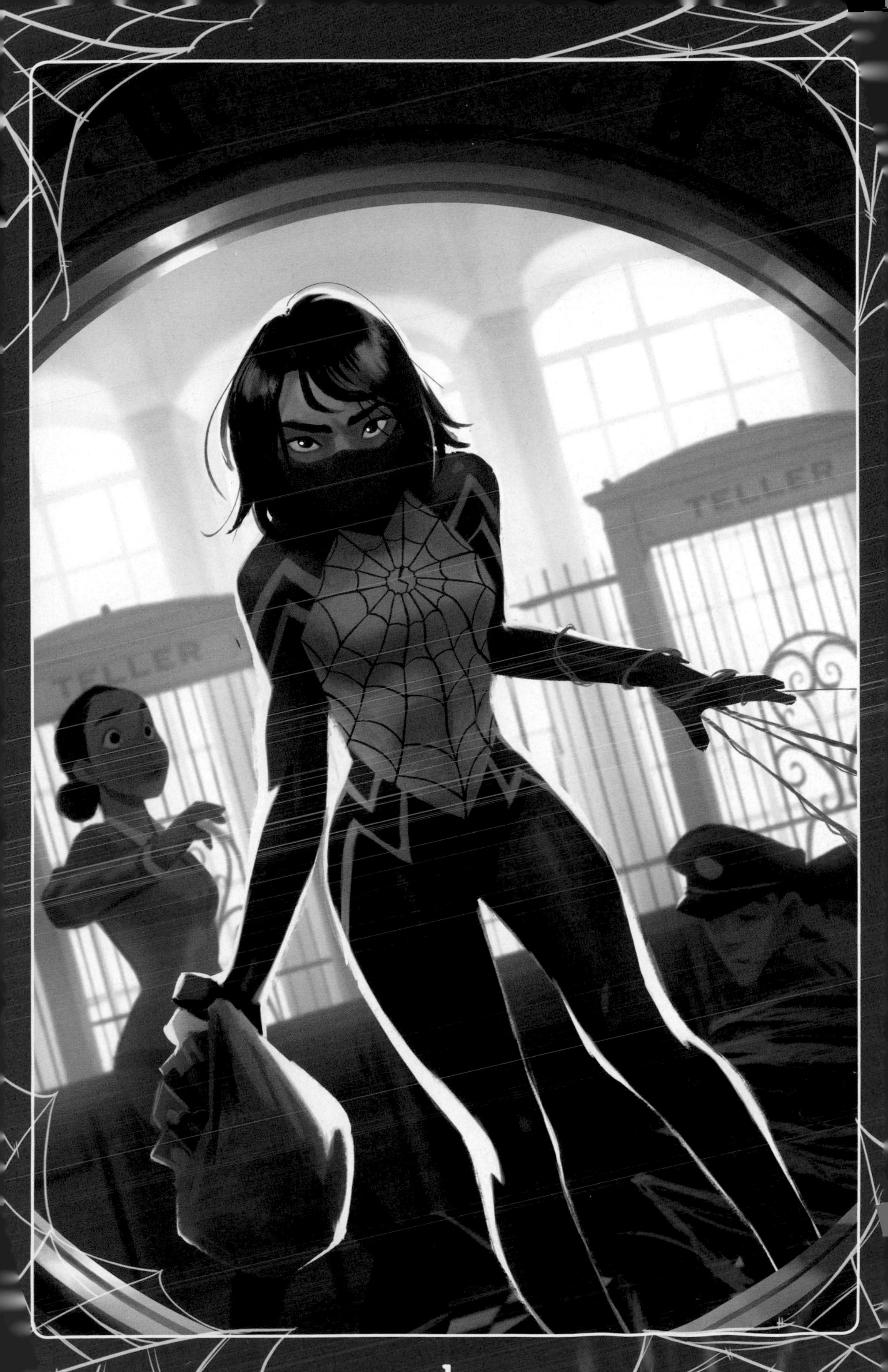
TELLER
TELLER
TELLER

1

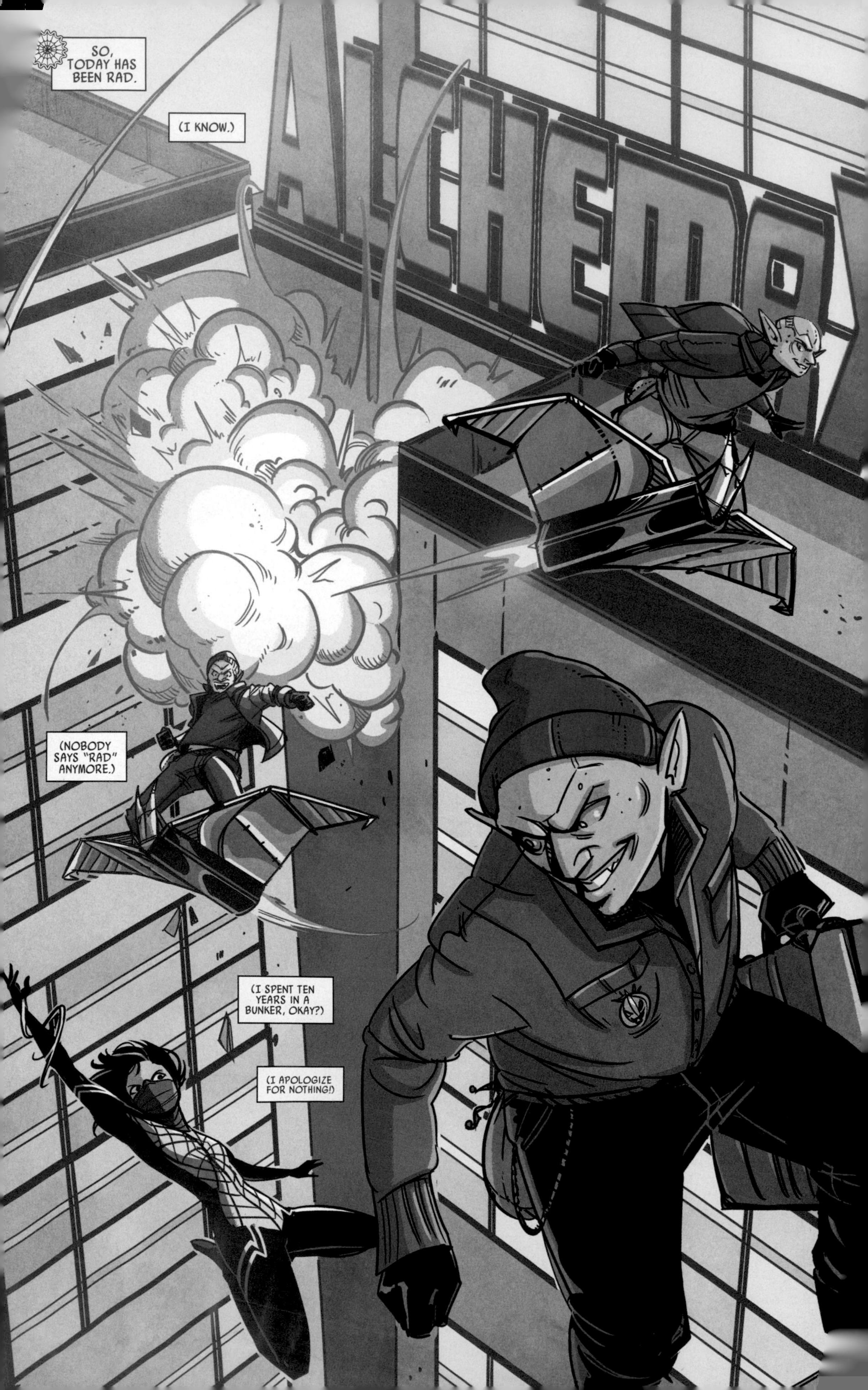
SO, TODAY HAS BEEN RAD.
(I KNOW.)
(NOBODY SAYS "RAD" ANYMORE.)
(I SPENT TEN YEARS IN A BUNKER, OKAY?)
(I APOLOGIZE FOR NOTHING!)

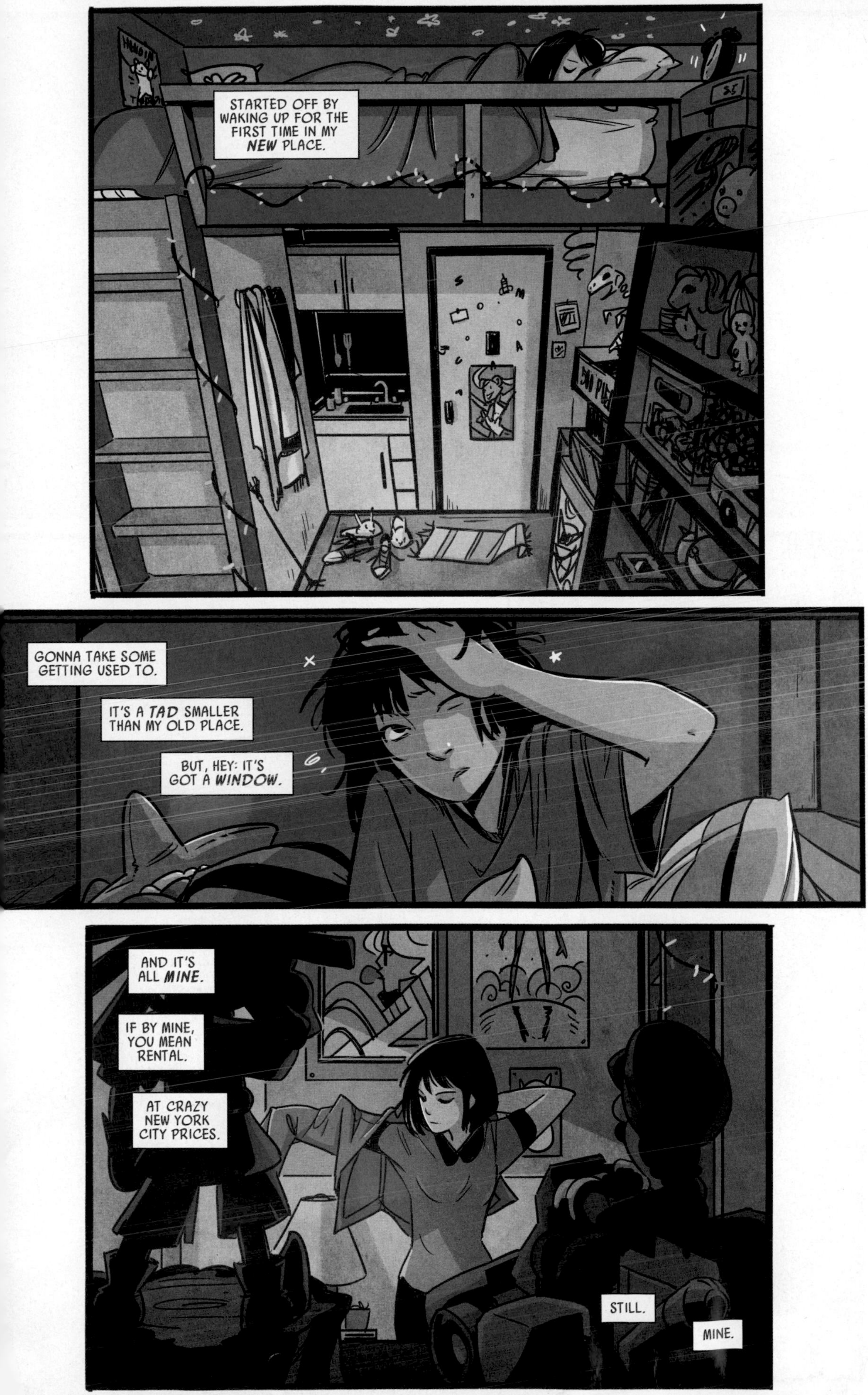
STARTED OFF BY WAKING UP FOR THE FIRST TIME IN MY *NEW* PLACE.
GONNA TAKE SOME GETTING USED TO.
IT'S A *TAD* SMALLER THAN MY OLD PLACE.
BUT, HEY: IT'S GOT A *WINDOW.*
AND IT'S ALL *MINE.*
IF BY MINE, YOU MEAN RENTAL.
AT CRAZY NEW YORK CITY PRICES.
STILL.
MINE.

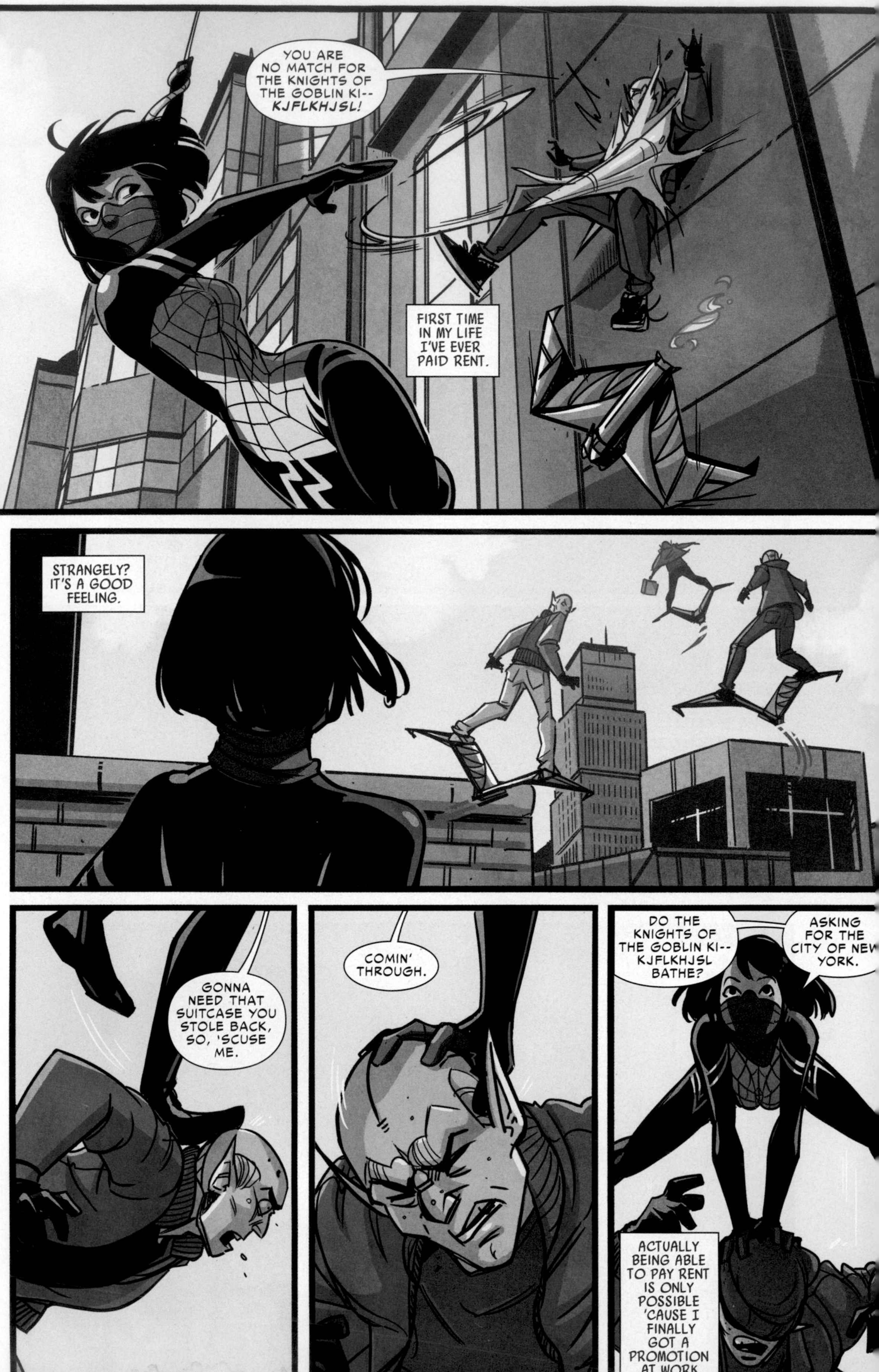
YOU ARE NO MATCH FOR THE KNIGHTS OF THE GOBLIN KI-- KJFLKHJSL!
FIRST TIME IN MY LIFE I'VE EVER PAID RENT.
STRANGELY? IT'S A GOOD FEELING.
GONNA NEED THAT SUITCASE YOU STOLE BACK, SO, 'SCUSE ME.
COMIN' THROUGH.
DO THE KNIGHTS OF THE GOBLIN KI-- KJFLKHJSL BATHE?
ASKING FOR THE CITY OF NEW YORK.
ACTUALLY BEING ABLE TO PAY RENT IS ONLY POSSIBLE 'CAUSE I FINALLY GOT A PROMOTION AT WORK.

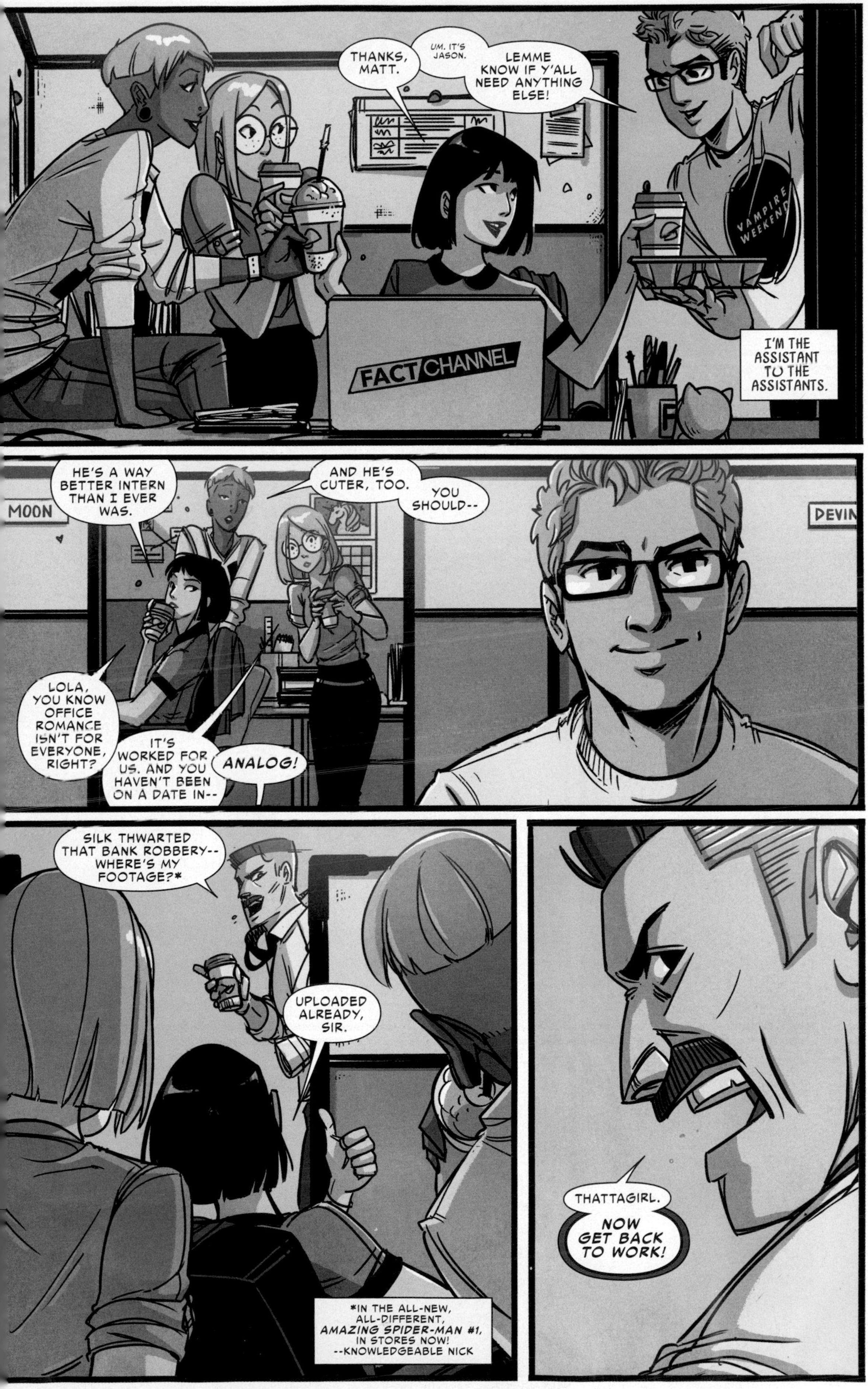
THANKS, MATT.
UM. IT'S JASON.
LEMME KNOW IF Y'ALL NEED ANYTHING ELSE!
FACT CHANNEL
VAMPIRE WEEKEND
I'M THE ASSISTANT TO THE ASSISTANTS.
MOON
HE'S A WAY BETTER INTERN THAN I EVER WAS.
AND HE'S CUTER, TOO.
YOU SHOULD--
DEVIN
LOLA, YOU KNOW OFFICE ROMANCE ISN'T FOR EVERYONE, RIGHT?
IT'S WORKED FOR US. AND YOU HAVEN'T BEEN ON A DATE IN--
ANALOG!
SILK THWARTED THAT BANK ROBBERY-- WHERE'S MY FOOTAGE?*
UPLOADED ALREADY, SIR.
*IN THE ALL-NEW, ALL-DIFFERENT, AMAZING SPIDER-MAN #1, IN STORES NOW! --KNOWLEDGEABLE NICK
THATTAGIRL.
NOW GET BACK TO WORK!

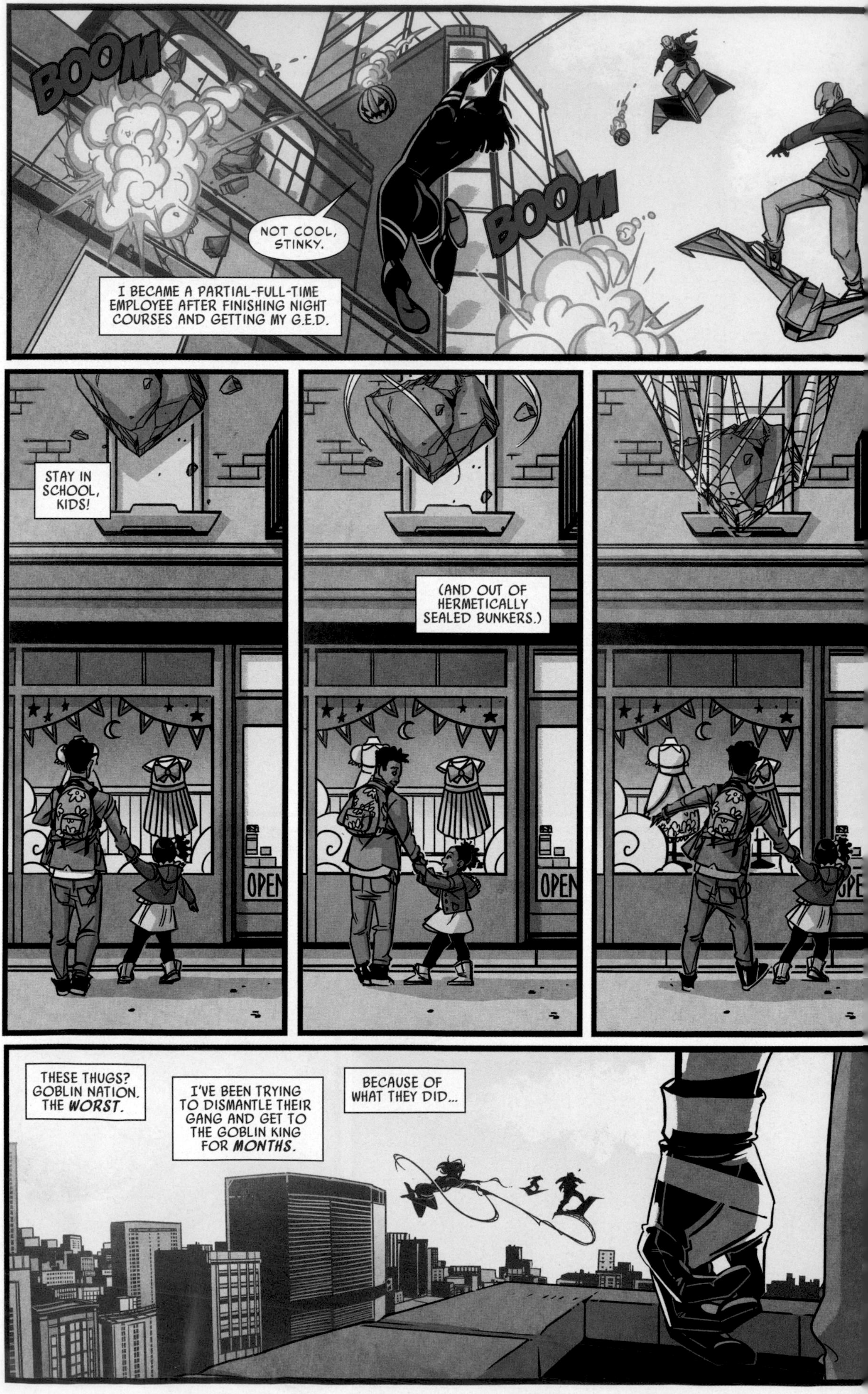
BOOM
NOT COOL, STINKY.
BOOM
I BECAME A PARTIAL-FULL-TIME EMPLOYEE AFTER FINISHING NIGHT COURSES AND GETTING MY G.E.D.
STAY IN SCHOOL, KIDS!
(AND OUT OF HERMETICALLY SEALED BUNKERS.)
OPEN
OPEN
THESE THUGS? GOBLIN NATION. THE *WORST.*
I'VE BEEN TRYING TO DISMANTLE THEIR GANG AND GET TO THE GOBLIN KING FOR *MONTHS.*
BECAUSE OF WHAT THEY DID...

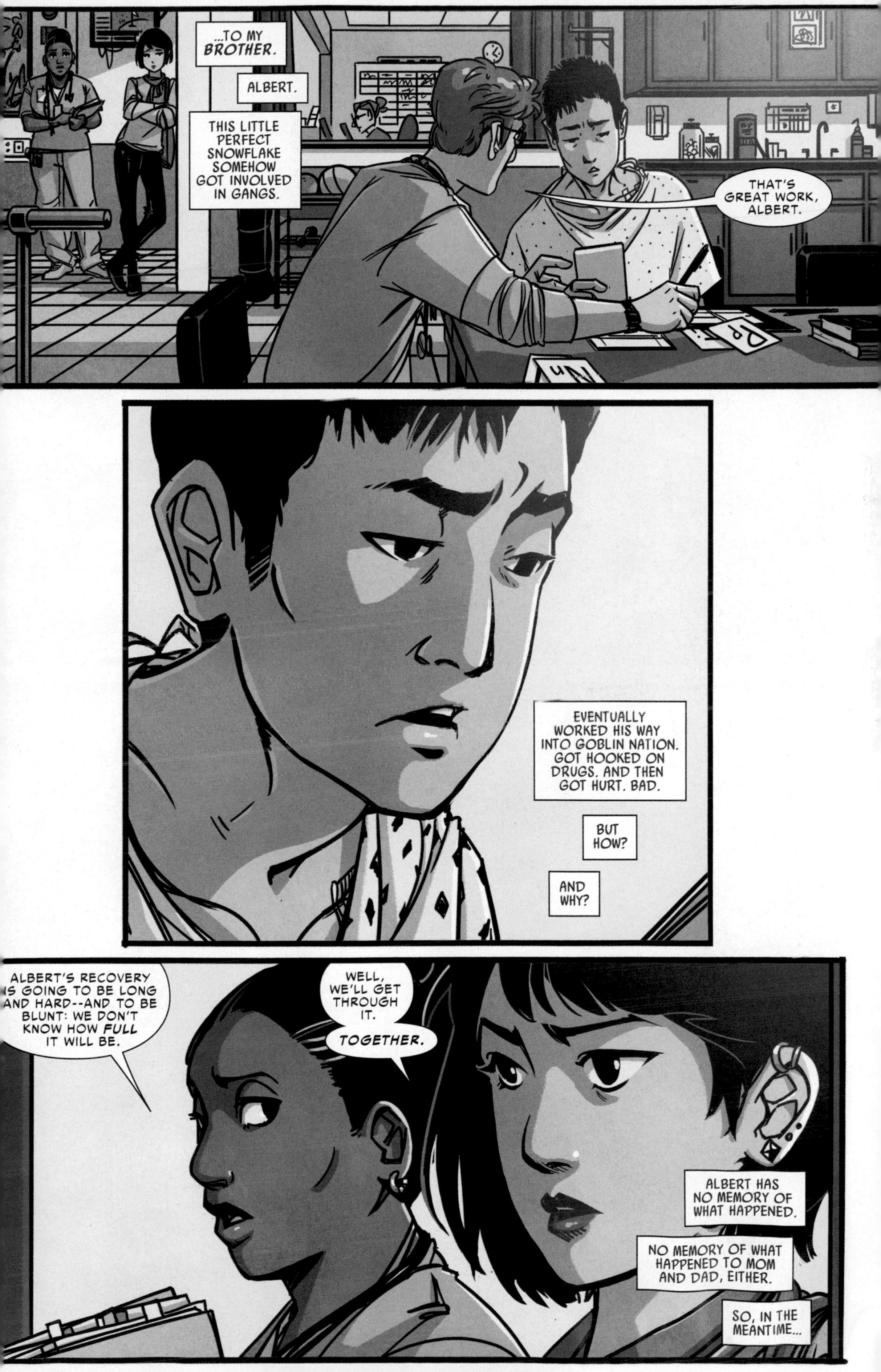
...TO MY BROTHER.
ALBERT.
THIS LITTLE PERFECT SNOWFLAKE SOMEHOW GOT INVOLVED IN GANGS.
THAT'S GREAT WORK, ALBERT.
EVENTUALLY WORKED HIS WAY INTO GOBLIN NATION. GOT HOOKED ON DRUGS. AND THEN GOT HURT. BAD.
BUT HOW?
AND WHY?
ALBERT'S RECOVERY IS GOING TO BE LONG AND HARD--AND TO BE BLUNT: WE DON'T KNOW HOW FULL IT WILL BE.
WELL, WE'LL GET THROUGH IT.
TOGETHER.
ALBERT HAS NO MEMORY OF WHAT HAPPENED.
NO MEMORY OF WHAT HAPPENED TO MOM AND DAD, EITHER.
SO, IN THE MEANTIME...

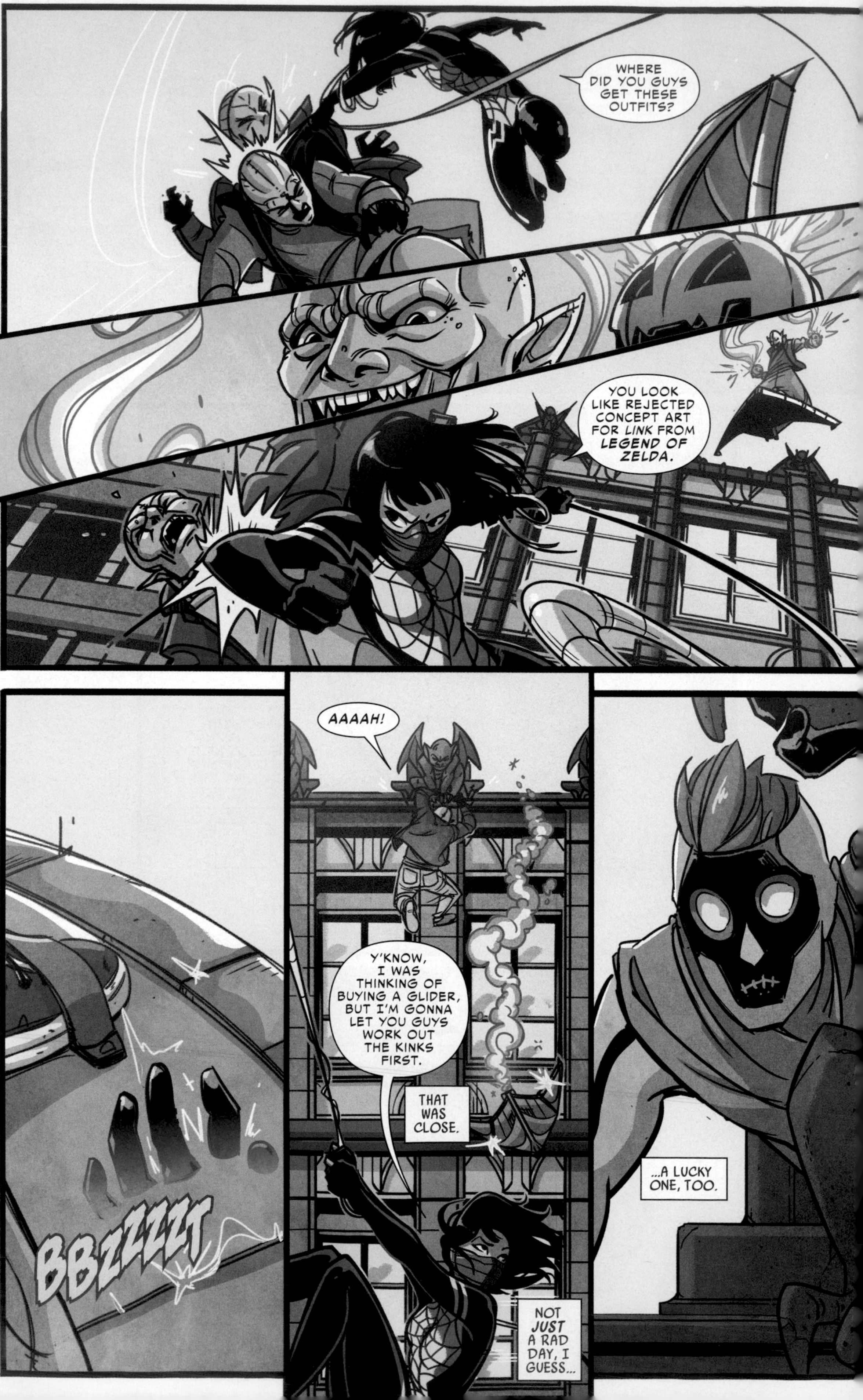
WHERE DID YOU GUYS GET THESE OUTFITS?
YOU LOOK LIKE REJECTED CONCEPT ART FOR *LINK* FROM ***LEGEND OF ZELDA.***
BBZZZZT
AAAAH!
Y'KNOW, I WAS THINKING OF BUYING A GLIDER, BUT I'M GONNA LET YOU GUYS WORK OUT THE KINKS FIRST.
THAT WAS CLOSE.
NOT *JUST* A RAD DAY, I GUESS...
...A LUCKY ONE, TOO.

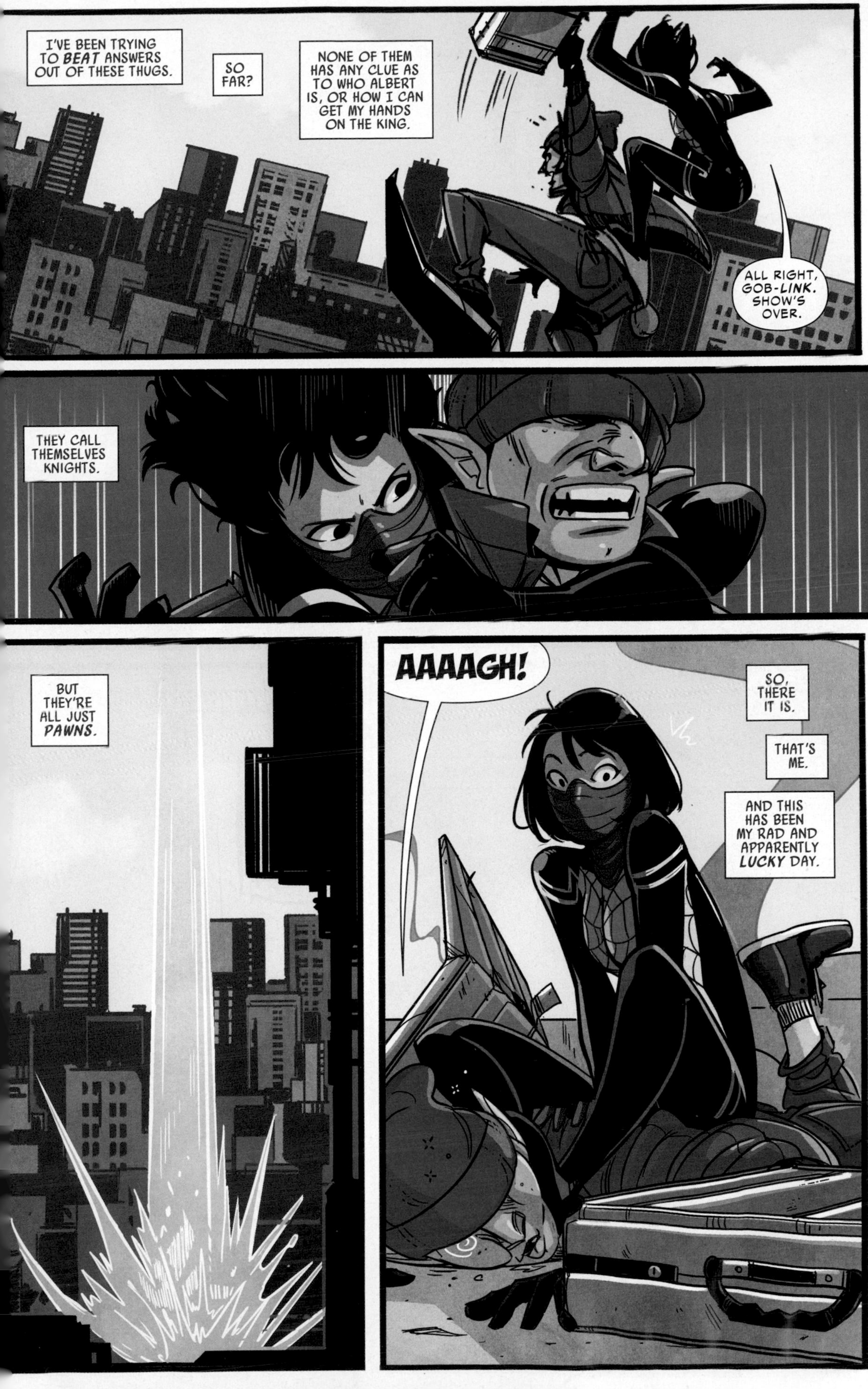
I'VE BEEN TRYING TO BEAT ANSWERS OUT OF THESE THUGS.
SO FAR?
NONE OF THEM HAS ANY CLUE AS TO WHO ALBERT IS, OR HOW I CAN GET MY HANDS ON THE KING.
ALL RIGHT, GOB-LINK. SHOW'S OVER.
THEY CALL THEMSELVES KNIGHTS.
BUT THEY'RE ALL JUST PAWNS.
AAAAGH!
SO, THERE IT IS.
THAT'S ME.
AND THIS HAS BEEN MY RAD AND APPARENTLY LUCKY DAY.

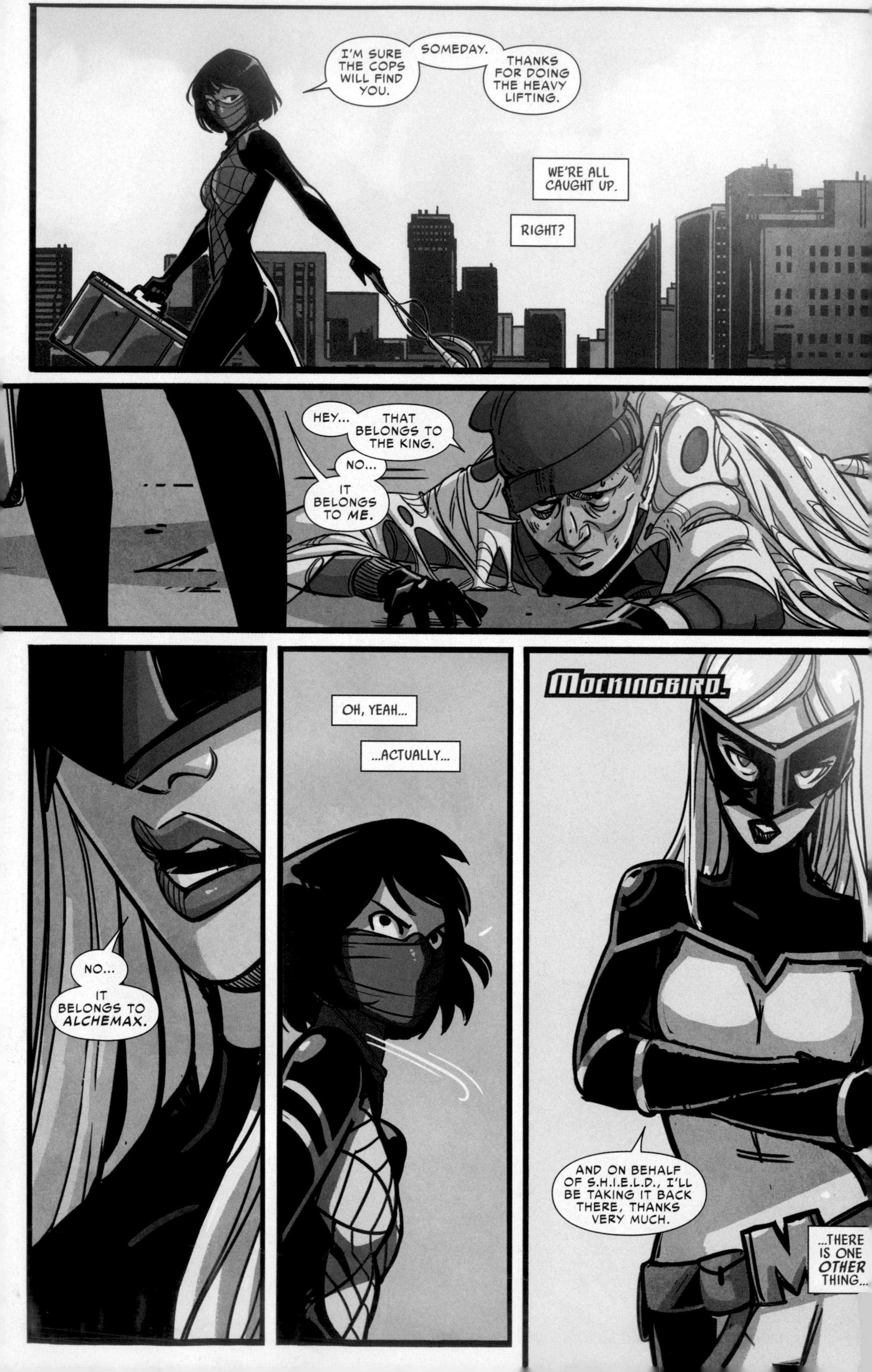

I'M SURE THE COPS WILL FIND YOU.
SOMEDAY.
THANKS FOR DOING THE HEAVY LIFTING.
WE'RE ALL CAUGHT UP.
RIGHT?
HEY... THAT BELONGS TO THE KING.
NO... IT BELONGS TO ME.
NO... IT BELONGS TO ALCHEMAX.
OH, YEAH...
...ACTUALLY...
MOCKINGBIRD.
AND ON BEHALF OF S.H.I.E.L.D., I'LL BE TAKING IT BACK THERE, THANKS VERY MUCH.
...THERE IS ONE OTHER THING...

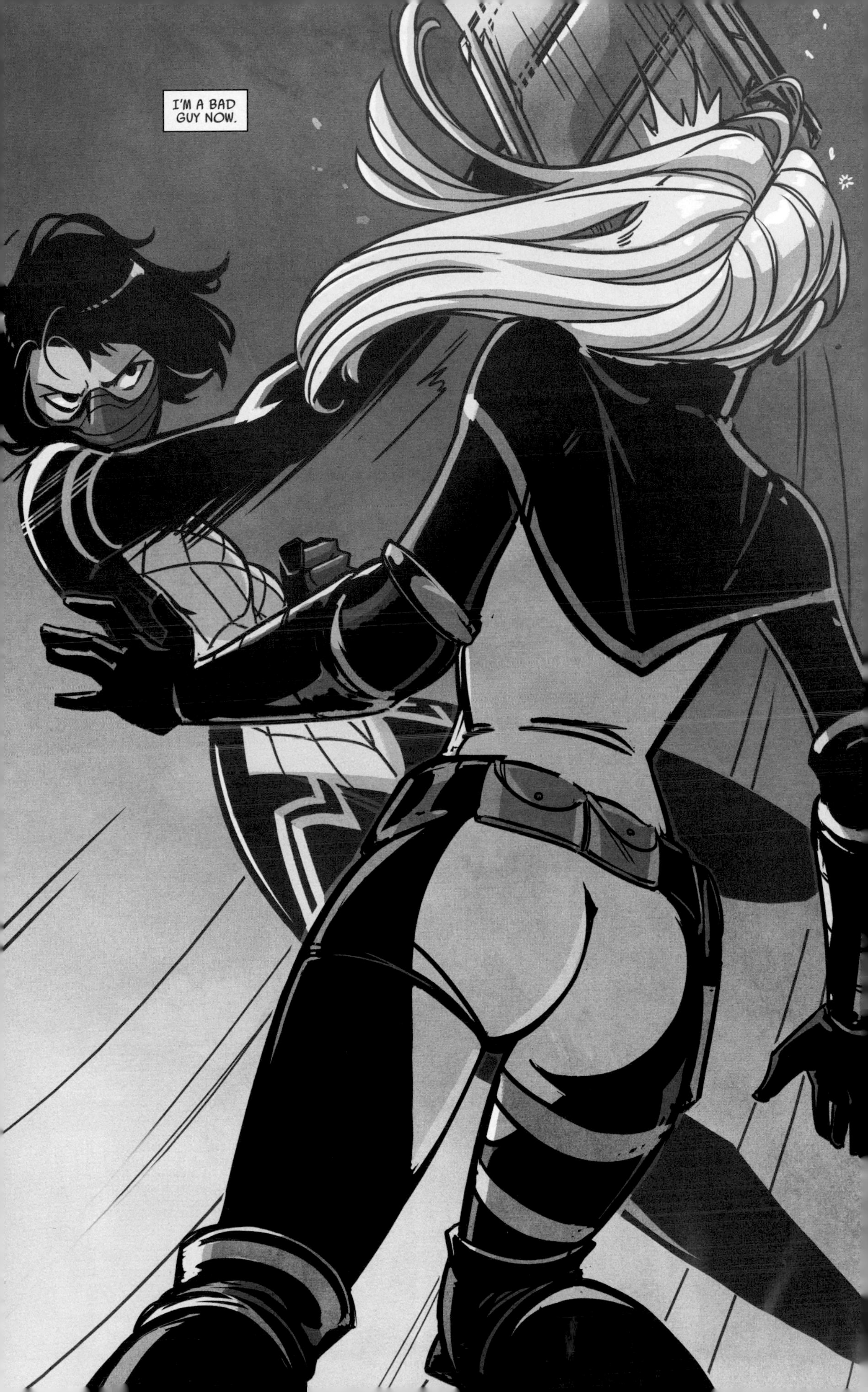
I'M A BAD GUY NOW.

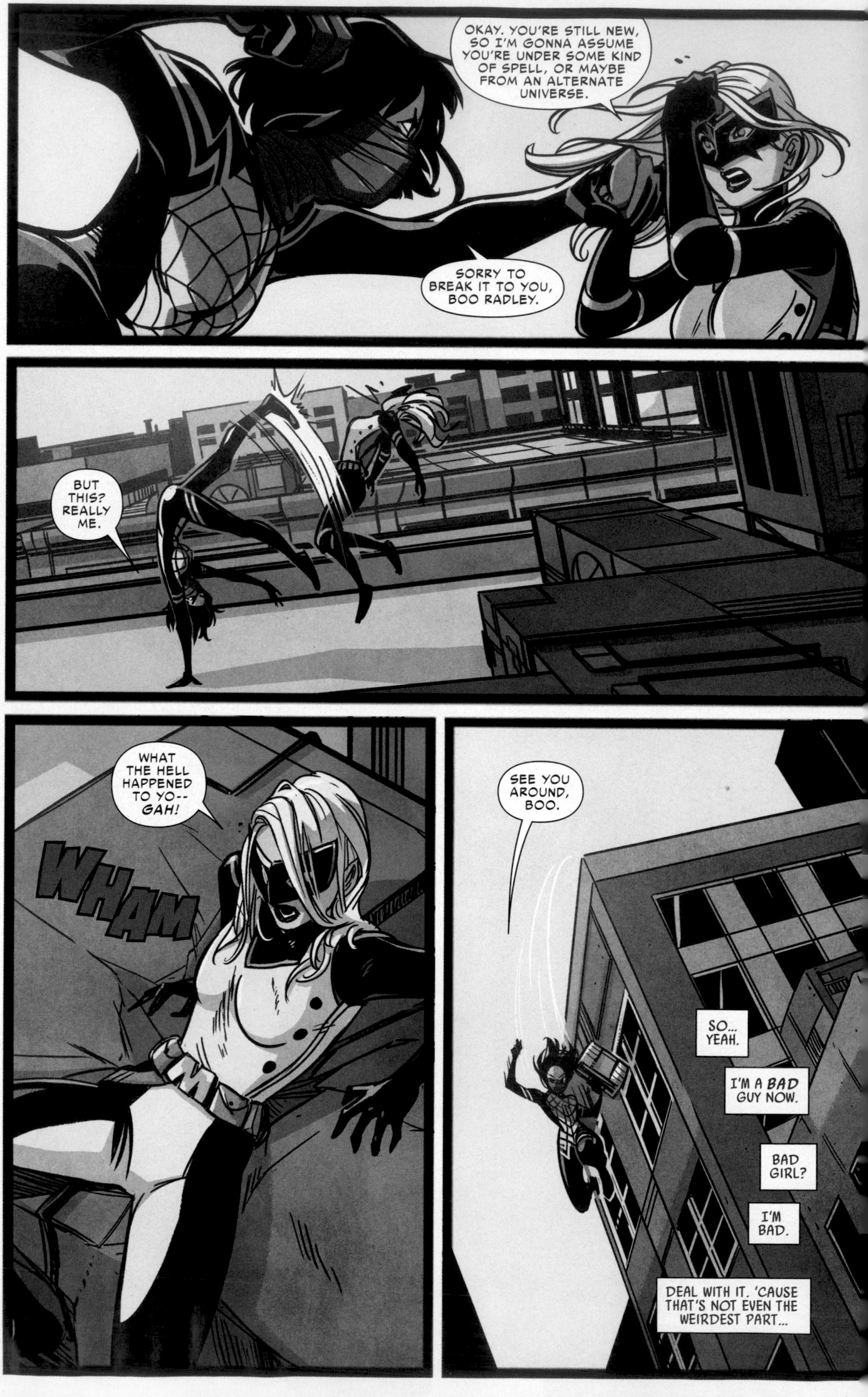
OKAY. YOU'RE STILL NEW, SO I'M GONNA ASSUME YOU'RE UNDER SOME KIND OF SPELL, OR MAYBE FROM AN ALTERNATE UNIVERSE.
SORRY TO BREAK IT TO YOU, BOO RADLEY.
BUT THIS? REALLY ME.
WHAT THE HELL HAPPENED TO YO-- GAH!
WHAM
SEE YOU AROUND, BOO.
SO... YEAH.
I'M A BAD GUY NOW.
BAD GIRL?
I'M BAD.
DEAL WITH IT. 'CAUSE THAT'S NOT EVEN THE WEIRDEST PART...

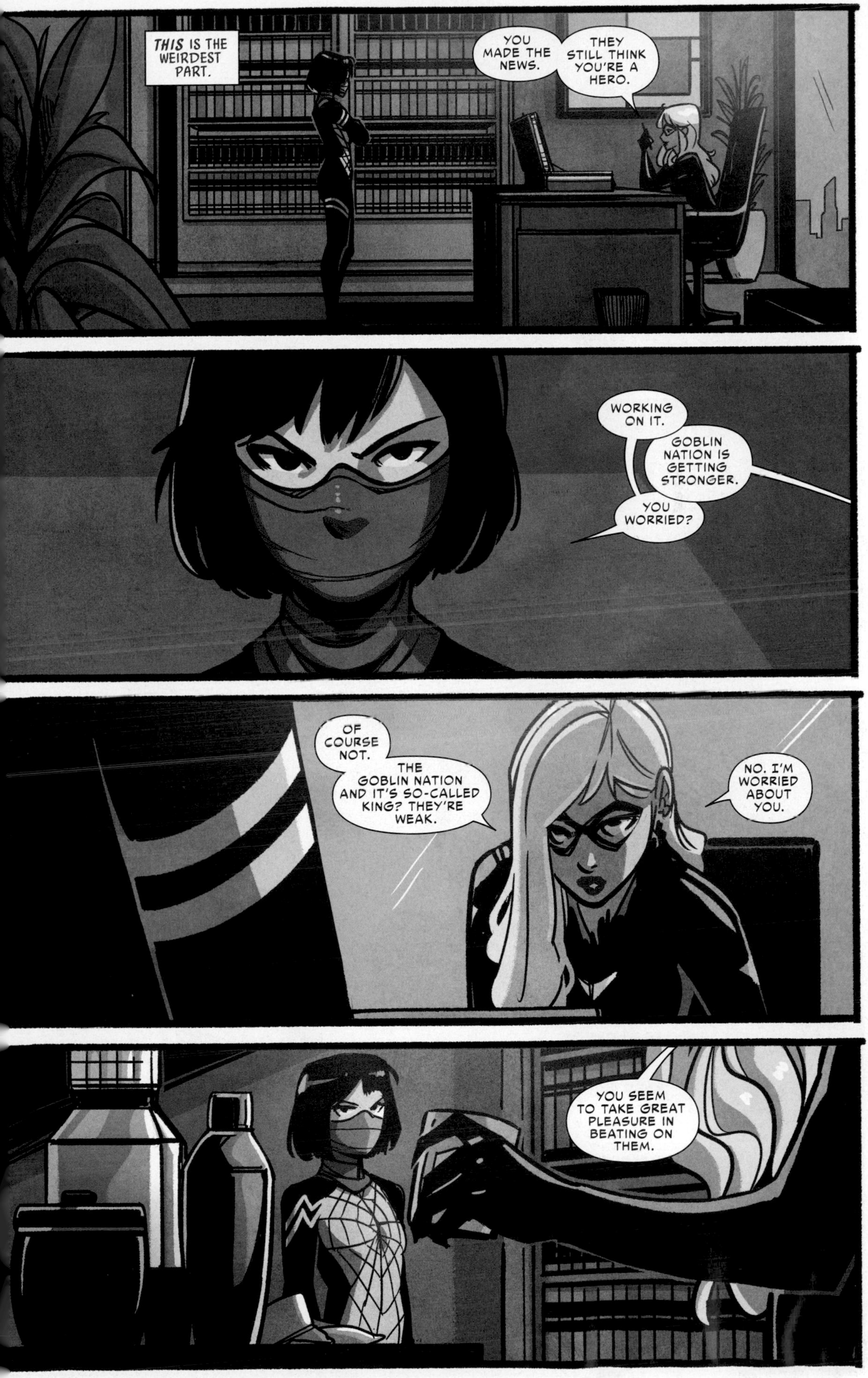
THIS IS THE WEIRDEST PART.
YOU MADE THE NEWS.
THEY STILL THINK YOU'RE A HERO.
WORKING ON IT.
GOBLIN NATION IS GETTING STRONGER.
YOU WORRIED?
OF COURSE NOT.
THE GOBLIN NATION AND IT'S SO-CALLED KING? THEY'RE WEAK.
NO. I'M WORRIED ABOUT YOU.
YOU SEEM TO TAKE GREAT PLEASURE IN BEATING ON THEM.

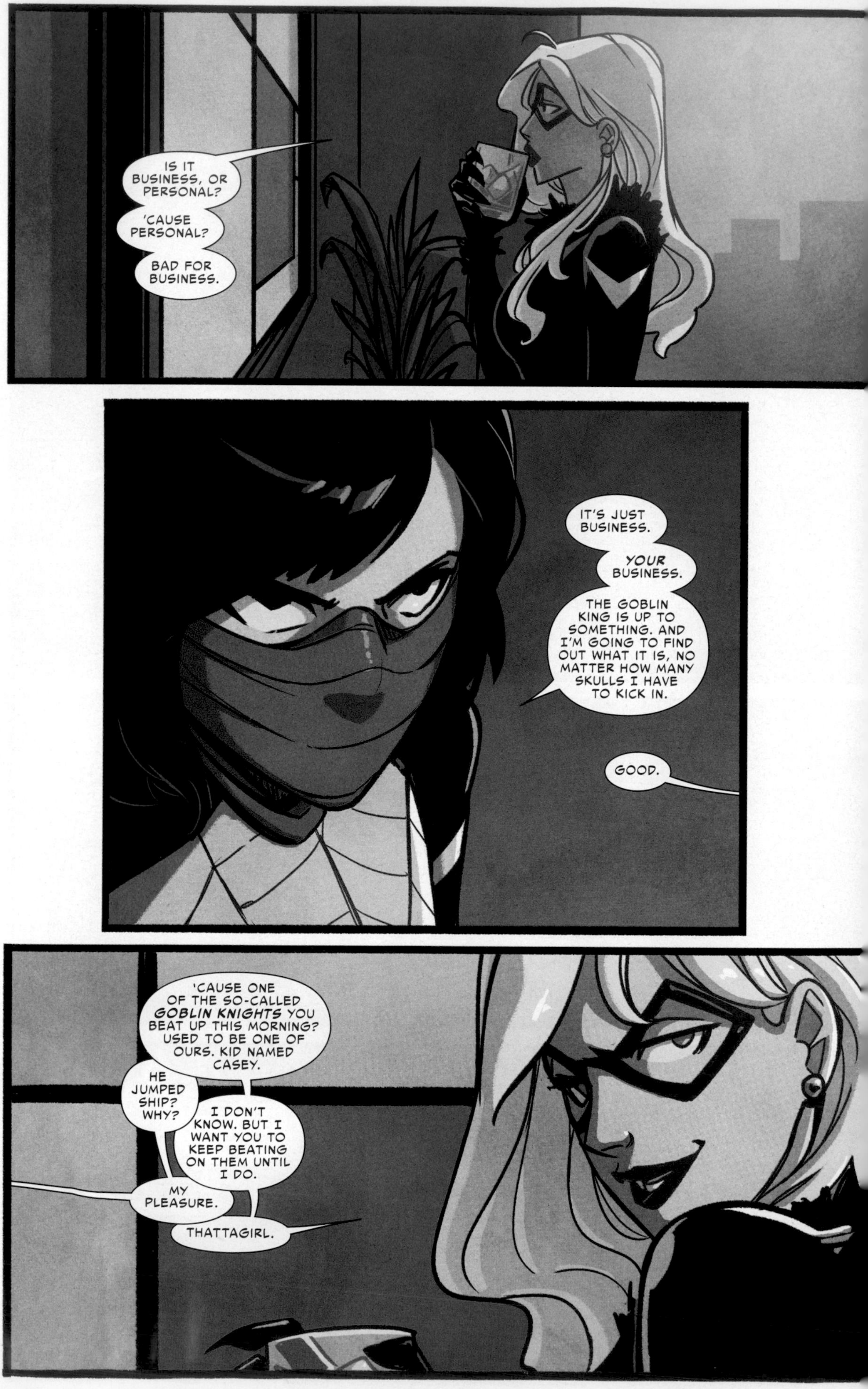
IS IT BUSINESS, OR PERSONAL?
'CAUSE PERSONAL?
BAD FOR BUSINESS.
IT'S JUST BUSINESS.
YOUR BUSINESS.
THE GOBLIN KING IS UP TO SOMETHING. AND I'M GOING TO FIND OUT WHAT IT IS, NO MATTER HOW MANY SKULLS I HAVE TO KICK IN.
GOOD.
'CAUSE ONE OF THE SO-CALLED ***GOBLIN KNIGHTS*** YOU BEAT UP THIS MORNING? USED TO BE ONE OF OURS. KID NAMED CASEY.
HE JUMPED SHIP? WHY?
I DON'T KNOW. BUT I WANT YOU TO KEEP BEATING ON THEM UNTIL I DO.
MY PLEASURE.
THATTAGIRL.

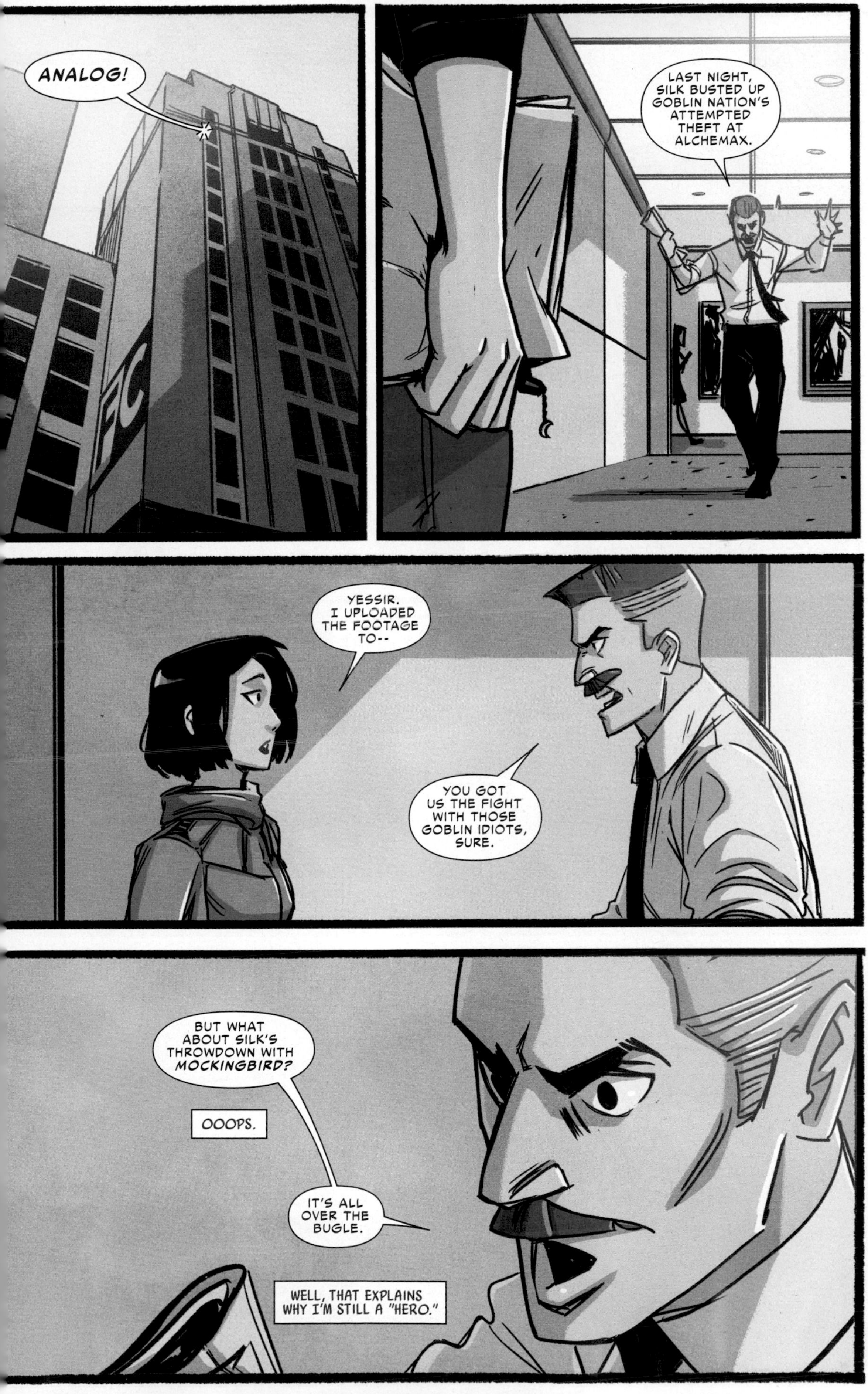
ANALOG!
LAST NIGHT, SILK BUSTED UP GOBLIN NATION'S ATTEMPTED THEFT AT ALCHEMAX.
YESSIR. I UPLOADED THE FOOTAGE TO--
YOU GOT US THE FIGHT WITH THOSE GOBLIN IDIOTS, SURE.
BUT WHAT ABOUT SILK'S THROWDOWN WITH MOCKINGBIRD?
OOOPS.
IT'S ALL OVER THE BUGLE.
WELL, THAT EXPLAINS WHY I'M STILL A "HERO."

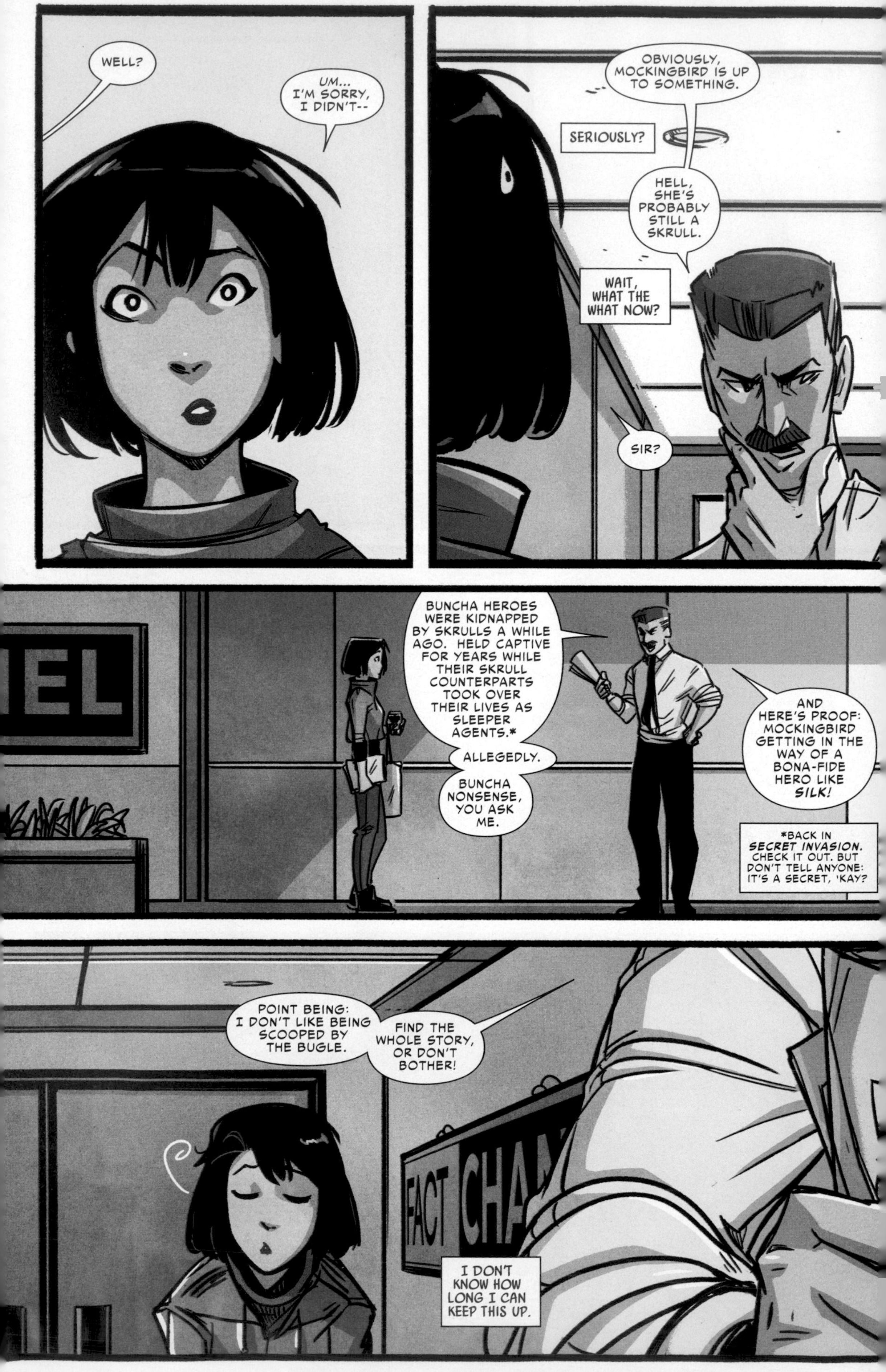
WELL?
UM... I'M SORRY, I DIDN'T--
OBVIOUSLY, MOCKINGBIRD IS UP TO SOMETHING.
SERIOUSLY?
HELL, SHE'S PROBABLY STILL A SKRULL.
WAIT, WHAT THE WHAT NOW?
SIR?
BUNCHA HEROES WERE KIDNAPPED BY SKRULLS A WHILE AGO. HELD CAPTIVE FOR YEARS WHILE THEIR SKRULL COUNTERPARTS TOOK OVER THEIR LIVES AS SLEEPER AGENTS.*
ALLEGEDLY.
BUNCHA NONSENSE, YOU ASK ME.
AND HERE'S PROOF: MOCKINGBIRD GETTING IN THE WAY OF A BONA-FIDE HERO LIKE SILK!
*BACK IN SECRET INVASION. CHECK IT OUT. BUT DON'T TELL ANYONE: IT'S A SECRET, 'KAY?
POINT BEING: I DON'T LIKE BEING SCOOPED BY THE BUGLE.
FIND THE WHOLE STORY, OR DON'T BOTHER!
FACT CHA
I DON'T KNOW HOW LONG I CAN KEEP THIS UP.

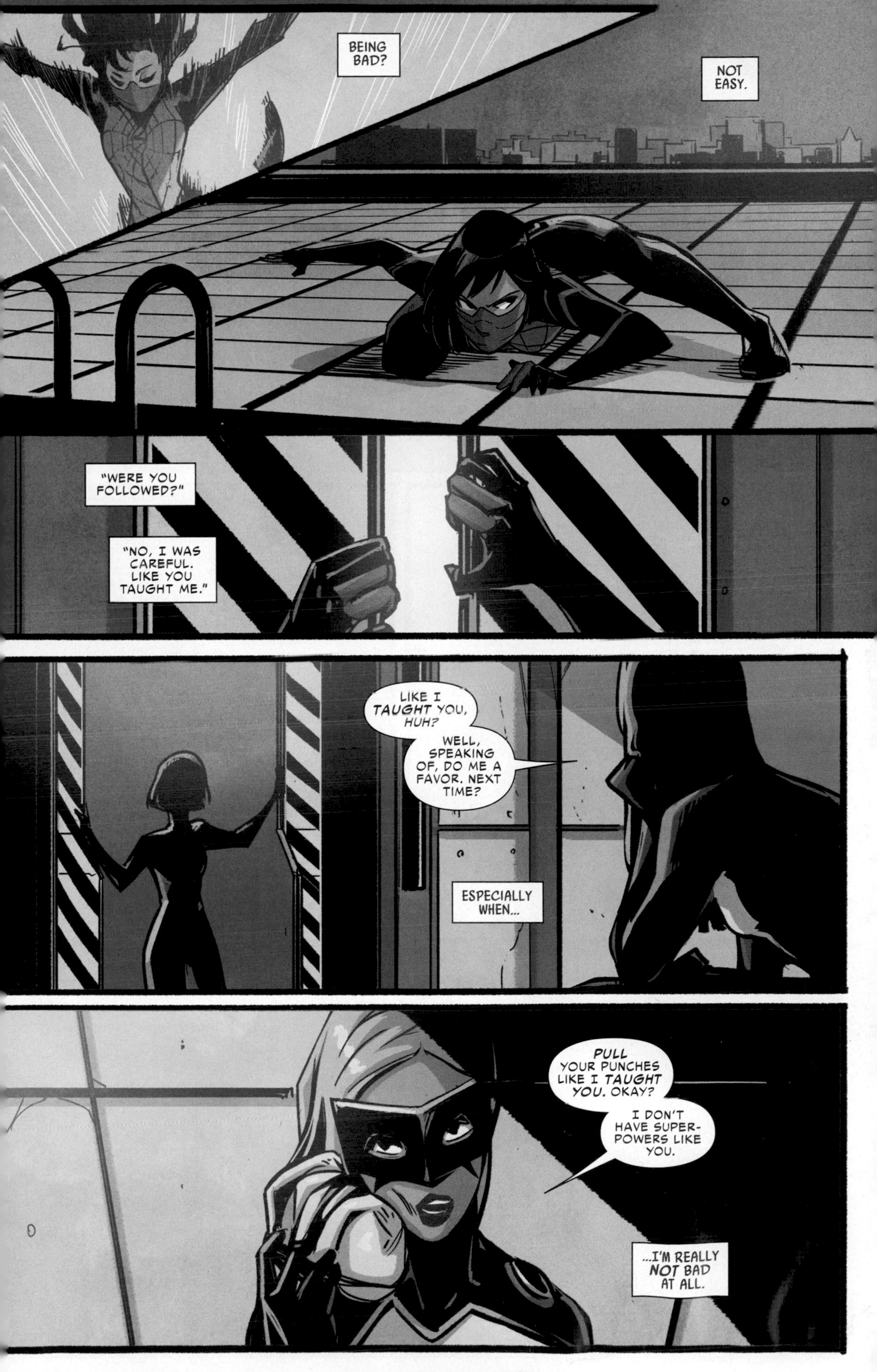
BEING BAD?
NOT EASY.
"WERE YOU FOLLOWED?"
"NO, I WAS CAREFUL. LIKE YOU TAUGHT ME."
LIKE I *TAUGHT* YOU, *HUH?*
WELL, SPEAKING OF, DO ME A FAVOR. NEXT TIME?
ESPECIALLY WHEN...
PULL YOUR PUNCHES LIKE I *TAUGHT YOU.* OKAY?
I DON'T HAVE SUPER-POWERS LIKE YOU.
...I'M REALLY *NOT* BAD AT ALL.

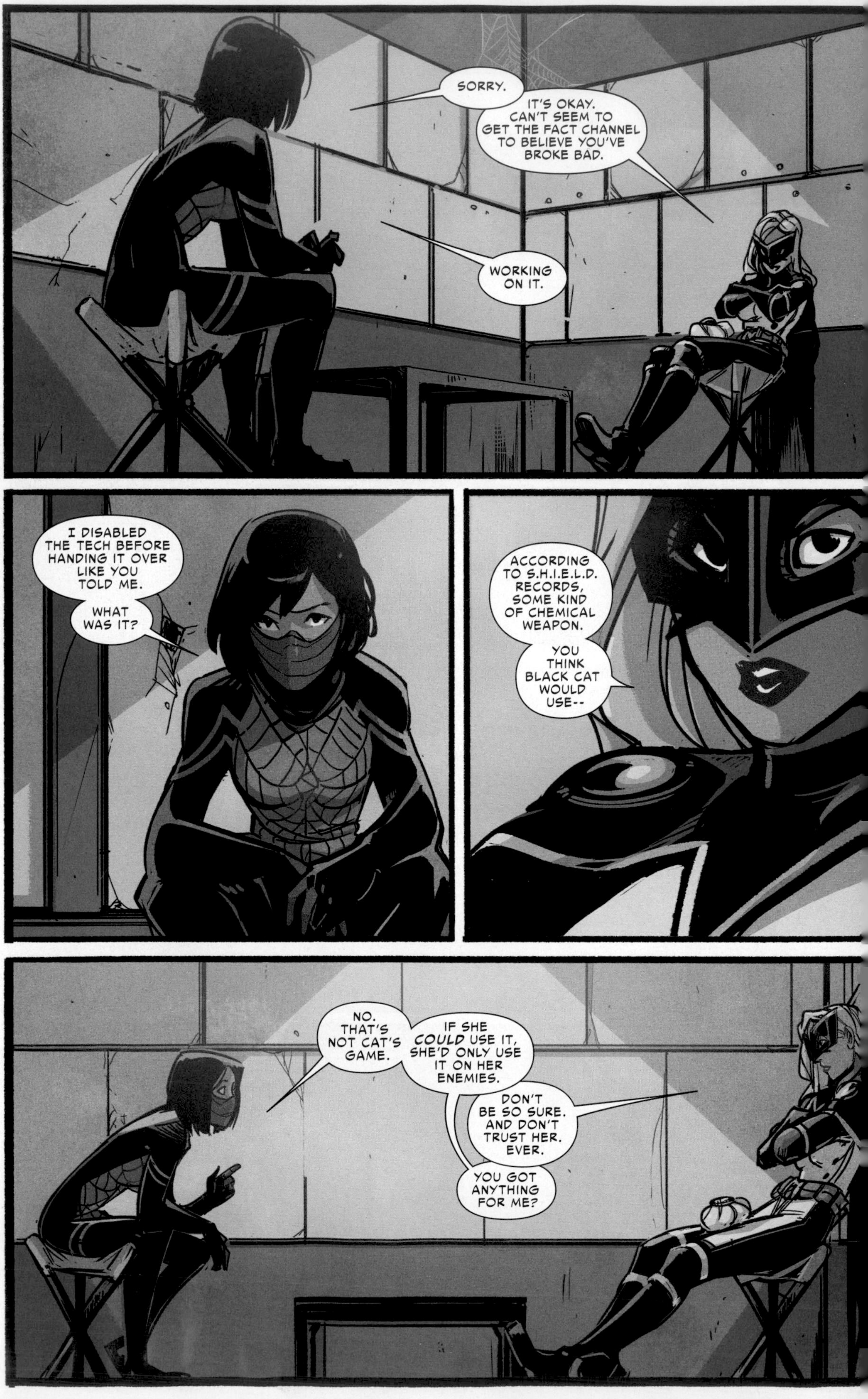
SORRY.
IT'S OKAY. CAN'T SEEM TO GET THE FACT CHANNEL TO BELIEVE YOU'VE BROKE BAD.
WORKING ON IT.
I DISABLED THE TECH BEFORE HANDING IT OVER LIKE YOU TOLD ME.
WHAT WAS IT?
ACCORDING TO S.H.I.E.L.D. RECORDS, SOME KIND OF CHEMICAL WEAPON.
YOU THINK BLACK CAT WOULD USE--
NO. THAT'S NOT CAT'S GAME.
IF SHE *COULD* USE IT, SHE'D ONLY USE IT ON HER ENEMIES.
DON'T BE SO SURE. AND DON'T TRUST HER. EVER.
YOU GOT ANYTHING FOR ME?

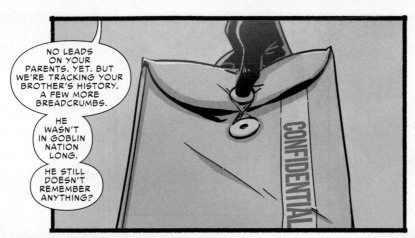

NO LEADS ON YOUR PARENTS. YET. BUT WE'RE TRACKING YOUR BROTHER'S HISTORY. A FEW MORE BREADCRUMBS.

HE WASN'T IN GOBLIN NATION LONG.

HE STILL DOESN'T REMEMBER ANYTHING?

NO. BUT HE'S GETTING BETTER. THANK YOU FOR GETTING HIM INTO THAT HOSPITAL. THEY'VE BEEN GREAT.

WE HOLD UP OUR END AT S.H.I.E.L.D.

ALRIGHT, I'M GONNA GO SLEEP THIS BRUISE AWAY. KEEP DIGGING INTO CAT.

HEY, BOO...

YOU WERE HELD CAPTIVE BY SKRULLS?

FOR YEARS. YEAH.

HOW...

HOW DID YOU GET OVER THAT?

I DIDN'T.

BE CAREFUL OUT THERE, KIDDO.

WORKING UNDERCOVER? ONLY PERSON TO WATCH YOUR BACK IS YOU.

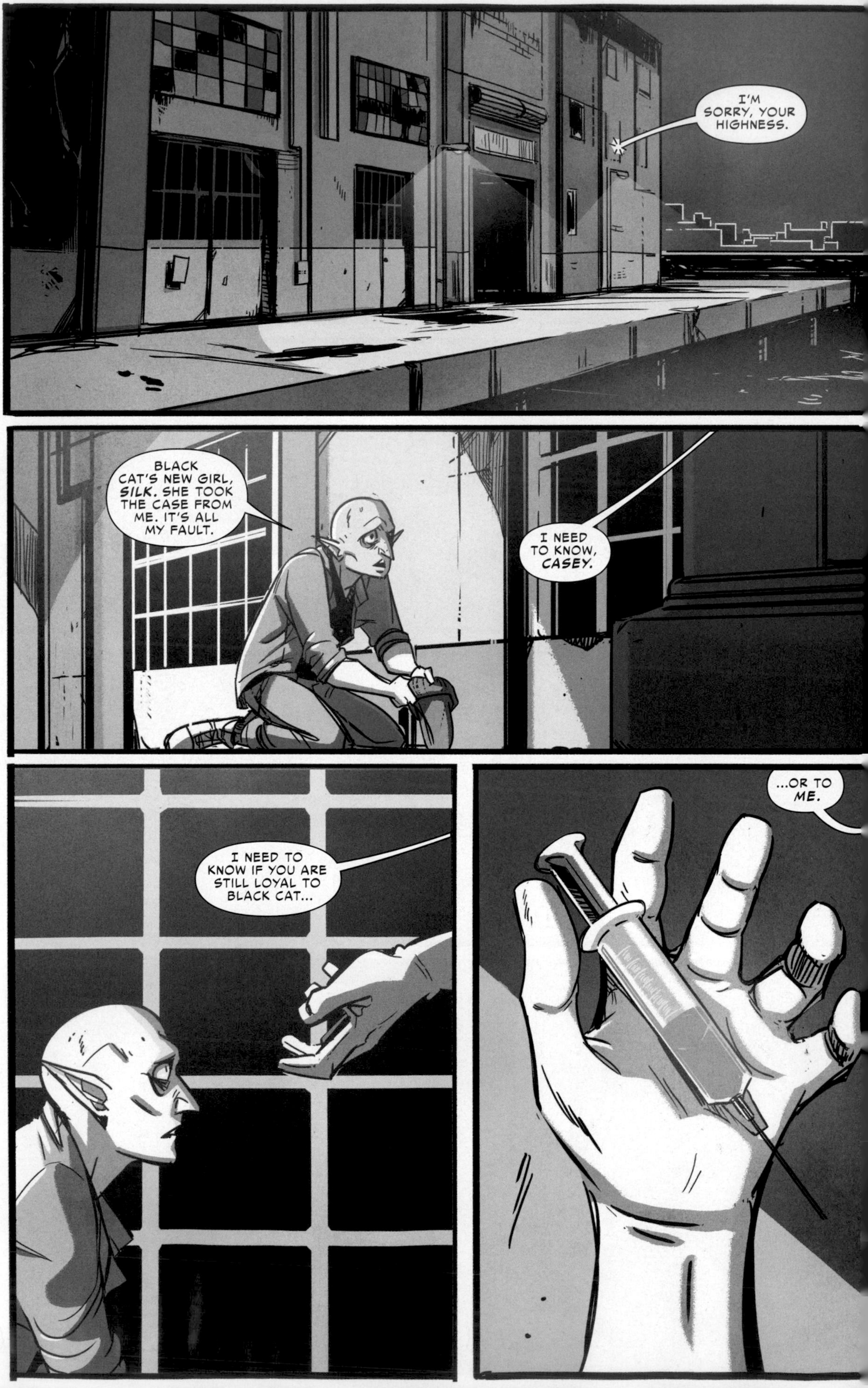
I'M SORRY, YOUR HIGHNESS.
BLACK CAT'S NEW GIRL, SILK. SHE TOOK THE CASE FROM ME. IT'S ALL MY FAULT.
I NEED TO KNOW, CASEY.
I NEED TO KNOW IF YOU ARE STILL LOYAL TO BLACK CAT...
...OR TO ME.

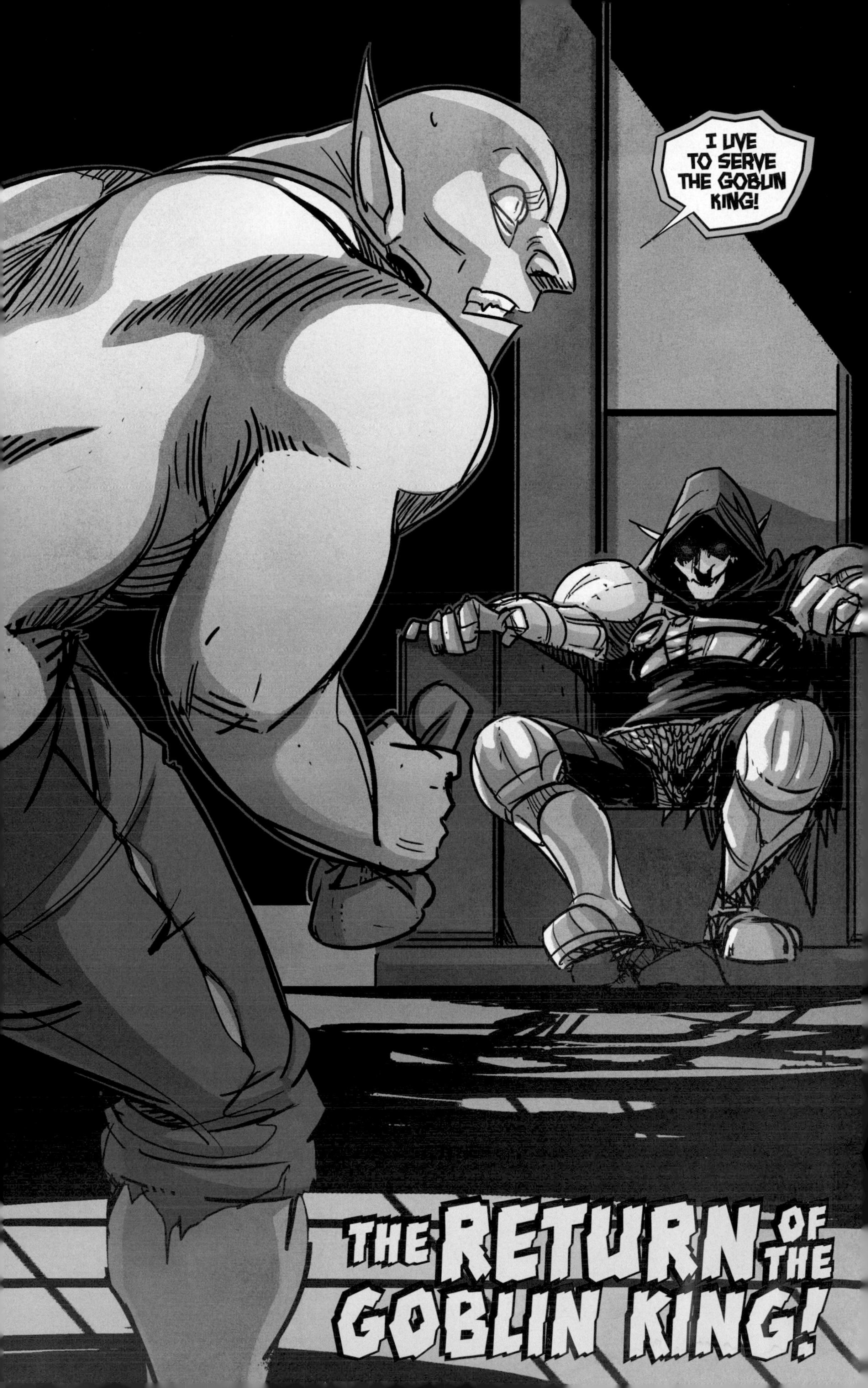
I LIVE TO SERVE THE GOBLIN KING!
THE RETURN OF THE GOBLIN KING!

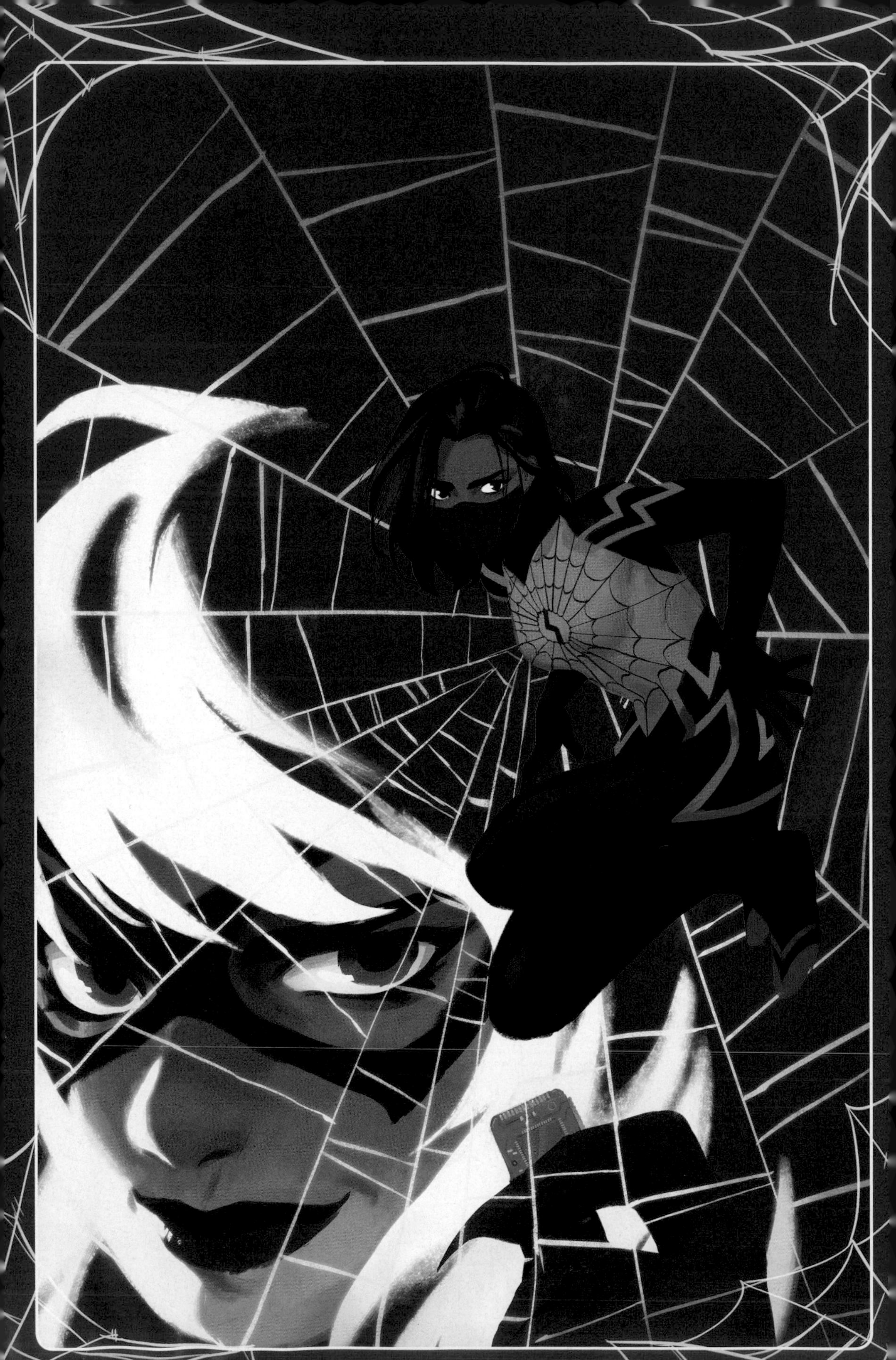

2

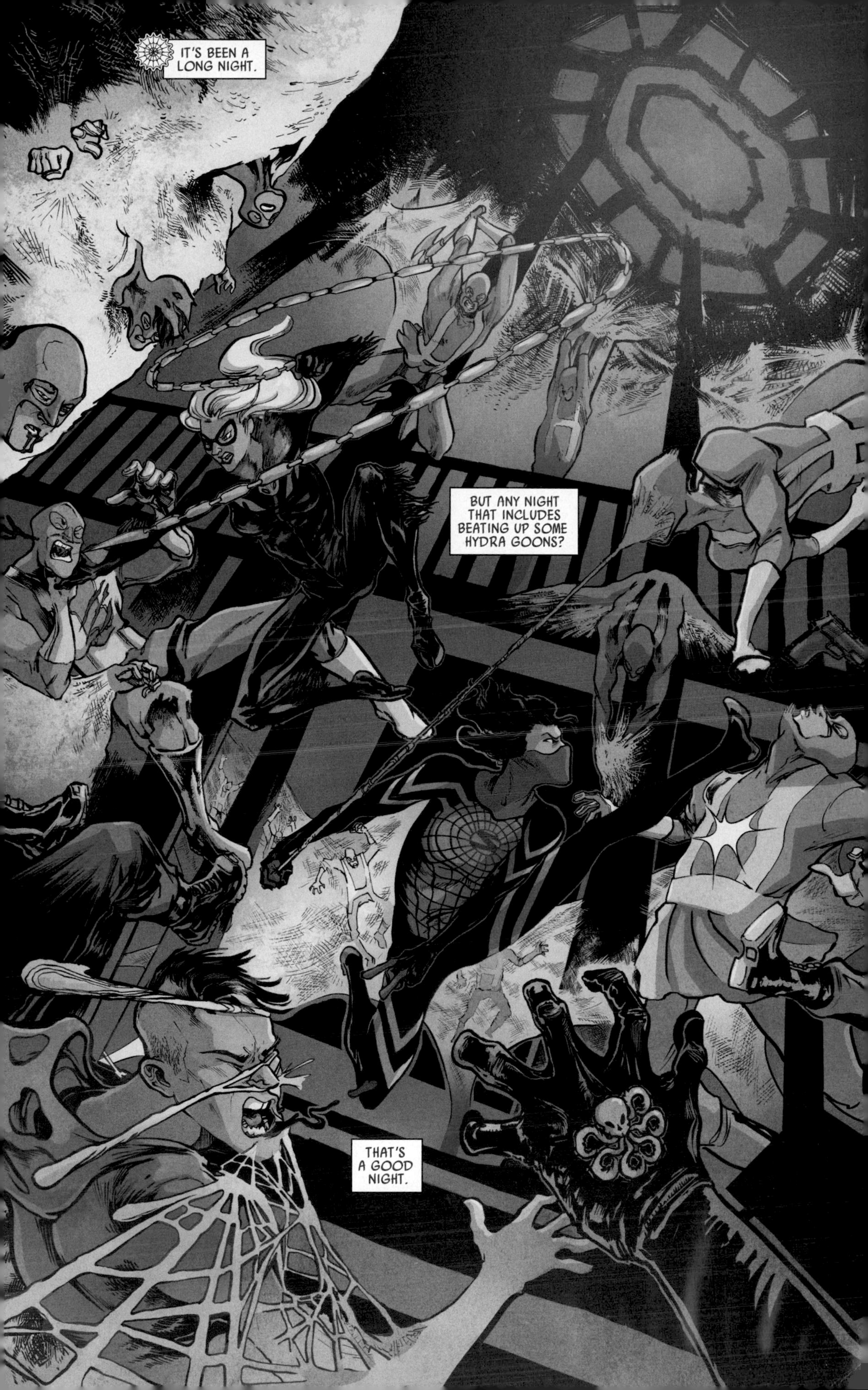
IT'S BEEN A LONG NIGHT.
BUT ANY NIGHT THAT INCLUDES BEATING UP SOME HYDRA GOONS?
THAT'S A GOOD NIGHT.

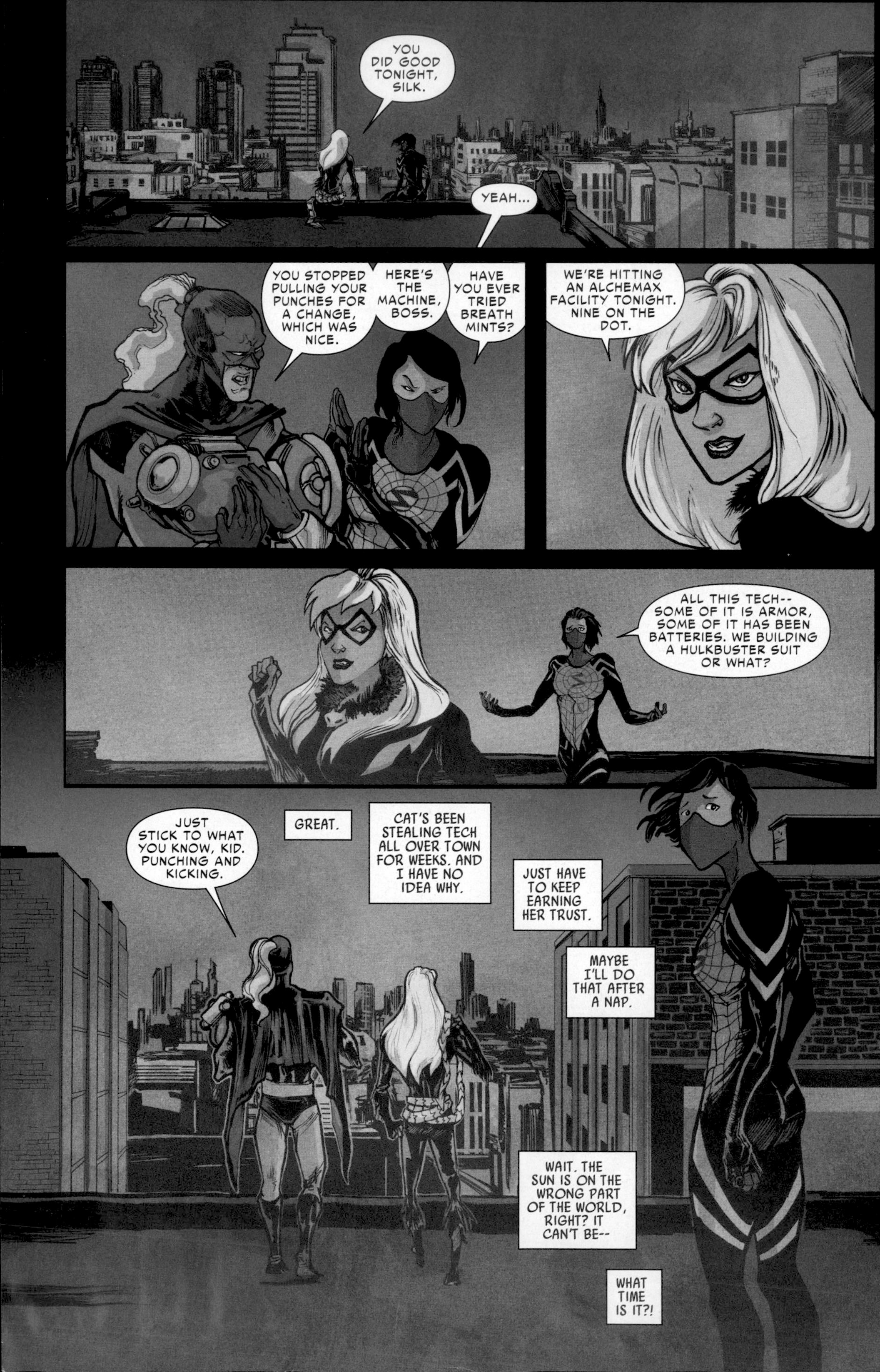

YOU DID GOOD TONIGHT, SILK.
YEAH...
YOU STOPPED PULLING YOUR PUNCHES FOR A CHANGE, WHICH WAS NICE.
HERE'S THE MACHINE, BOSS.
HAVE YOU EVER TRIED BREATH MINTS?
WE'RE HITTING AN ALCHEMAX FACILITY TONIGHT. NINE ON THE DOT.
ALL THIS TECH-- SOME OF IT IS ARMOR, SOME OF IT HAS BEEN BATTERIES. WE BUILDING A HULKBUSTER SUIT OR WHAT?
JUST STICK TO WHAT YOU KNOW, KID. PUNCHING AND KICKING.
GREAT.
CAT'S BEEN STEALING TECH ALL OVER TOWN FOR WEEKS. AND I HAVE NO IDEA WHY.
JUST HAVE TO KEEP EARNING HER TRUST.
MAYBE I'LL DO THAT AFTER A NAP.
WAIT. THE SUN IS ON THE WRONG PART OF THE WORLD, RIGHT? IT CAN'T BE--
WHAT TIME IS IT?!

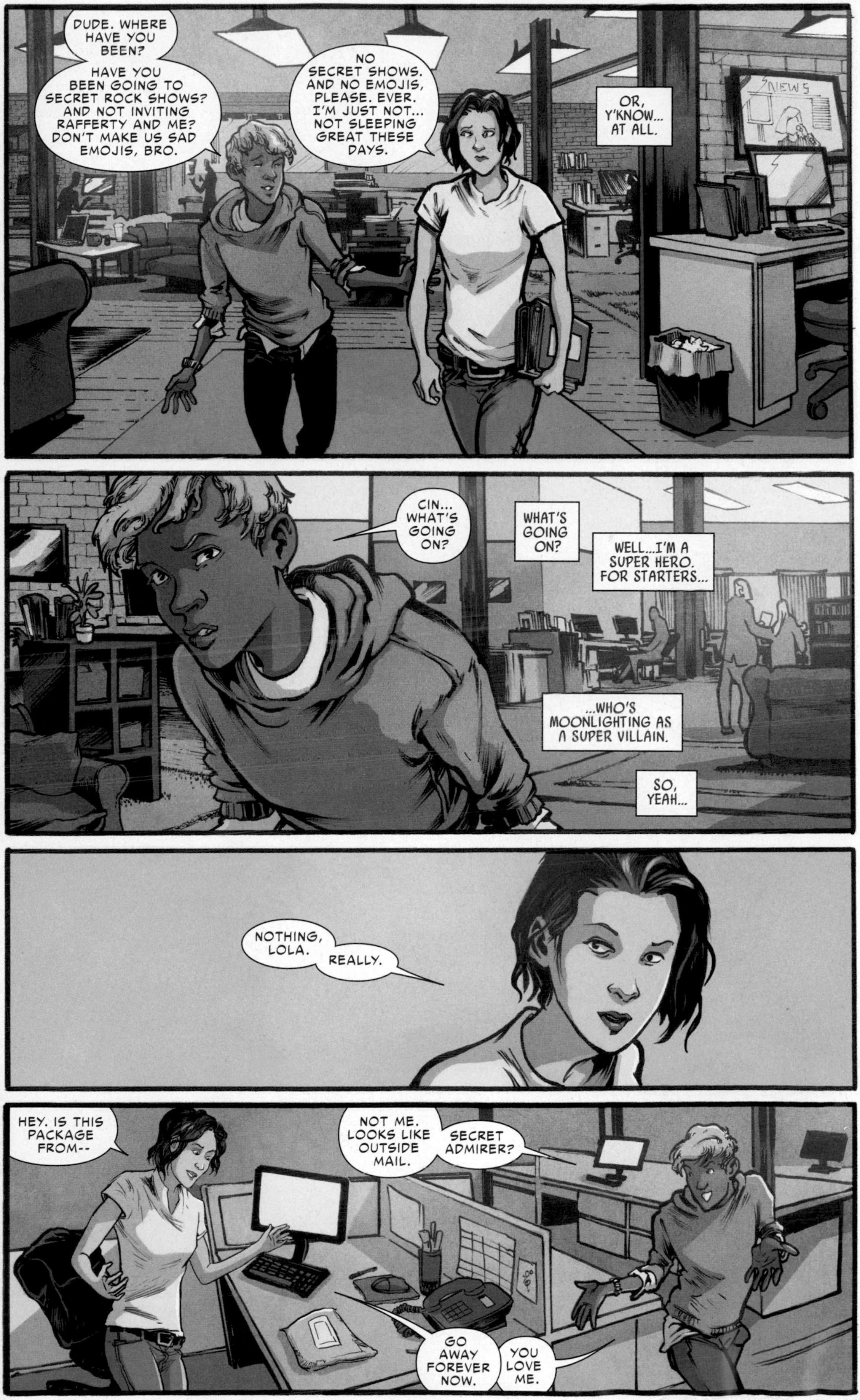
DUDE. WHERE HAVE YOU BEEN?
HAVE YOU BEEN GOING TO SECRET ROCK SHOWS? AND NOT INVITING RAFFERTY AND ME? DON'T MAKE US SAD EMOJIS, BRO.
NO SECRET SHOWS. AND NO EMOJIS, PLEASE. EVER. I'M JUST NOT... NOT SLEEPING GREAT THESE DAYS.
OR, Y'KNOW... AT ALL.
NEWS
CIN... WHAT'S GOING ON?
WHAT'S GOING ON?
WELL...I'M A SUPER HERO. FOR STARTERS...
...WHO'S MOONLIGHTING AS A SUPER VILLAIN.
SO, YEAH...
NOTHING, LOLA.
REALLY.
HEY. IS THIS PACKAGE FROM--
NOT ME. LOOKS LIKE OUTSIDE MAIL.
SECRET ADMIRER?
GO AWAY FOREVER NOW.
YOU LOVE ME.

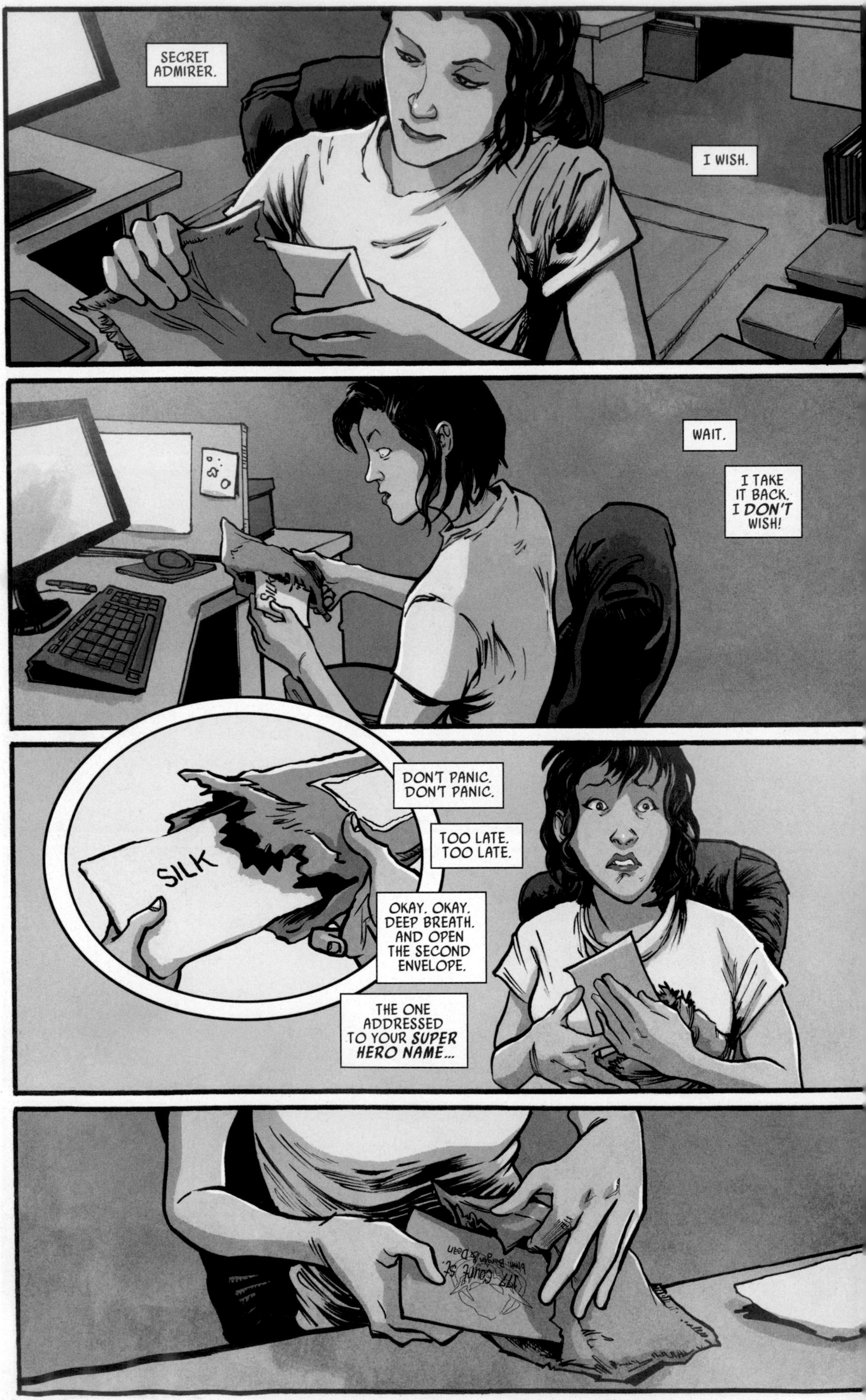
SECRET ADMIRER.
I WISH.
WAIT.
I TAKE IT BACK. I *DON'T* WISH!
SILK
DON'T PANIC. DON'T PANIC.
TOO LATE. TOO LATE.
OKAY. OKAY. DEEP BREATH. AND OPEN THE SECOND ENVELOPE.
THE ONE ADDRESSED TO YOUR *SUPER HERO NAME*...

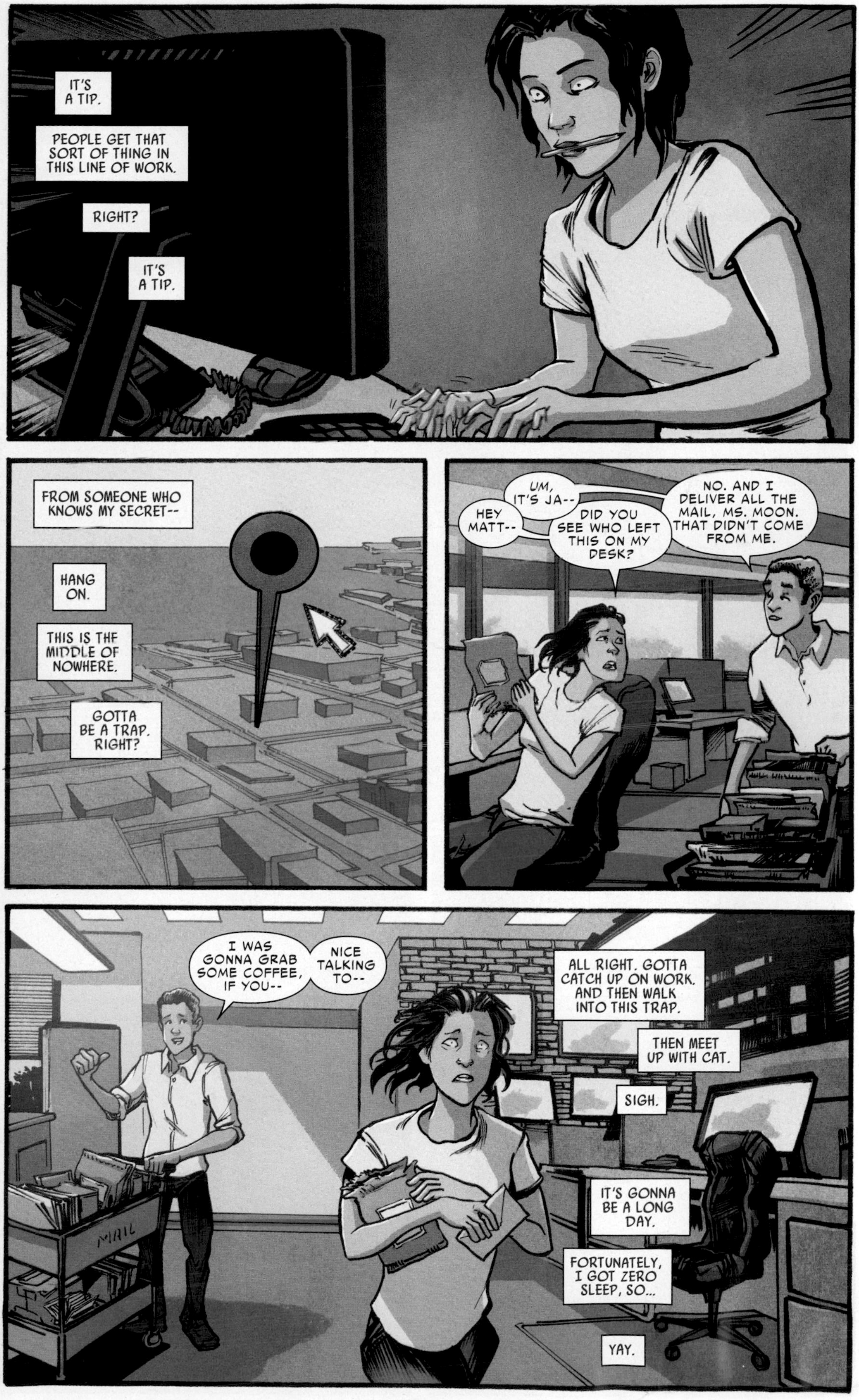
IT'S A TIP.
PEOPLE GET THAT SORT OF THING IN THIS LINE OF WORK.
RIGHT?
IT'S A TIP.
FROM SOMEONE WHO KNOWS MY SECRET--
HANG ON.
THIS IS THE MIDDLE OF NOWHERE.
GOTTA BE A TRAP. RIGHT?
HEY MATT--
UM, IT'S JA--
DID YOU SEE WHO LEFT THIS ON MY DESK?
NO. AND I DELIVER ALL THE MAIL, MS. MOON. THAT DIDN'T COME FROM ME.
I WAS GONNA GRAB SOME COFFEE, IF YOU--
NICE TALKING TO--
ALL RIGHT. GOTTA CATCH UP ON WORK. AND THEN WALK INTO THIS TRAP.
THEN MEET UP WITH CAT.
SIGH.
IT'S GONNA BE A LONG DAY.
FORTUNATELY, I GOT ZERO SLEEP, SO...
YAY.
MAIL

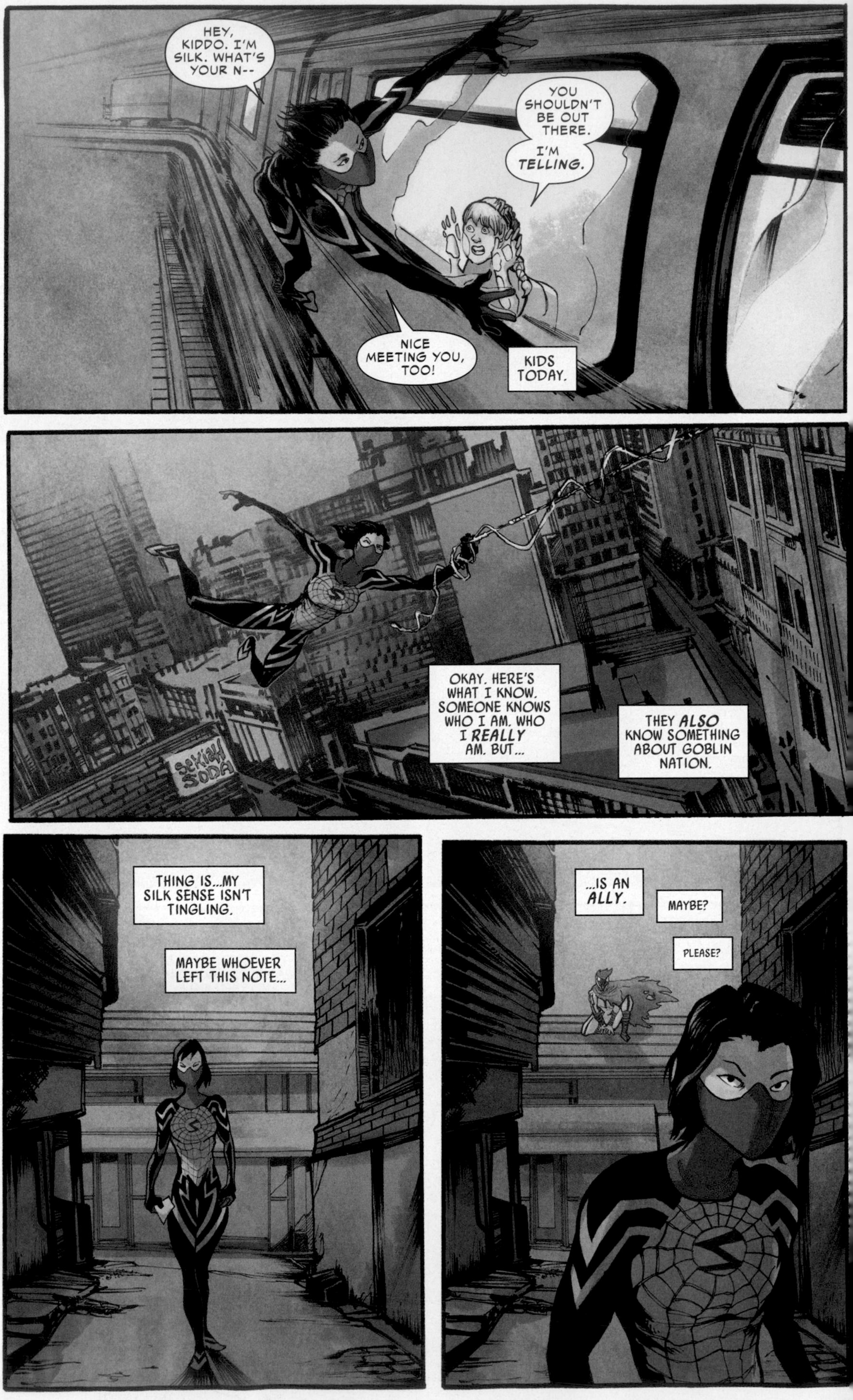
HEY, KIDDO. I'M SILK. WHAT'S YOUR N--
YOU SHOULDN'T BE OUT THERE.
I'M TELLING.
NICE MEETING YOU, TOO!
KIDS TODAY.
OKAY. HERE'S WHAT I KNOW. SOMEONE KNOWS WHO I AM. WHO I REALLY AM. BUT...
THEY ALSO KNOW SOMETHING ABOUT GOBLIN NATION.
SEKIAH SODA
THING IS...MY SILK SENSE ISN'T TINGLING.
MAYBE WHOEVER LEFT THIS NOTE...
...IS AN ALLY.
MAYBE?
PLEASE?

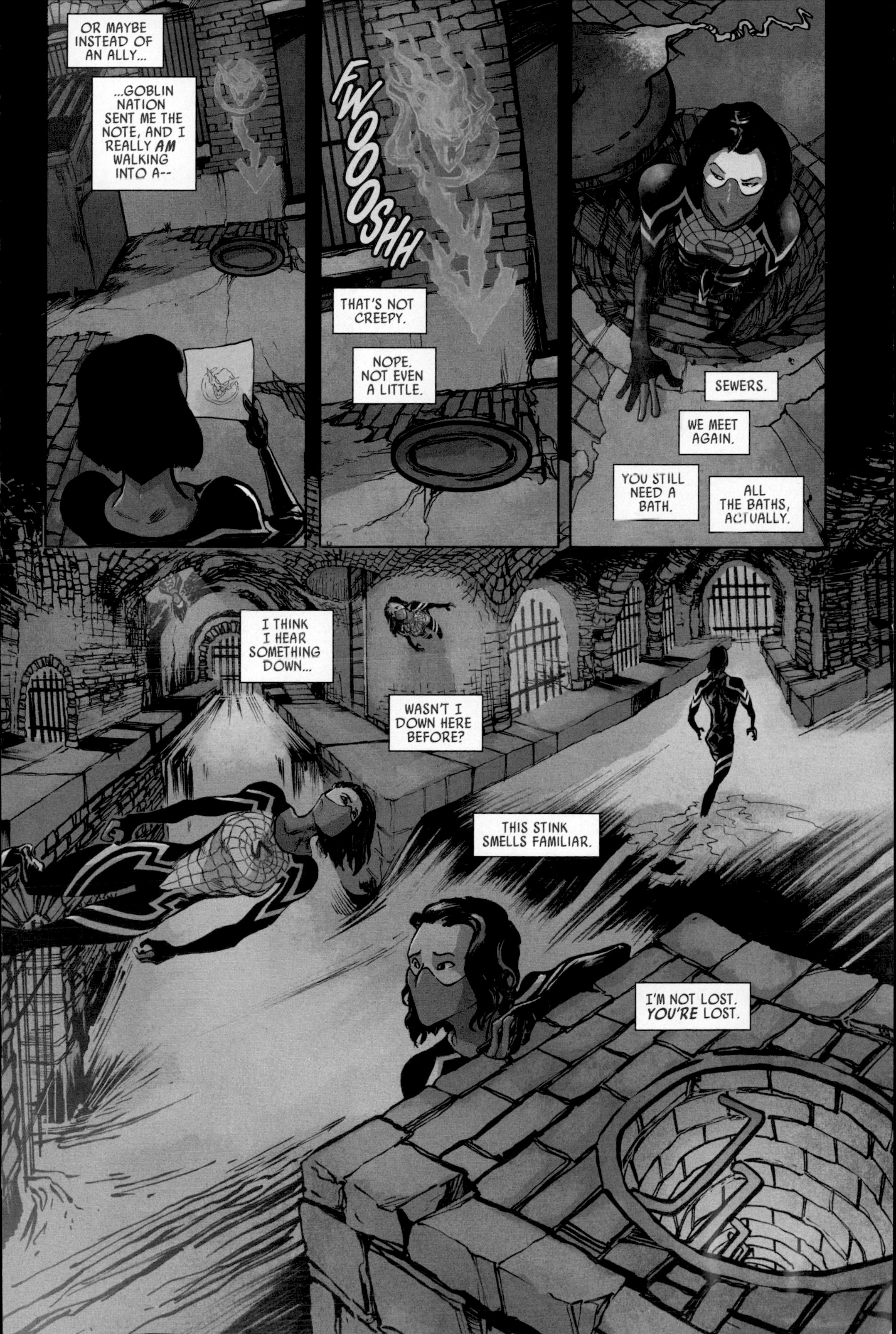
OR MAYBE INSTEAD OF AN ALLY...
...GOBLIN NATION SENT ME THE NOTE, AND I REALLY AM WALKING INTO A--
FWOOOSHH
THAT'S NOT CREEPY.
NOPE. NOT EVEN A LITTLE.
SEWERS.
WE MEET AGAIN.
YOU STILL NEED A BATH.
ALL THE BATHS, ACTUALLY.
I THINK I HEAR SOMETHING DOWN...
WASN'T I DOWN HERE BEFORE?
THIS STINK SMELLS FAMILIAR.
I'M NOT LOST. YOU'RE LOST.

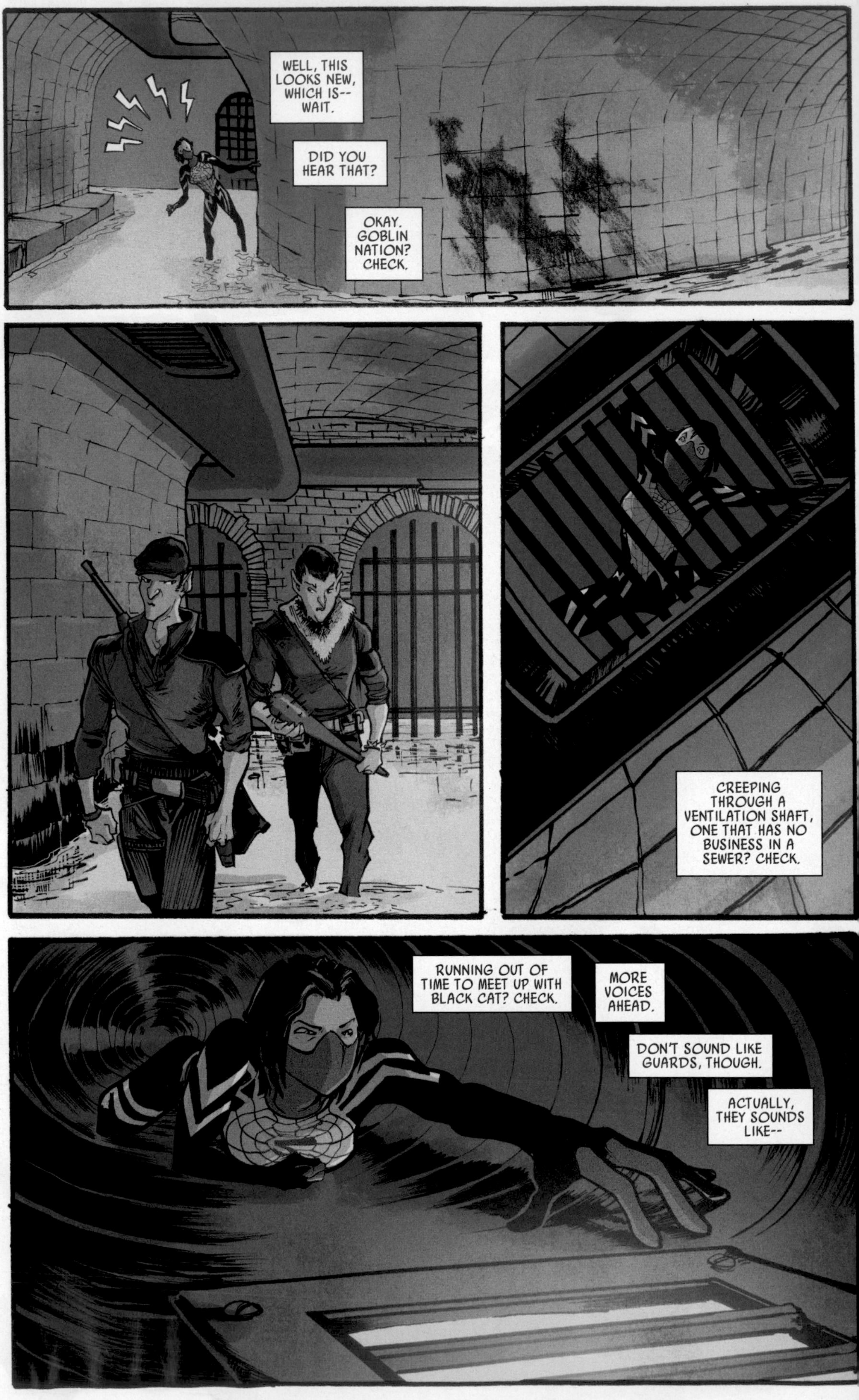
WELL, THIS LOOKS NEW, WHICH IS-- WAIT.
DID YOU HEAR THAT?
OKAY. GOBLIN NATION? CHECK.
CREEPING THROUGH A VENTILATION SHAFT, ONE THAT HAS NO BUSINESS IN A SEWER? CHECK.
RUNNING OUT OF TIME TO MEET UP WITH BLACK CAT? CHECK.
MORE VOICES AHEAD.
DON'T SOUND LIKE GUARDS, THOUGH.
ACTUALLY, THEY SOUNDS LIKE--

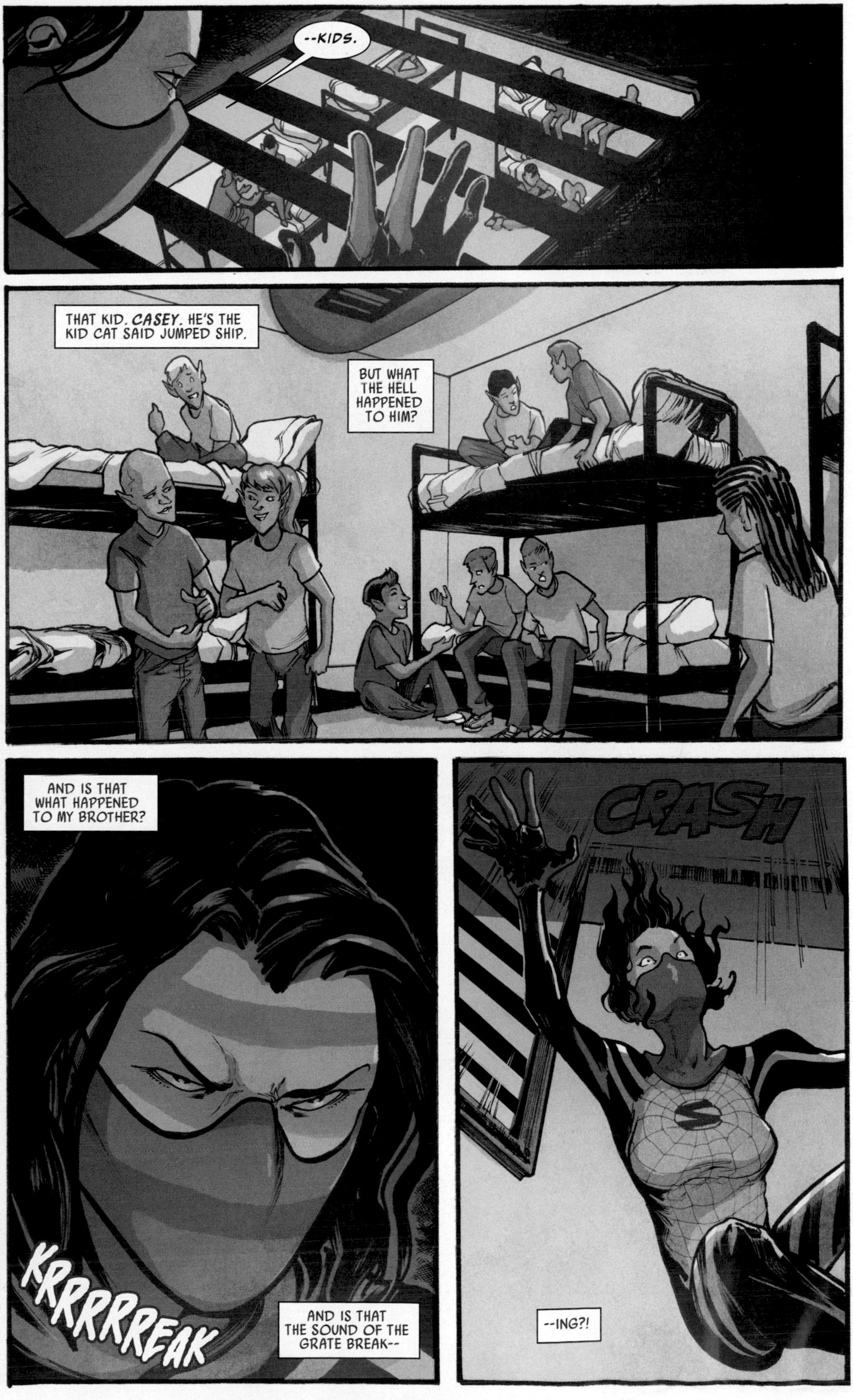
--KIDS.
THAT KID. CASEY. HE'S THE KID CAT SAID JUMPED SHIP.
BUT WHAT THE HELL HAPPENED TO HIM?
AND IS THAT WHAT HAPPENED TO MY BROTHER?
KRRRRREAK
AND IS THAT THE SOUND OF THE GRATE BREAK--
CRASH
--ING?!

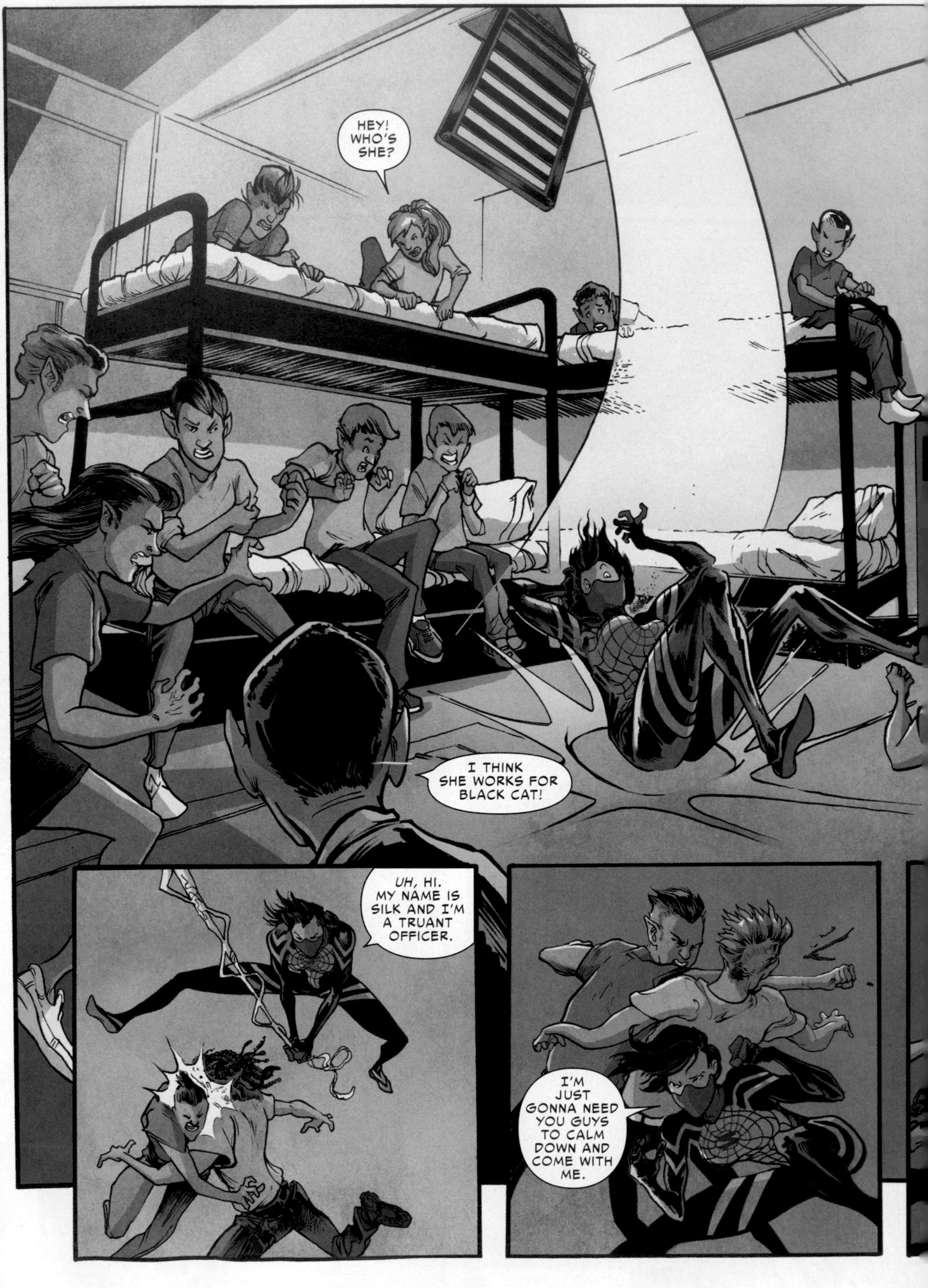
HEY! WHO'S SHE?
I THINK SHE WORKS FOR BLACK CAT!
UH, HI. MY NAME IS SILK AND I'M A TRUANT OFFICER.
I'M JUST GONNA NEED YOU GUYS TO CALM DOWN AND COME WITH ME.

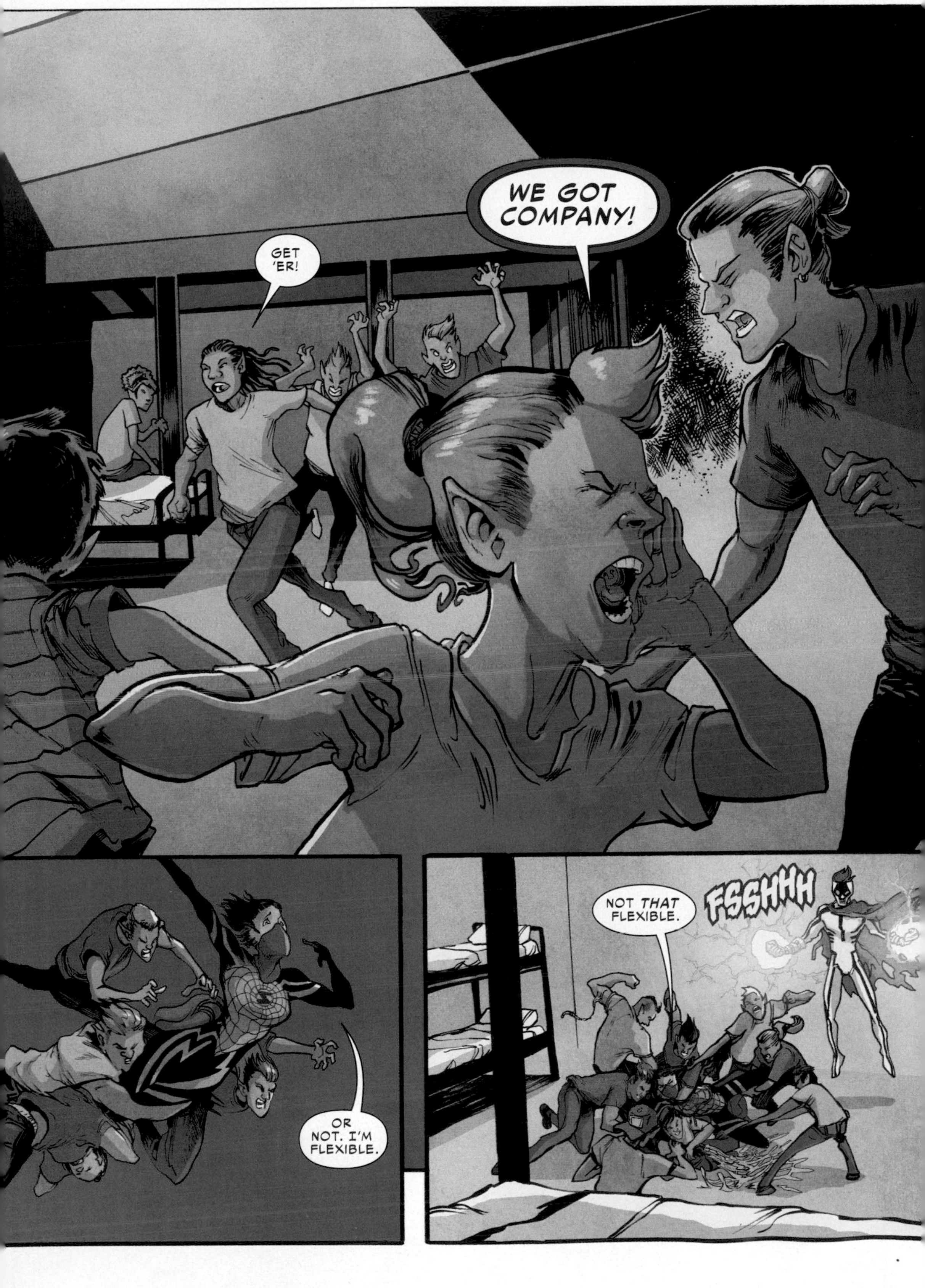
GET 'ER!
WE GOT COMPANY!
OR NOT. I'M FLEXIBLE.
NOT THAT FLEXIBLE.
FSSHHH

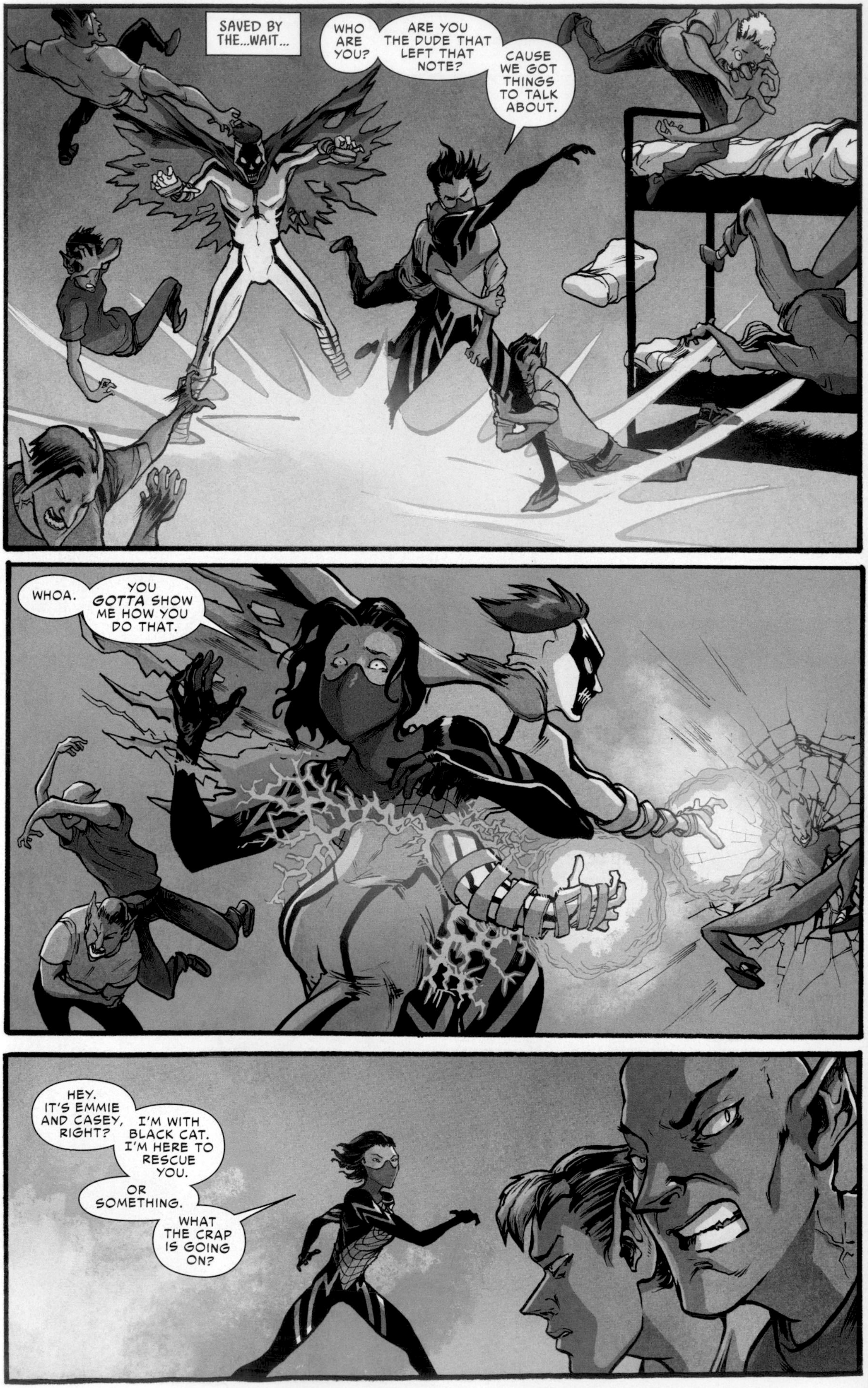
SAVED BY THE...WAIT...
WHO ARE YOU?
ARE YOU THE DUDE THAT LEFT THAT NOTE?
CAUSE WE GOT THINGS TO TALK ABOUT.
WHOA.
YOU GOTTA SHOW ME HOW YOU DO THAT.
HEY. IT'S EMMIE AND CASEY, RIGHT?
I'M WITH BLACK CAT. I'M HERE TO RESCUE YOU.
OR SOMETHING.
WHAT THE CRAP IS GOING ON?

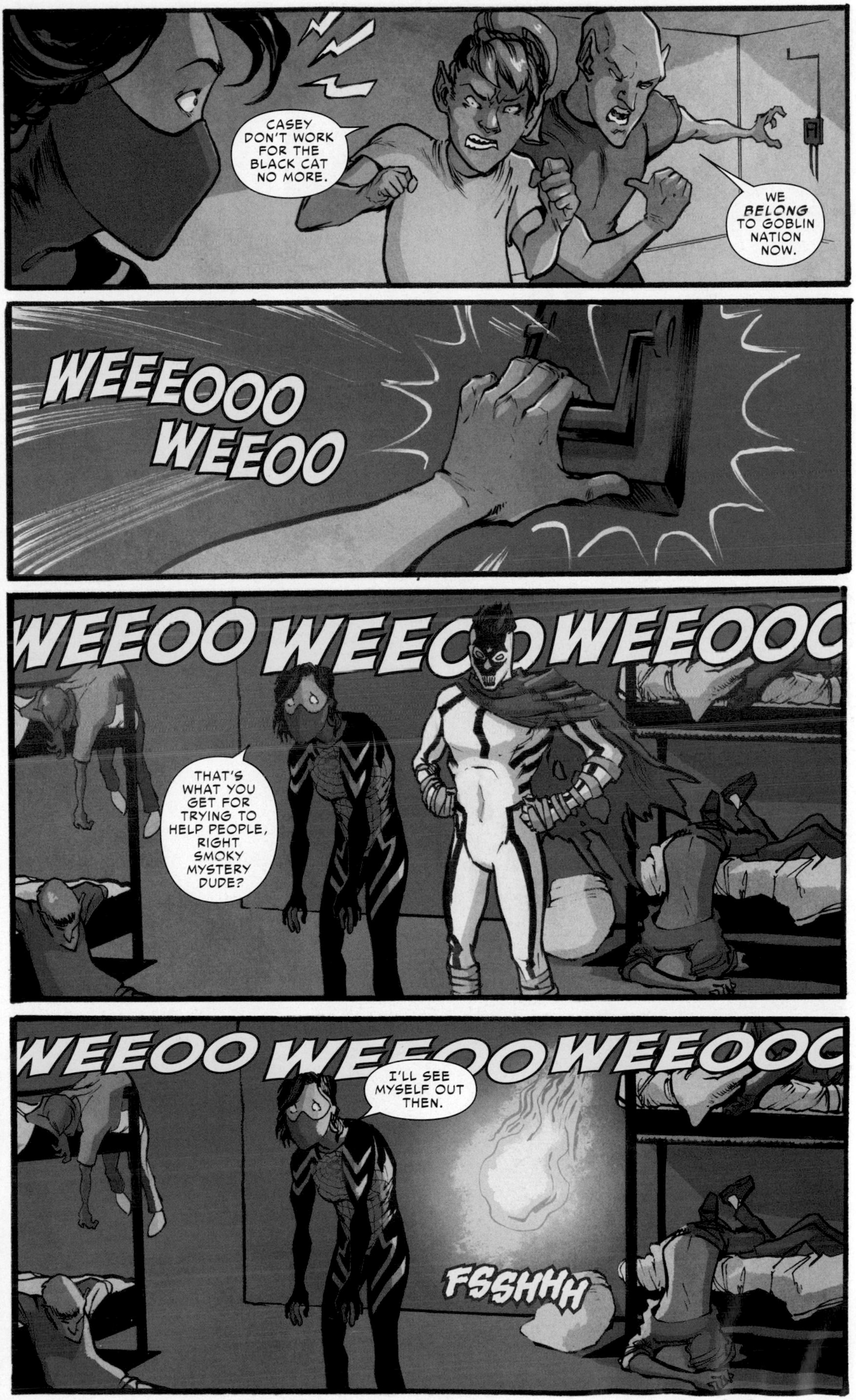
CASEY DON'T WORK FOR THE BLACK CAT NO MORE.
WE *BELONG* TO GOBLIN NATION NOW.
WEEEOOO WEEOO
WEEOO WEEOO WEEOOO
THAT'S WHAT YOU GET FOR TRYING TO HELP PEOPLE, RIGHT SMOKY MYSTERY DUDE?
WEEOO WEEOO WEEOOO
I'LL SEE MYSELF OUT THEN.
FSSHHH

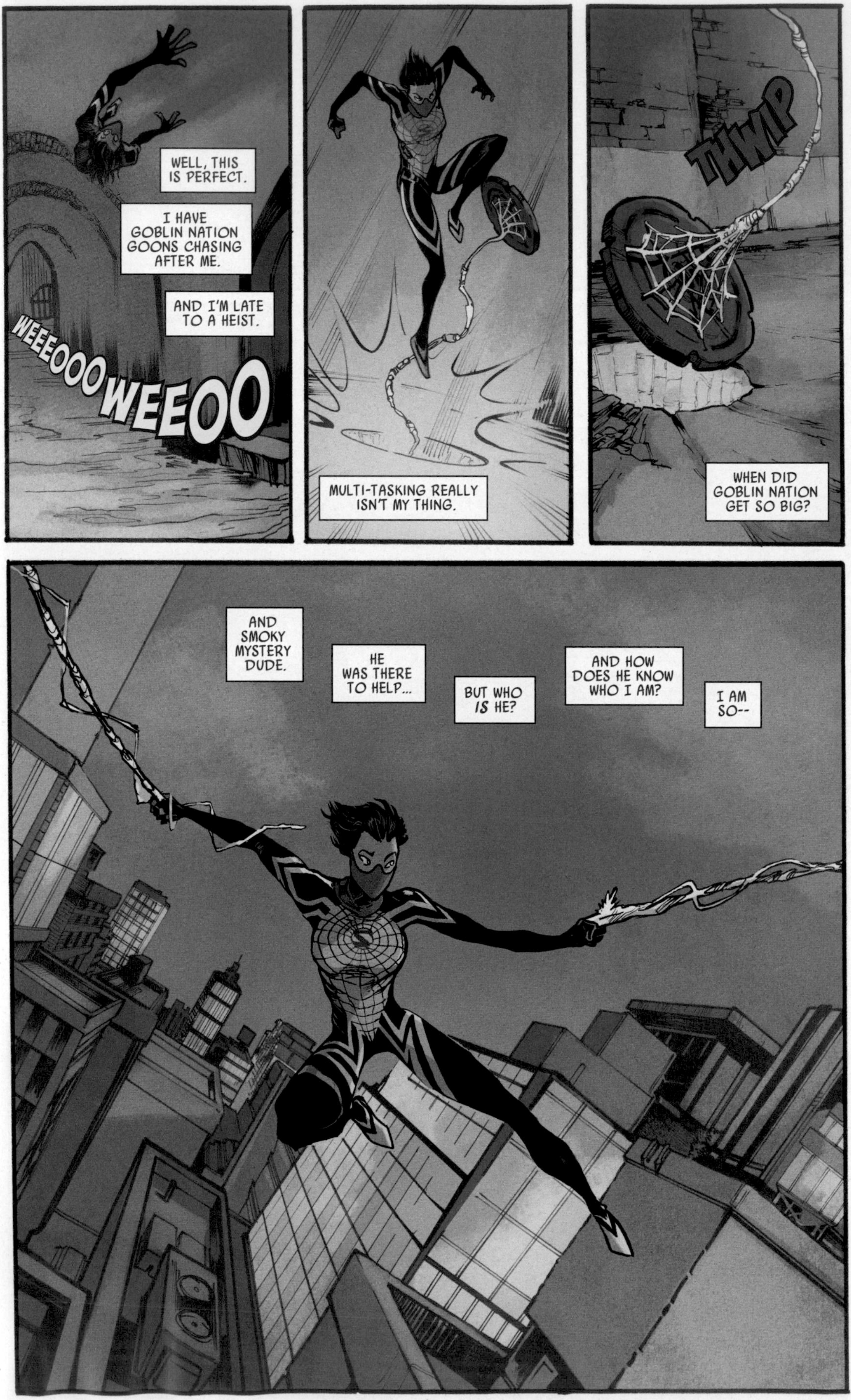
WELL, THIS IS PERFECT.
I HAVE GOBLIN NATION GOONS CHASING AFTER ME.
AND I'M LATE TO A HEIST.
WEEEOOOWEEOO
MULTI-TASKING REALLY ISN'T MY THING.
THWIP
WHEN DID GOBLIN NATION GET SO BIG?
AND SMOKY MYSTERY DUDE.
HE WAS THERE TO HELP...
BUT WHO *IS* HE?
AND HOW DOES HE KNOW WHO I AM?
I AM SO--

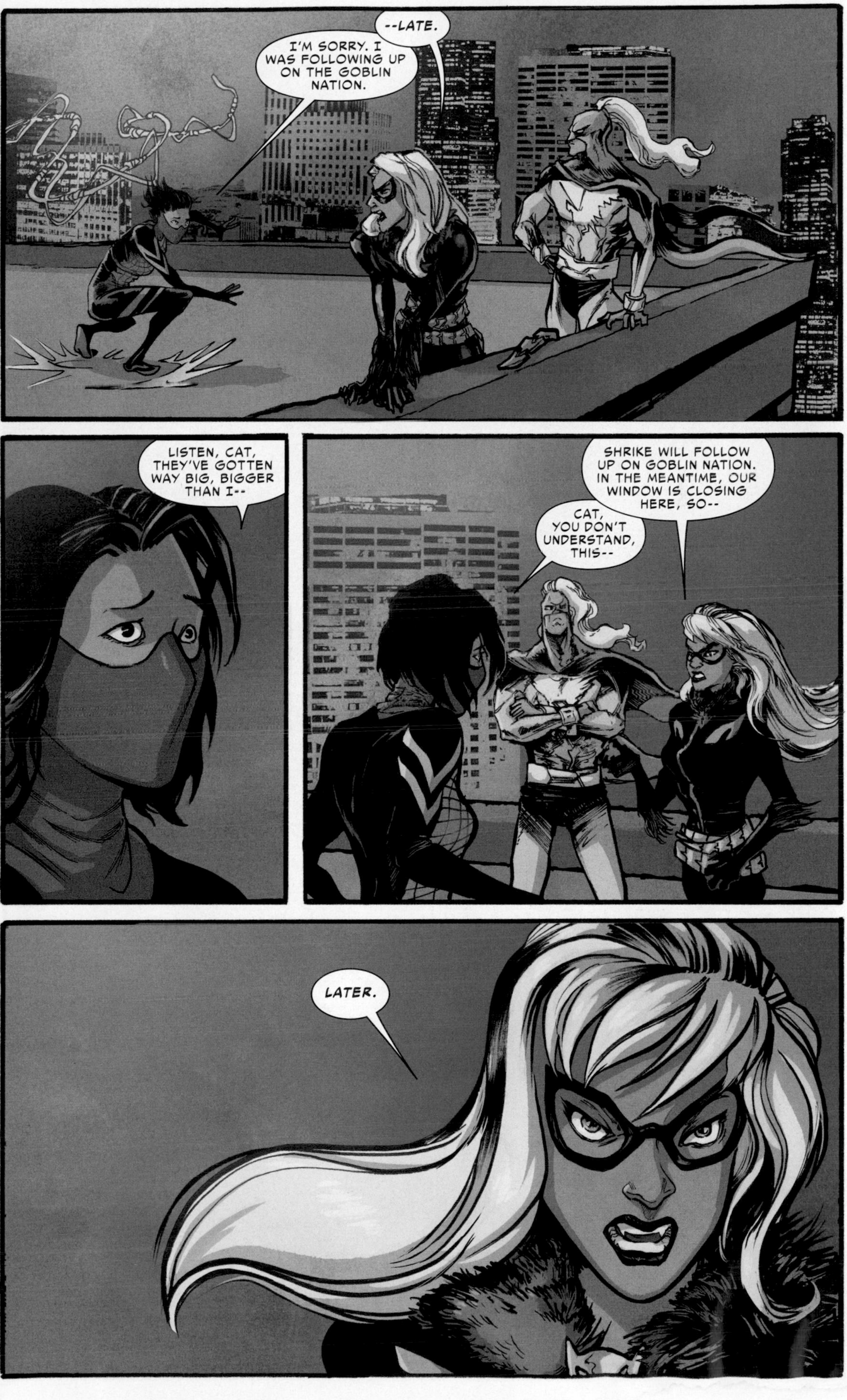

I'M SORRY. I WAS FOLLOWING UP ON THE GOBLIN NATION.
--LATE.
LISTEN, CAT, THEY'VE GOTTEN WAY BIG, BIGGER THAN I--
CAT, YOU DON'T UNDERSTAND, THIS--
SHRIKE WILL FOLLOW UP ON GOBLIN NATION. IN THE MEANTIME, OUR WINDOW IS CLOSING HERE, SO--
LATER.

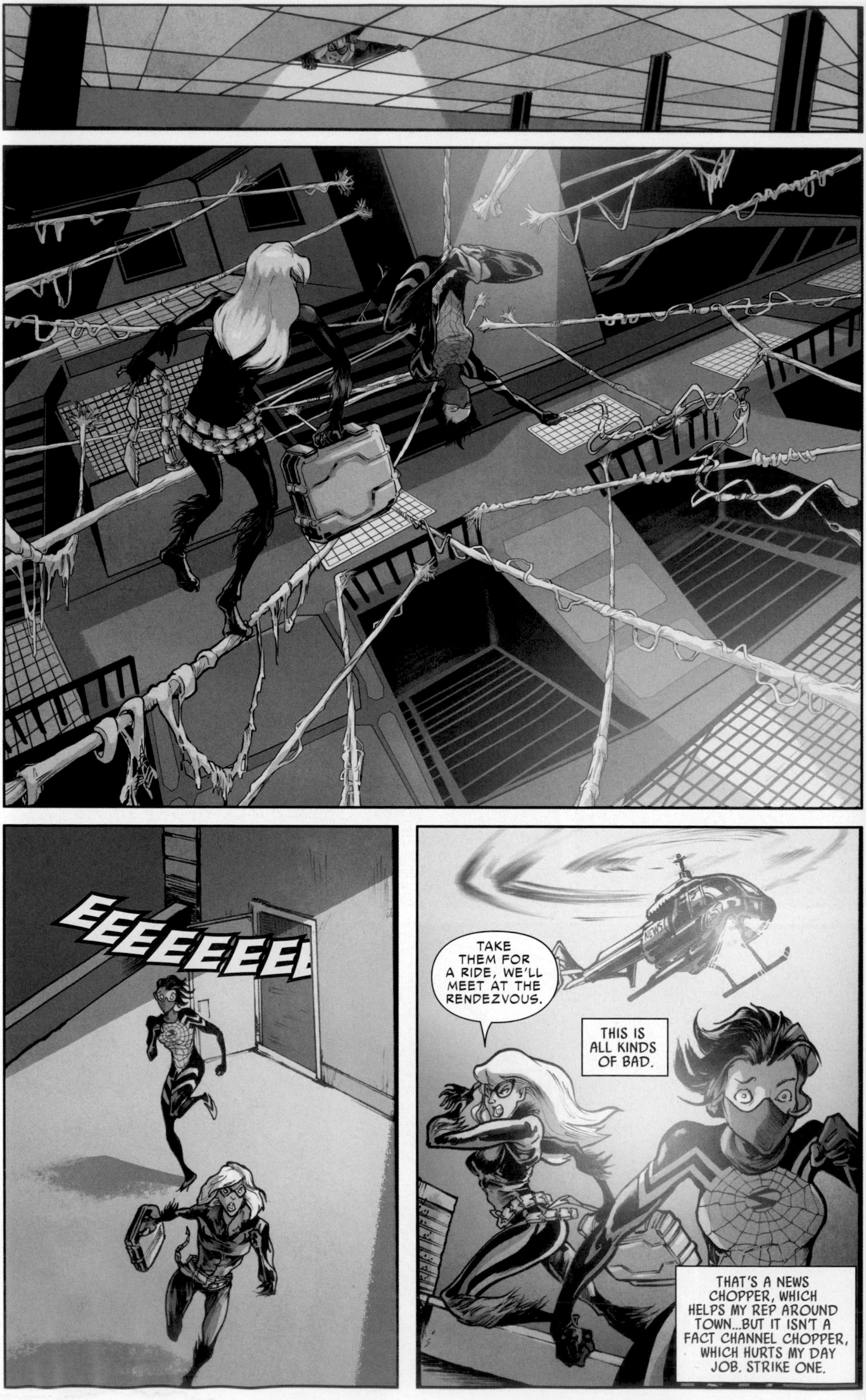
EEEEEEEEE
TAKE THEM FOR A RIDE, WE'LL MEET AT THE RENDEZVOUS.
THIS IS ALL KINDS OF BAD.
THAT'S A NEWS CHOPPER, WHICH HELPS MY REP AROUND TOWN...BUT IT ISN'T A FACT CHANNEL CHOPPER, WHICH HURTS MY DAY JOB. STRIKE ONE.

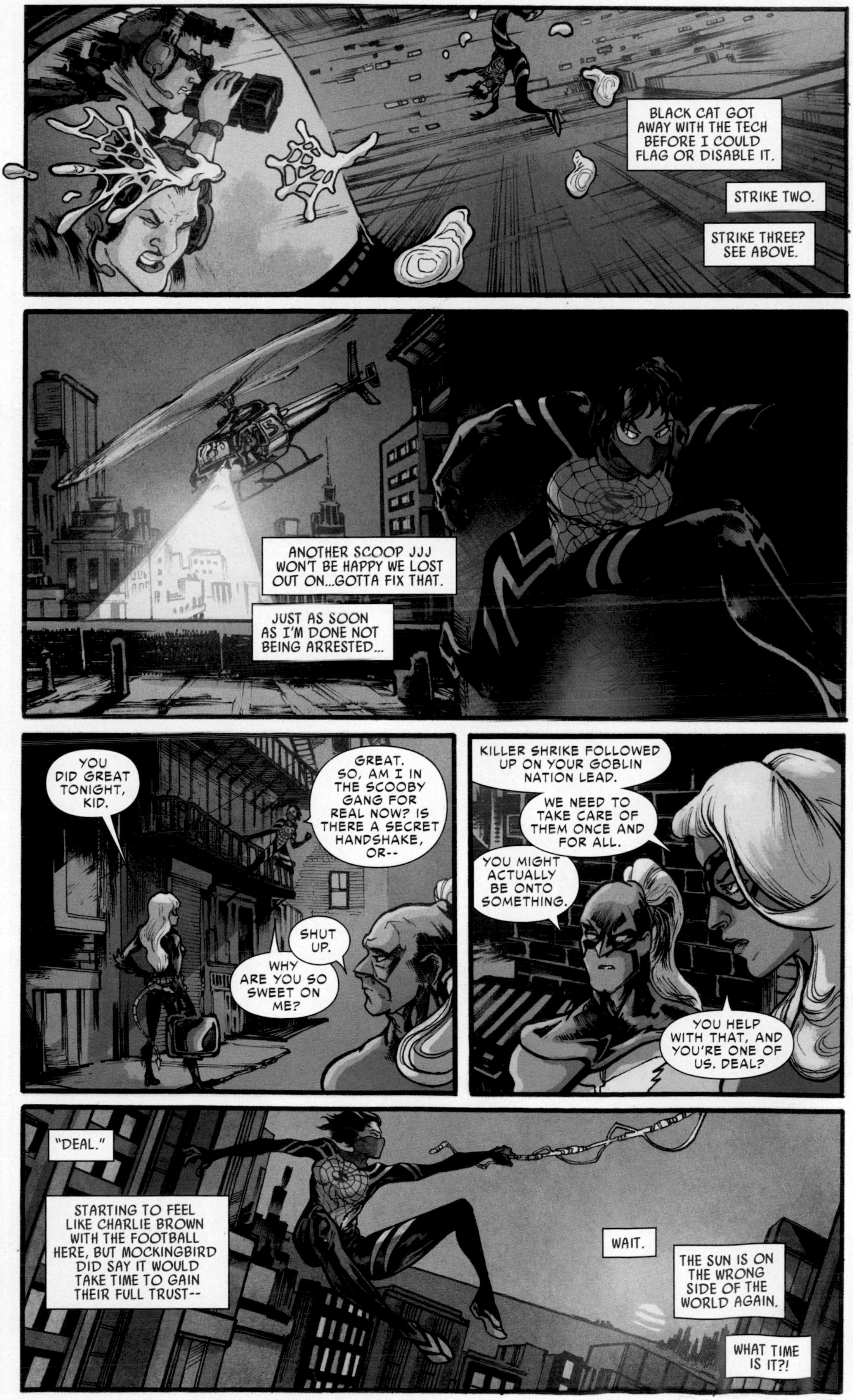
BLACK CAT GOT AWAY WITH THE TECH BEFORE I COULD FLAG OR DISABLE IT.
STRIKE TWO.
STRIKE THREE? SEE ABOVE.
ANOTHER SCOOP JJJ WON'T BE HAPPY WE LOST OUT ON...GOTTA FIX THAT.
JUST AS SOON AS I'M DONE NOT BEING ARRESTED...
YOU DID GREAT TONIGHT, KID.
GREAT. SO, AM I IN THE SCOOBY GANG FOR REAL NOW? IS THERE A SECRET HANDSHAKE, OR--
SHUT UP.
WHY ARE YOU SO SWEET ON ME?
KILLER SHRIKE FOLLOWED UP ON YOUR GOBLIN NATION LEAD.
WE NEED TO TAKE CARE OF THEM ONCE AND FOR ALL.
YOU MIGHT ACTUALLY BE ONTO SOMETHING.
YOU HELP WITH THAT, AND YOU'RE ONE OF US. DEAL?
"DEAL."
STARTING TO FEEL LIKE CHARLIE BROWN WITH THE FOOTBALL HERE, BUT MOCKINGBIRD DID SAY IT WOULD TAKE TIME TO GAIN THEIR FULL TRUST--
WAIT.
THE SUN IS ON THE WRONG SIDE OF THE WORLD AGAIN.
WHAT TIME IS IT?!

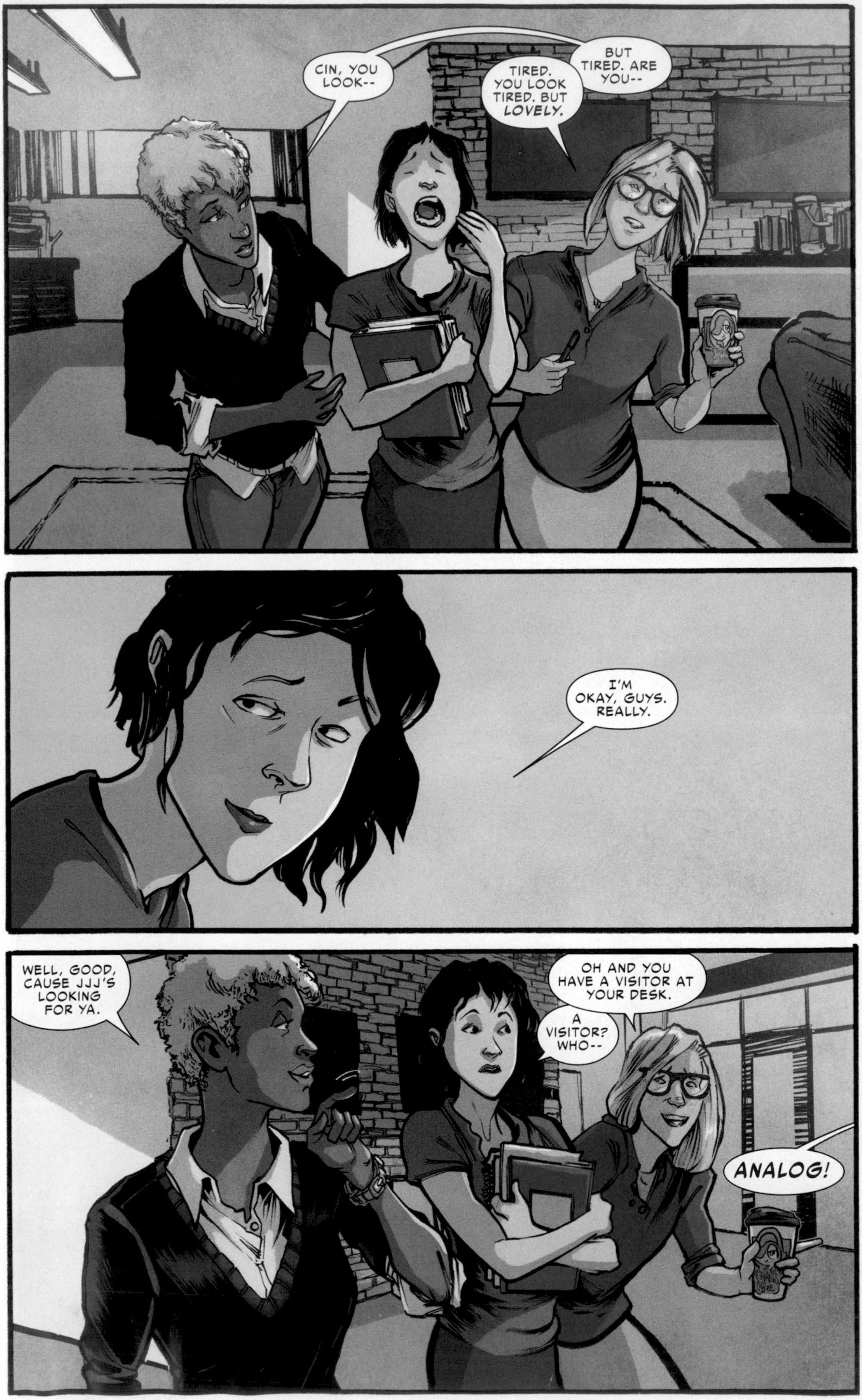
CIN, YOU LOOK--
TIRED. YOU LOOK TIRED. BUT *LOVELY.*
BUT TIRED. ARE YOU--
I'M OKAY, GUYS. REALLY.
WELL, GOOD, CAUSE JJJ'S LOOKING FOR YA.
OH AND YOU HAVE A VISITOR AT YOUR DESK.
A VISITOR? WHO--
ANALOG!

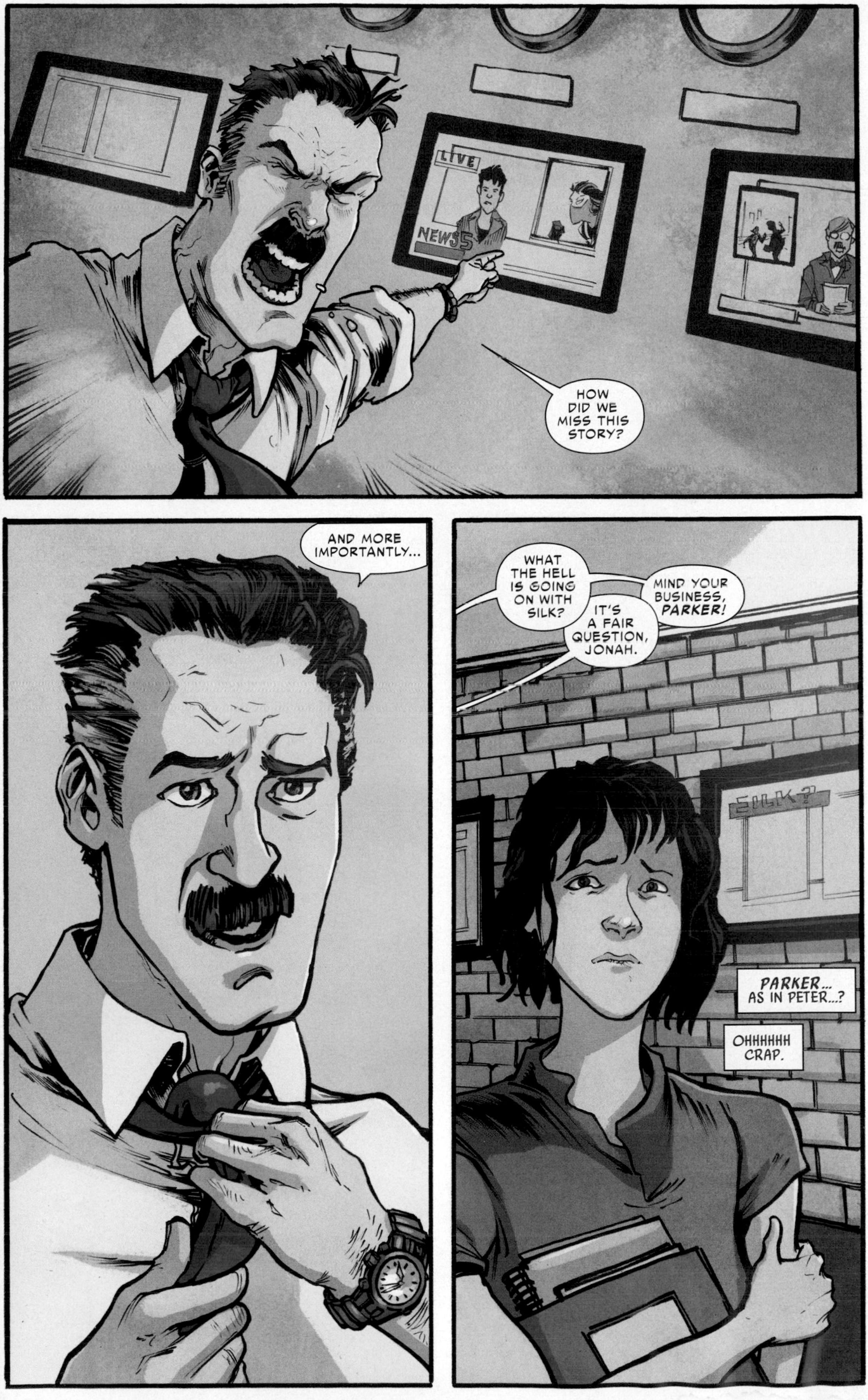
LIVE
NEWS5
HOW DID WE MISS THIS STORY?
AND MORE IMPORTANTLY...
WHAT THE HELL IS GOING ON WITH SILK?
MIND YOUR BUSINESS, PARKER!
IT'S A FAIR QUESTION, JONAH.
SILK?
PARKER... AS IN PETER...?
OHHHHHH CRAP.

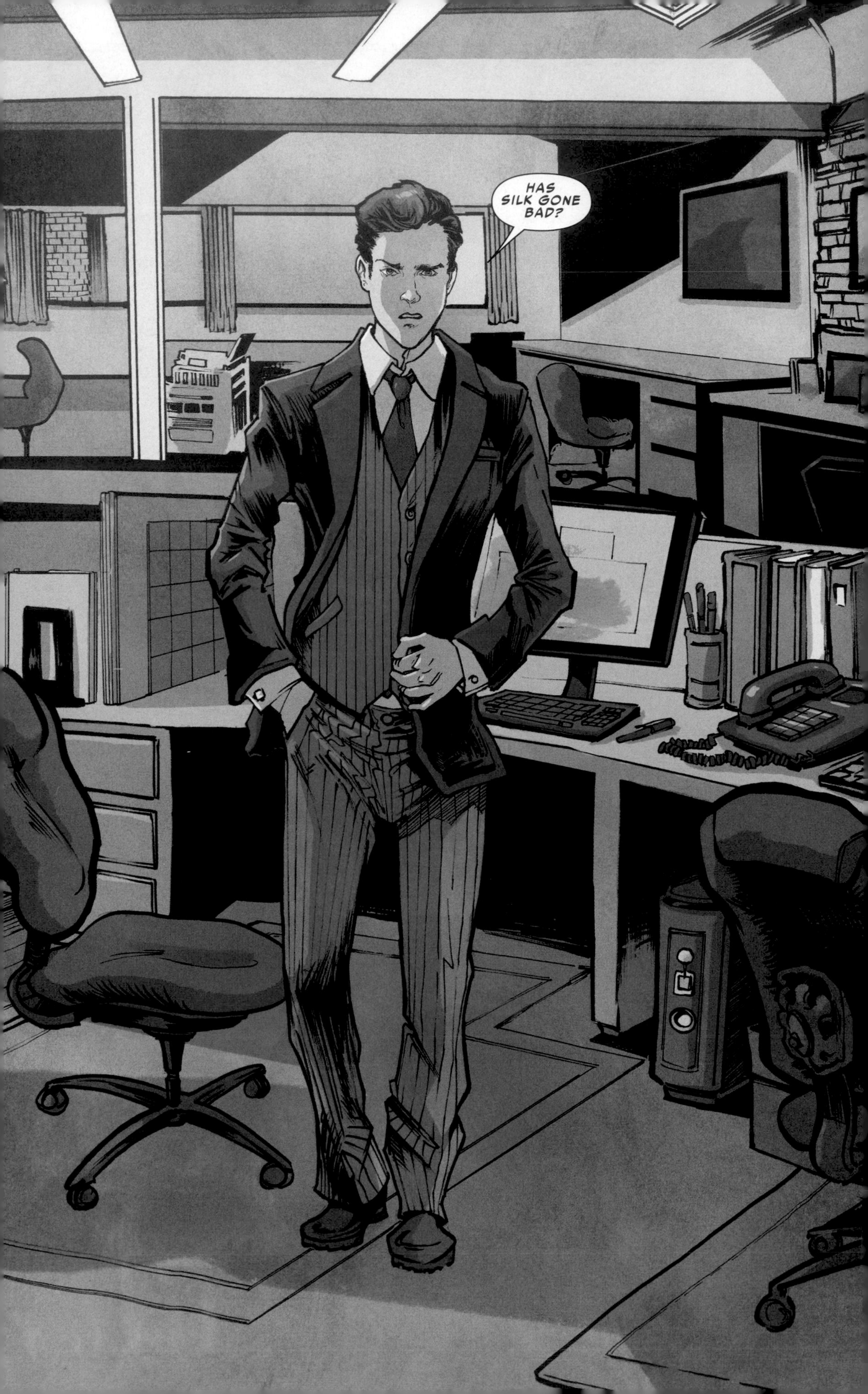
HAS SILK GONE BAD?

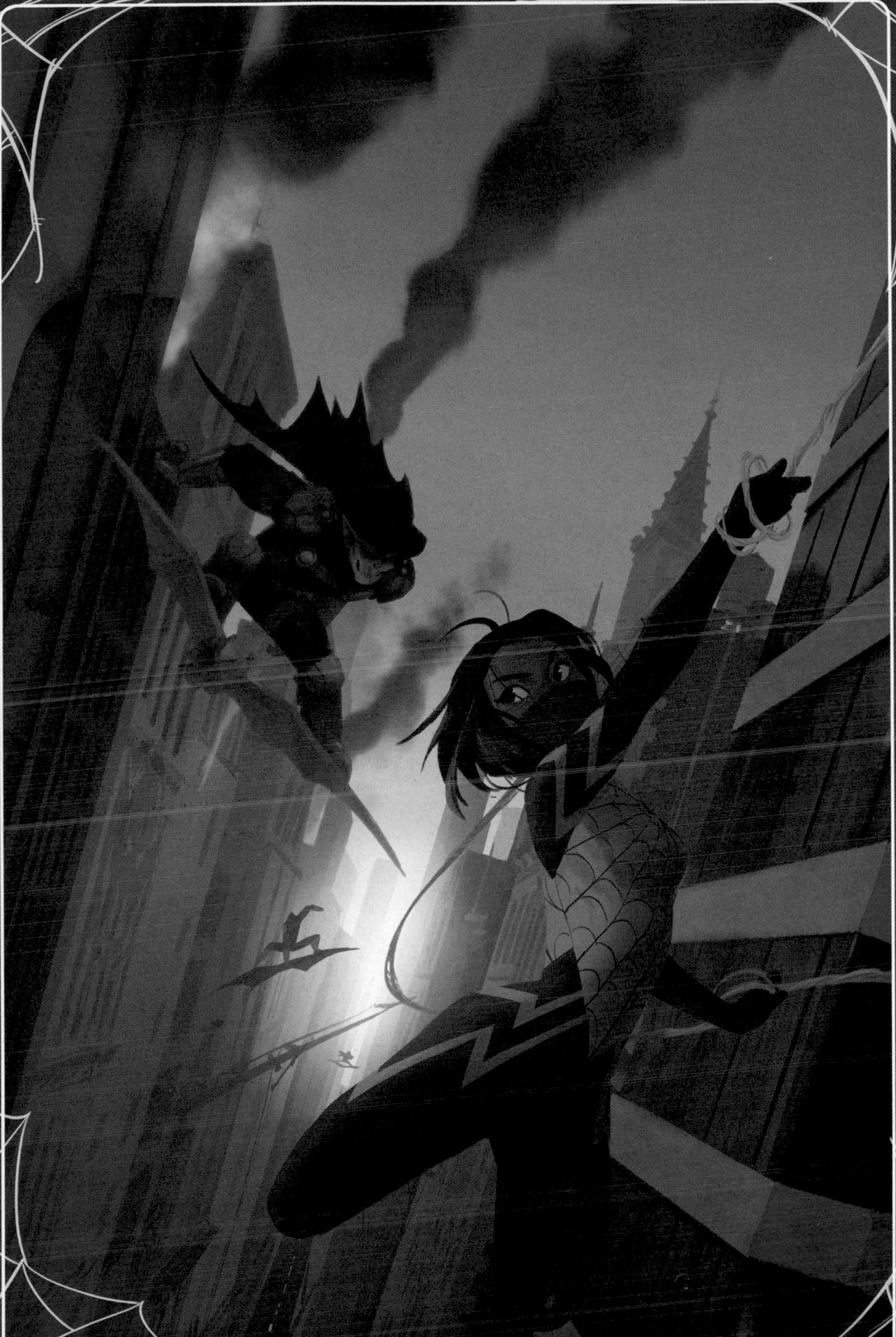

3

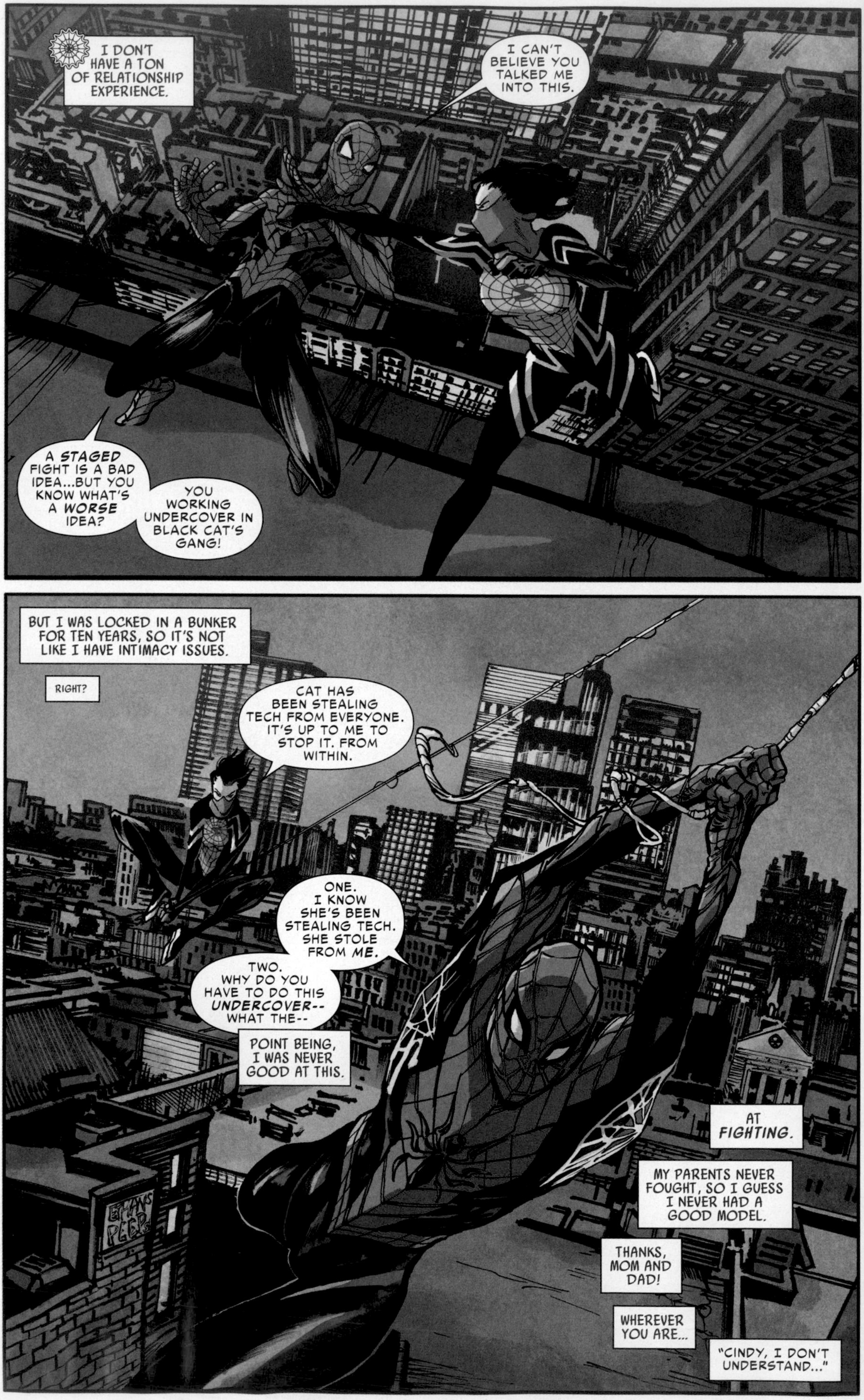
I DON'T HAVE A TON OF RELATIONSHIP EXPERIENCE.
I CAN'T BELIEVE YOU TALKED ME INTO THIS.
A STAGED FIGHT IS A BAD IDEA...BUT YOU KNOW WHAT'S A WORSE IDEA?
YOU WORKING UNDERCOVER IN BLACK CAT'S GANG!
BUT I WAS LOCKED IN A BUNKER FOR TEN YEARS, SO IT'S NOT LIKE I HAVE INTIMACY ISSUES.
RIGHT?
CAT HAS BEEN STEALING TECH FROM EVERYONE. IT'S UP TO ME TO STOP IT. FROM WITHIN.
ONE. I KNOW SHE'S BEEN STEALING TECH. SHE STOLE FROM ME.
TWO. WHY DO YOU HAVE TO DO THIS UNDERCOVER-- WHAT THE--
POINT BEING, I WAS NEVER GOOD AT THIS.
AT FIGHTING.
MY PARENTS NEVER FOUGHT, SO I GUESS I NEVER HAD A GOOD MODEL.
THANKS, MOM AND DAD!
WHEREVER YOU ARE...
"CINDY, I DON'T UNDERSTAND..."

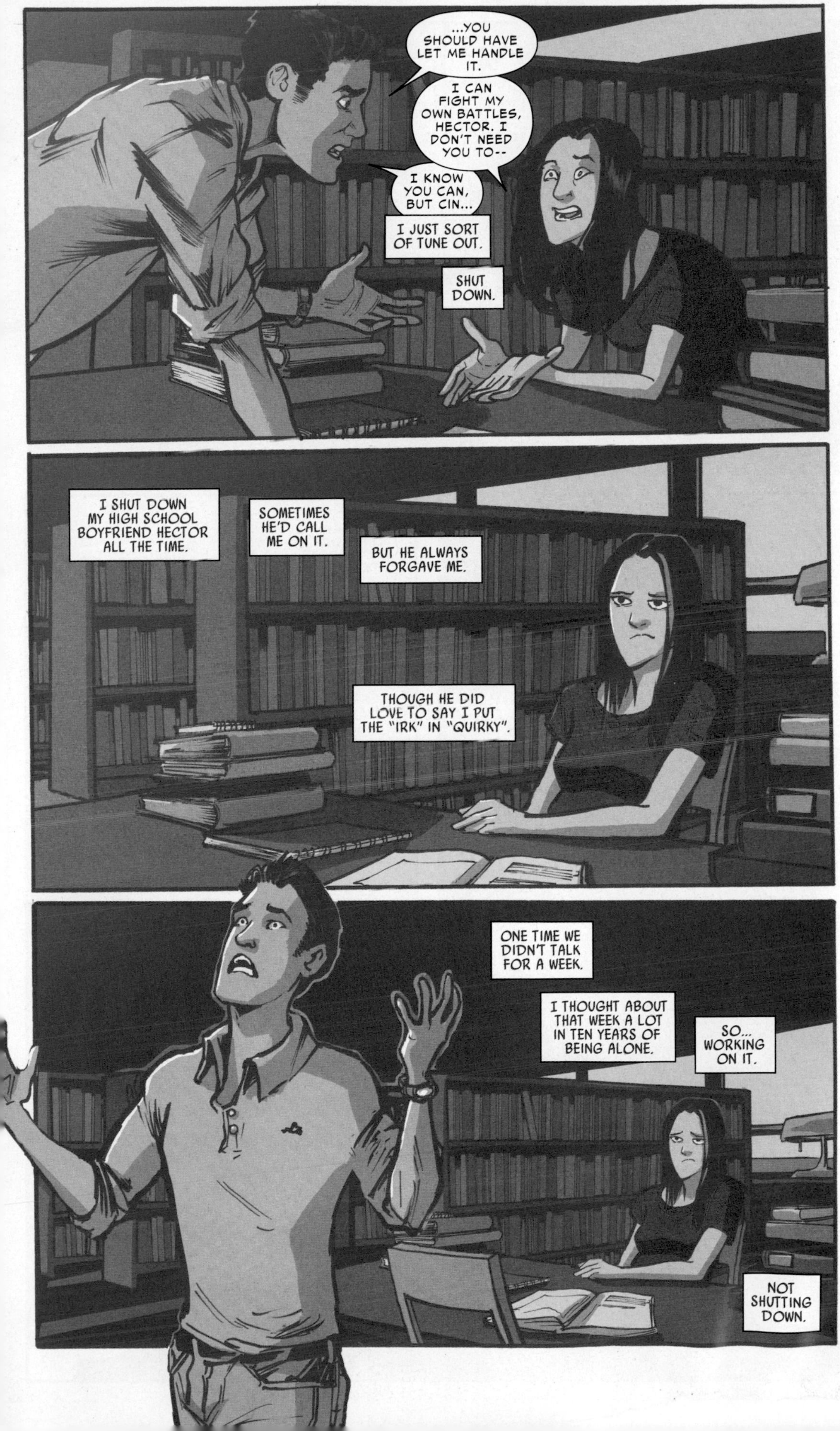
...YOU SHOULD HAVE LET ME HANDLE IT.
I CAN FIGHT MY OWN BATTLES, HECTOR. I DON'T NEED YOU TO--
I KNOW YOU CAN, BUT CIN...
I JUST SORT OF TUNE OUT.
SHUT DOWN.
I SHUT DOWN MY HIGH SCHOOL BOYFRIEND HECTOR ALL THE TIME.
SOMETIMES HE'D CALL ME ON IT.
BUT HE ALWAYS FORGAVE ME.
THOUGH HE DID LOVE TO SAY I PUT THE "IRK" IN "QUIRKY".
ONE TIME WE DIDN'T TALK FOR A WEEK.
I THOUGHT ABOUT THAT WEEK A LOT IN TEN YEARS OF BEING ALONE.
SO... WORKING ON IT.
NOT SHUTTING DOWN.

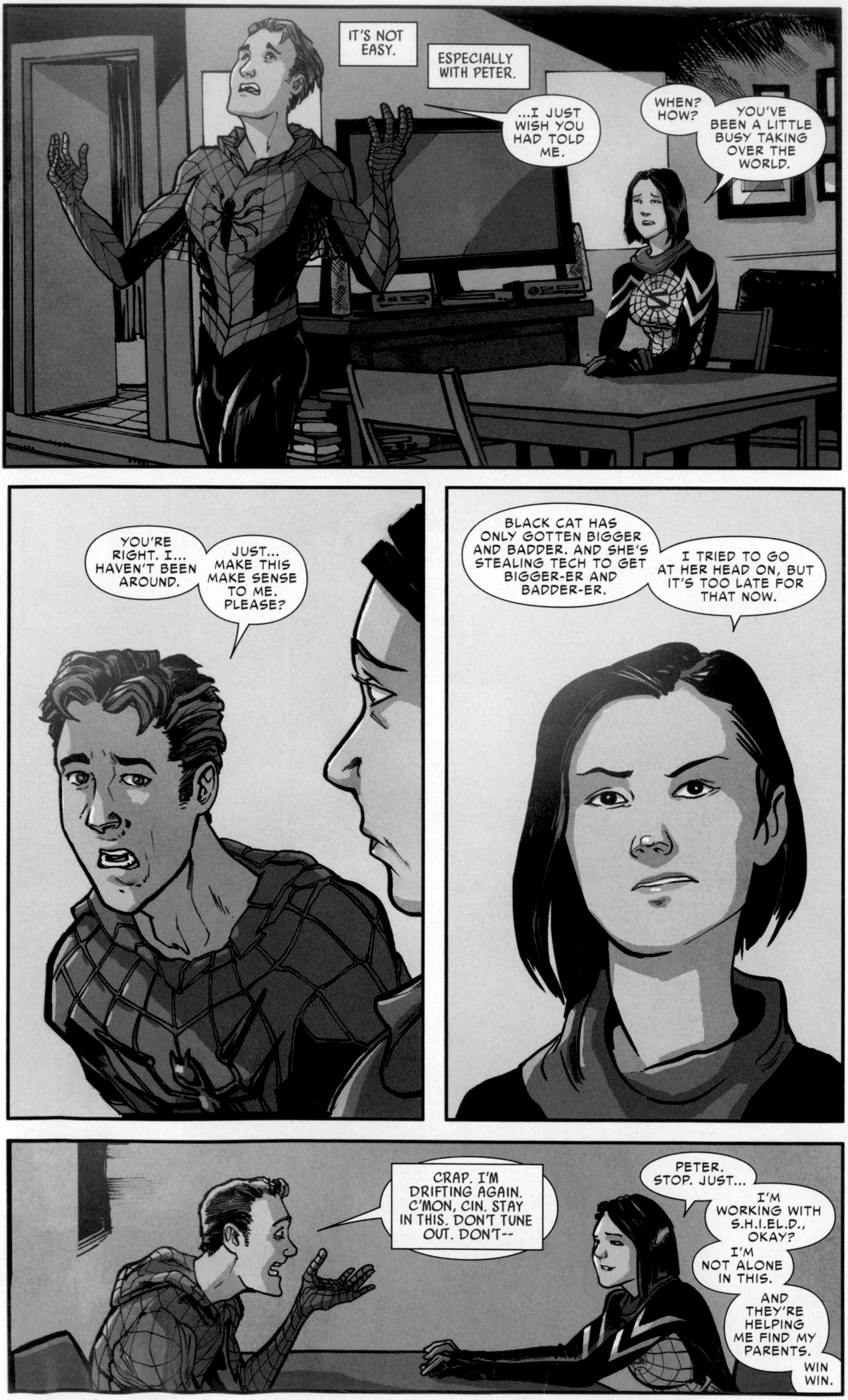
IT'S NOT EASY.
ESPECIALLY WITH PETER.
...I JUST WISH YOU HAD TOLD ME.
WHEN? HOW?
YOU'VE BEEN A LITTLE BUSY TAKING OVER THE WORLD.
YOU'RE RIGHT. I... HAVEN'T BEEN AROUND.
JUST... MAKE THIS MAKE SENSE TO ME. PLEASE?
BLACK CAT HAS ONLY GOTTEN BIGGER AND BADDER. AND SHE'S STEALING TECH TO GET BIGGER-ER AND BADDER-ER.
I TRIED TO GO AT HER HEAD ON, BUT IT'S TOO LATE FOR THAT NOW.
CRAP. I'M DRIFTING AGAIN. C'MON, CIN. STAY IN THIS. DON'T TUNE OUT. DON'T--
PETER. STOP. JUST...
I'M WORKING WITH S.H.I.E.L.D., OKAY?
I'M NOT ALONE IN THIS.
AND THEY'RE HELPING ME FIND MY PARENTS.
WIN WIN.

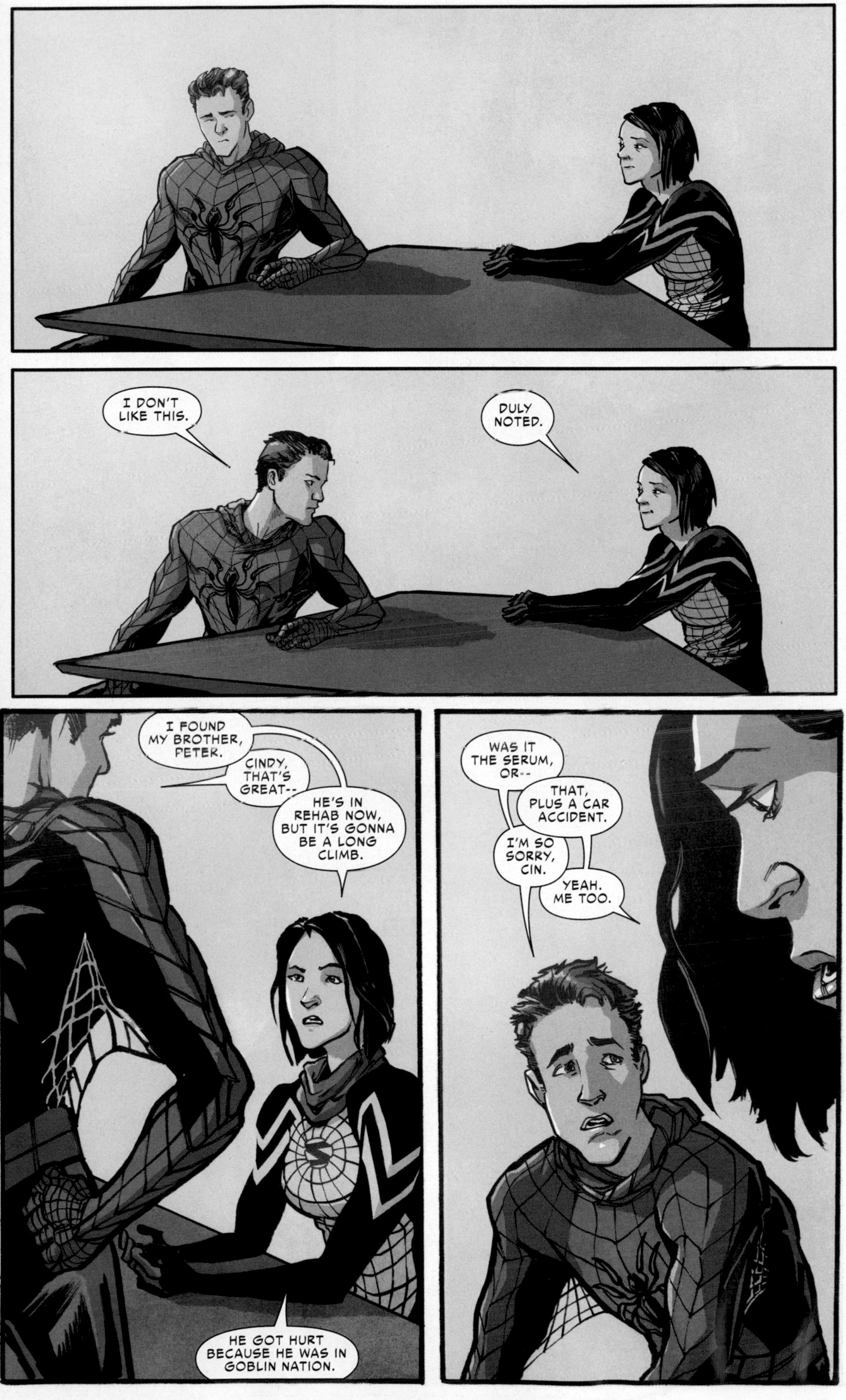
I DON'T LIKE THIS.
DULY NOTED.
I FOUND MY BROTHER, PETER.
CINDY, THAT'S GREAT--
HE'S IN REHAB NOW, BUT IT'S GONNA BE A LONG CLIMB.
HE GOT HURT BECAUSE HE WAS IN GOBLIN NATION.
WAS IT THE SERUM, OR--
THAT, PLUS A CAR ACCIDENT.
I'M SO SORRY, CIN.
YEAH. ME TOO.

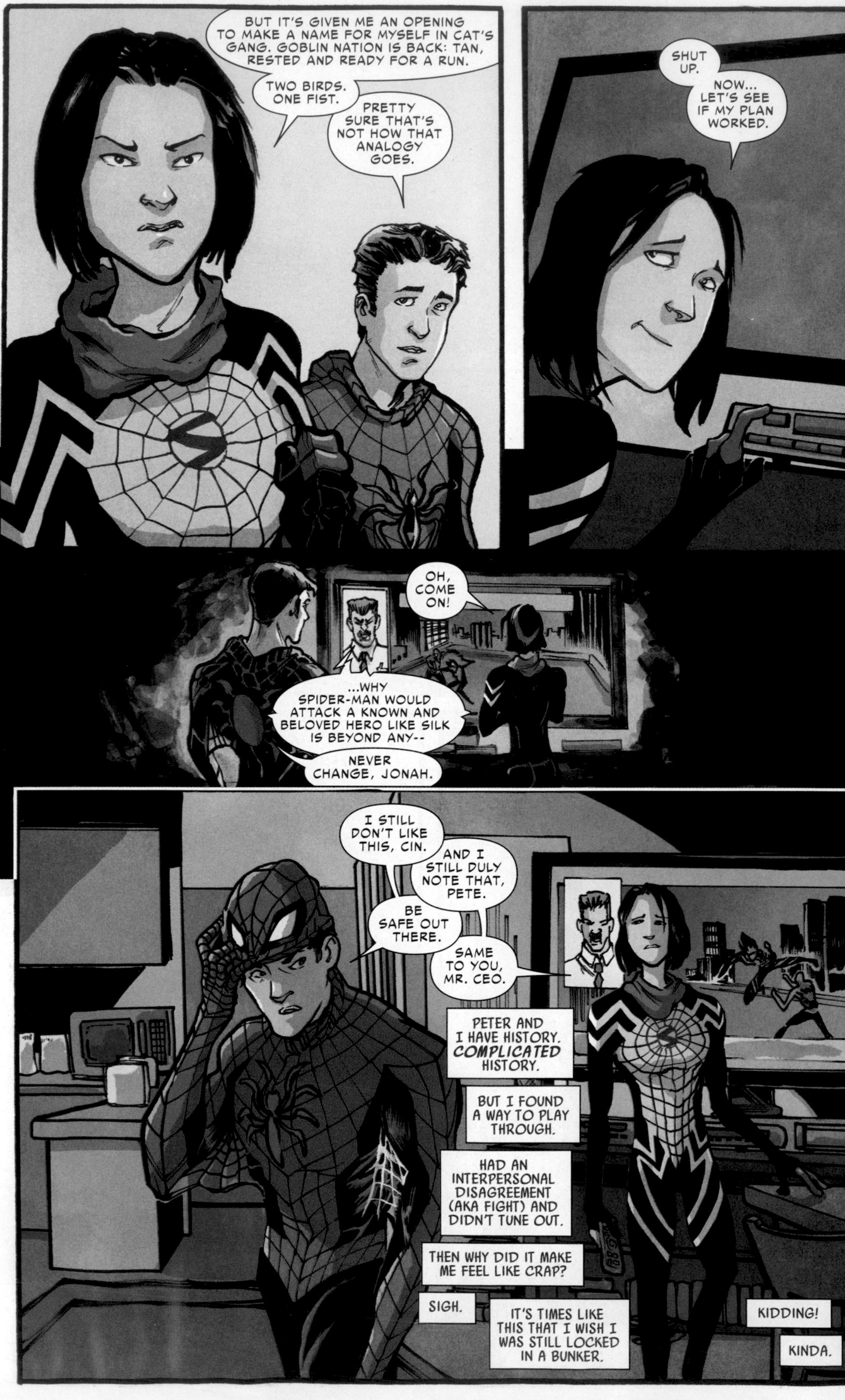
BUT IT'S GIVEN ME AN OPENING TO MAKE A NAME FOR MYSELF IN CAT'S GANG. GOBLIN NATION IS BACK: TAN, RESTED AND READY FOR A RUN.
TWO BIRDS. ONE FIST.
PRETTY SURE THAT'S NOT HOW THAT ANALOGY GOES.
SHUT UP.
NOW... LET'S SEE IF MY PLAN WORKED.
OH, COME ON!
...WHY SPIDER-MAN WOULD ATTACK A KNOWN AND BELOVED HERO LIKE SILK IS BEYOND ANY--
NEVER CHANGE, JONAH.
I STILL DON'T LIKE THIS, CIN.
AND I STILL DULY NOTE THAT, PETE.
BE SAFE OUT THERE.
SAME TO YOU, MR. CEO.
PETER AND I HAVE HISTORY. *COMPLICATED* HISTORY.
BUT I FOUND A WAY TO PLAY THROUGH.
HAD AN INTERPERSONAL DISAGREEMENT (AKA FIGHT) AND DIDN'T TUNE OUT.
THEN WHY DID IT MAKE ME FEEL LIKE CRAP?
SIGH.
IT'S TIMES LIKE THIS THAT I WISH I WAS STILL LOCKED IN A BUNKER.
KIDDING!
KINDA.

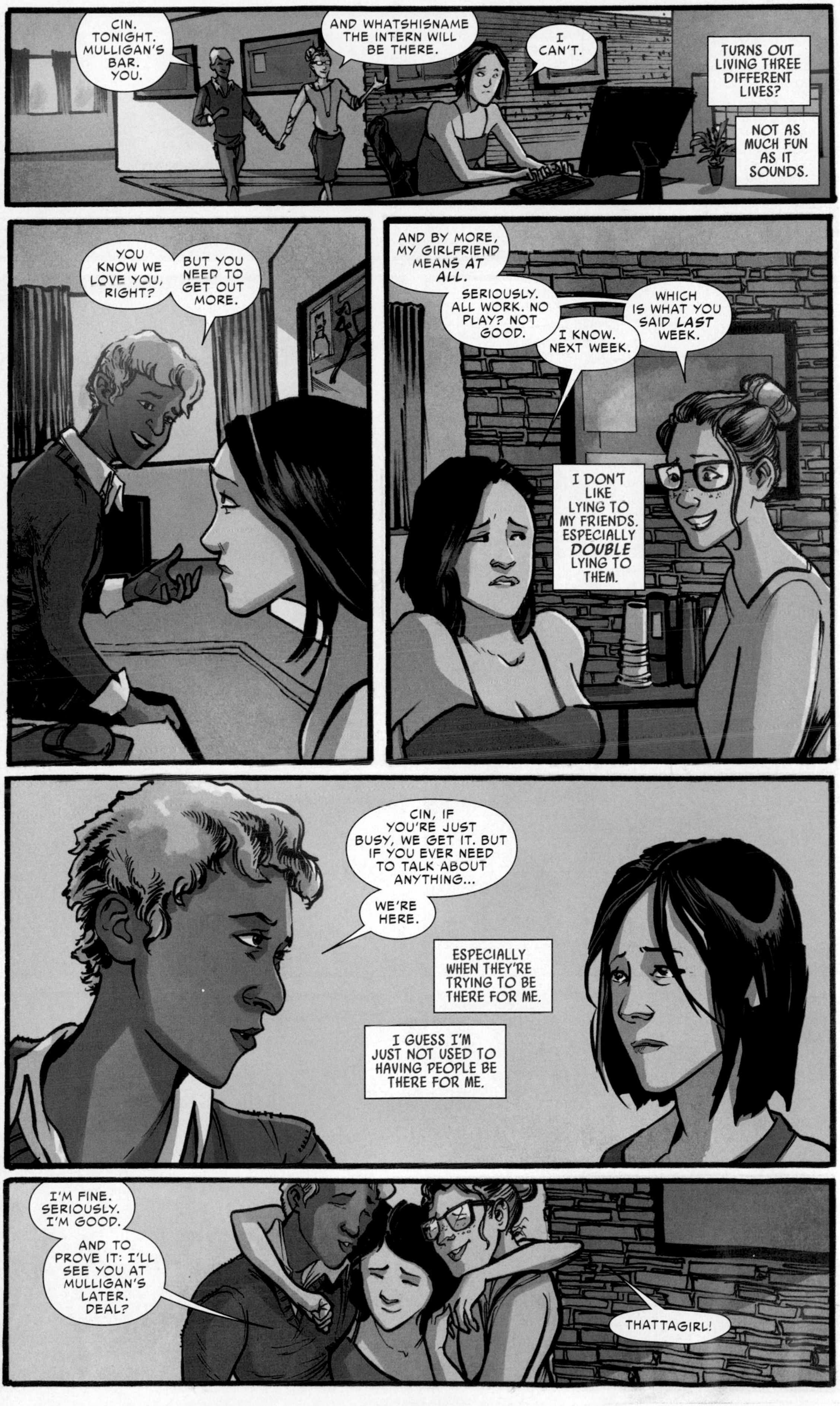
CIN. TONIGHT. MULLIGAN'S BAR. YOU.
AND WHATSHISNAME THE INTERN WILL BE THERE.
I CAN'T.
TURNS OUT LIVING THREE DIFFERENT LIVES?
NOT AS MUCH FUN AS IT SOUNDS.
YOU KNOW WE LOVE YOU, RIGHT?
BUT YOU NEED TO GET OUT MORE.
AND BY MORE, MY GIRLFRIEND MEANS AT ALL.
SERIOUSLY. ALL WORK. NO PLAY? NOT GOOD.
I KNOW. NEXT WEEK.
WHICH IS WHAT YOU SAID LAST WEEK.
I DON'T LIKE LYING TO MY FRIENDS. ESPECIALLY DOUBLE LYING TO THEM.
CIN, IF YOU'RE JUST BUSY, WE GET IT. BUT IF YOU EVER NEED TO TALK ABOUT ANYTHING...
WE'RE HERE.
ESPECIALLY WHEN THEY'RE TRYING TO BE THERE FOR ME.
I GUESS I'M JUST NOT USED TO HAVING PEOPLE BE THERE FOR ME.
I'M FINE. SERIOUSLY. I'M GOOD.
AND TO PROVE IT: I'LL SEE YOU AT MULLIGAN'S LATER. DEAL?
THATTAGIRL!

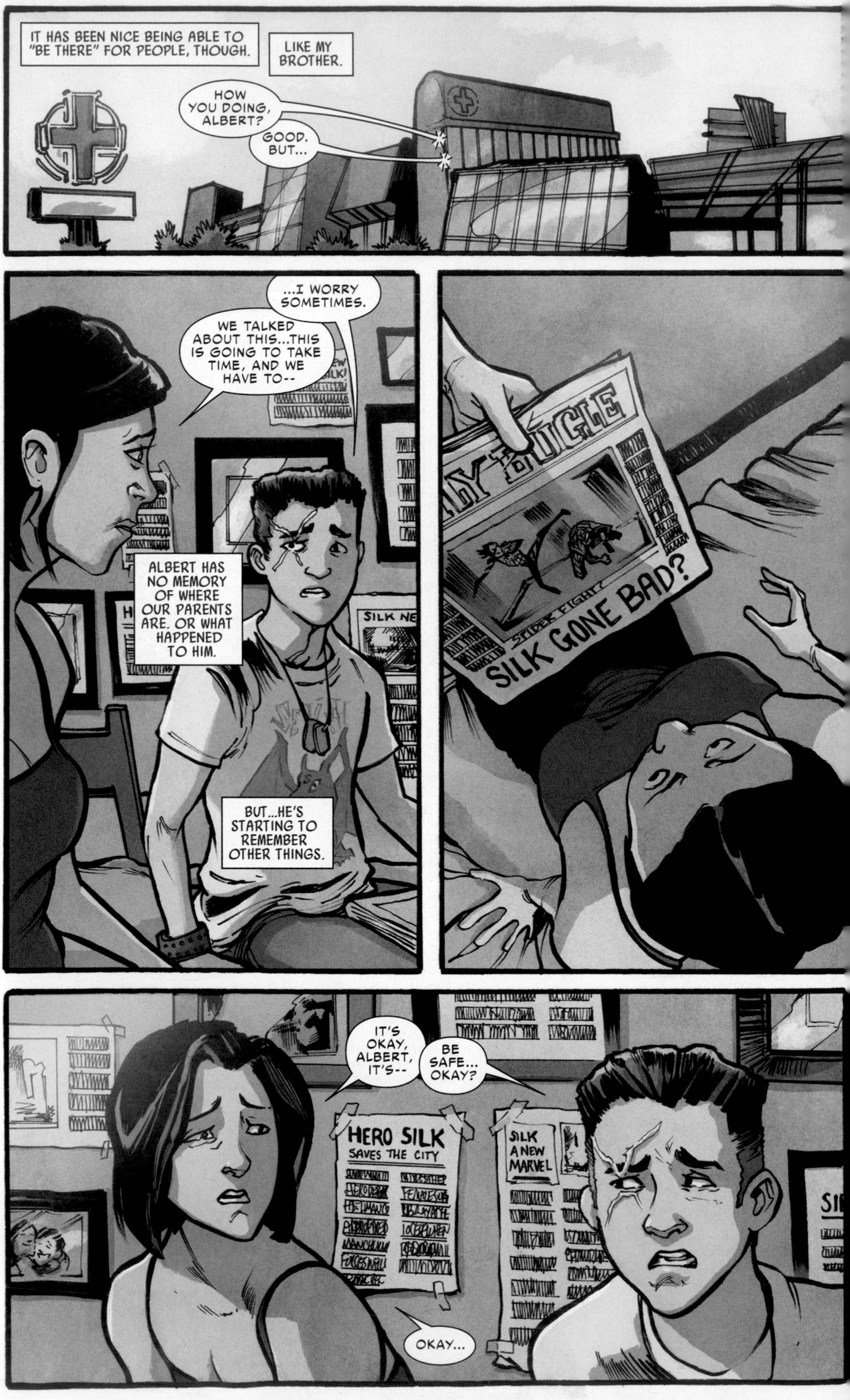

IT HAS BEEN NICE BEING ABLE TO "BE THERE" FOR PEOPLE, THOUGH.
LIKE MY BROTHER.
HOW YOU DOING, ALBERT?
GOOD. BUT...
...I WORRY SOMETIMES.
WE TALKED ABOUT THIS...THIS IS GOING TO TAKE TIME, AND WE HAVE TO--
ALBERT HAS NO MEMORY OF WHERE OUR PARENTS ARE. OR WHAT HAPPENED TO HIM.
BUT...HE'S STARTING TO REMEMBER OTHER THINGS.
SILK GONE BAD?
SPIDER FIGHT
IT'S OKAY, ALBERT, IT'S--
BE SAFE... OKAY?
HERO SILK
SAVES THE CITY
SILK A NEW MARVEL
OKAY...

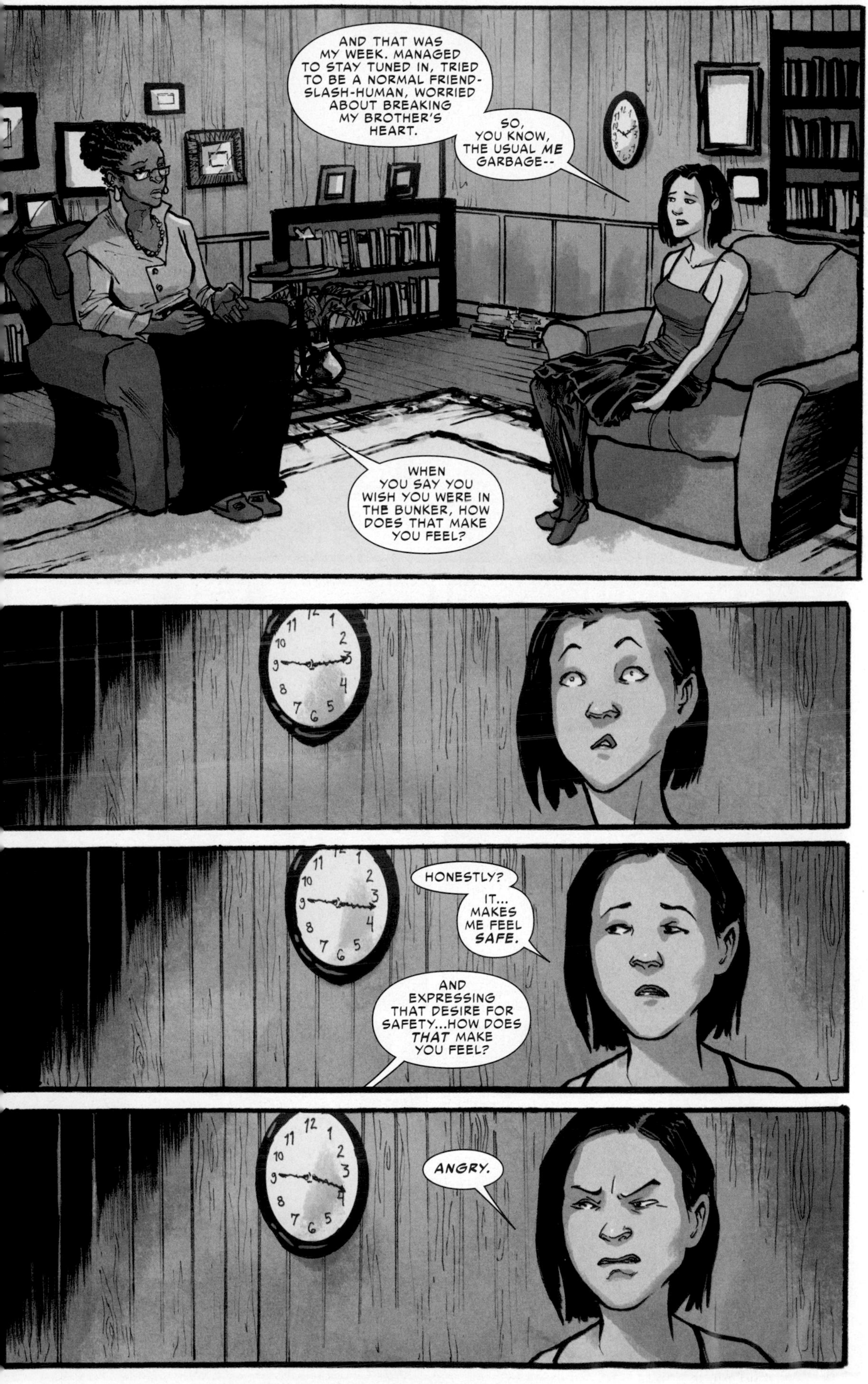
AND THAT WAS MY WEEK. MANAGED TO STAY TUNED IN, TRIED TO BE A NORMAL FRIEND-SLASH-HUMAN, WORRIED ABOUT BREAKING MY BROTHER'S HEART.
SO, YOU KNOW, THE USUAL *ME* GARBAGE--
WHEN YOU SAY YOU WISH YOU WERE IN THE BUNKER, HOW DOES THAT MAKE YOU FEEL?
HONESTLY?
IT... MAKES ME FEEL *SAFE.*
AND EXPRESSING THAT DESIRE FOR SAFETY...HOW DOES *THAT* MAKE YOU FEEL?
ANGRY.

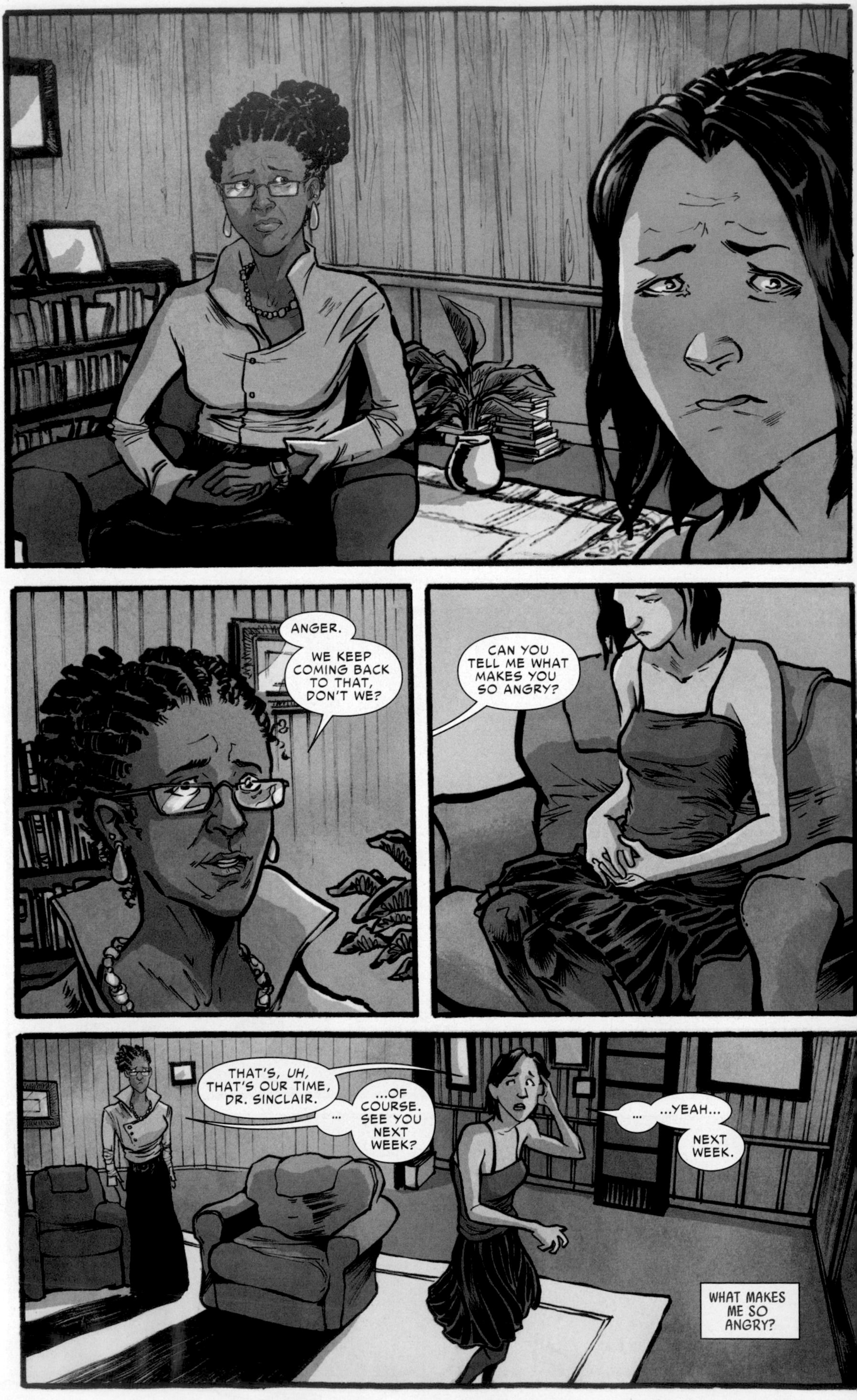
ANGER.
WE KEEP COMING BACK TO THAT, DON'T WE?
CAN YOU TELL ME WHAT MAKES YOU SO ANGRY?
THAT'S, UH, THAT'S OUR TIME, DR. SINCLAIR.
...
...OF COURSE. SEE YOU NEXT WEEK?
...
...YEAH...
NEXT WEEK.
WHAT MAKES ME SO ANGRY?

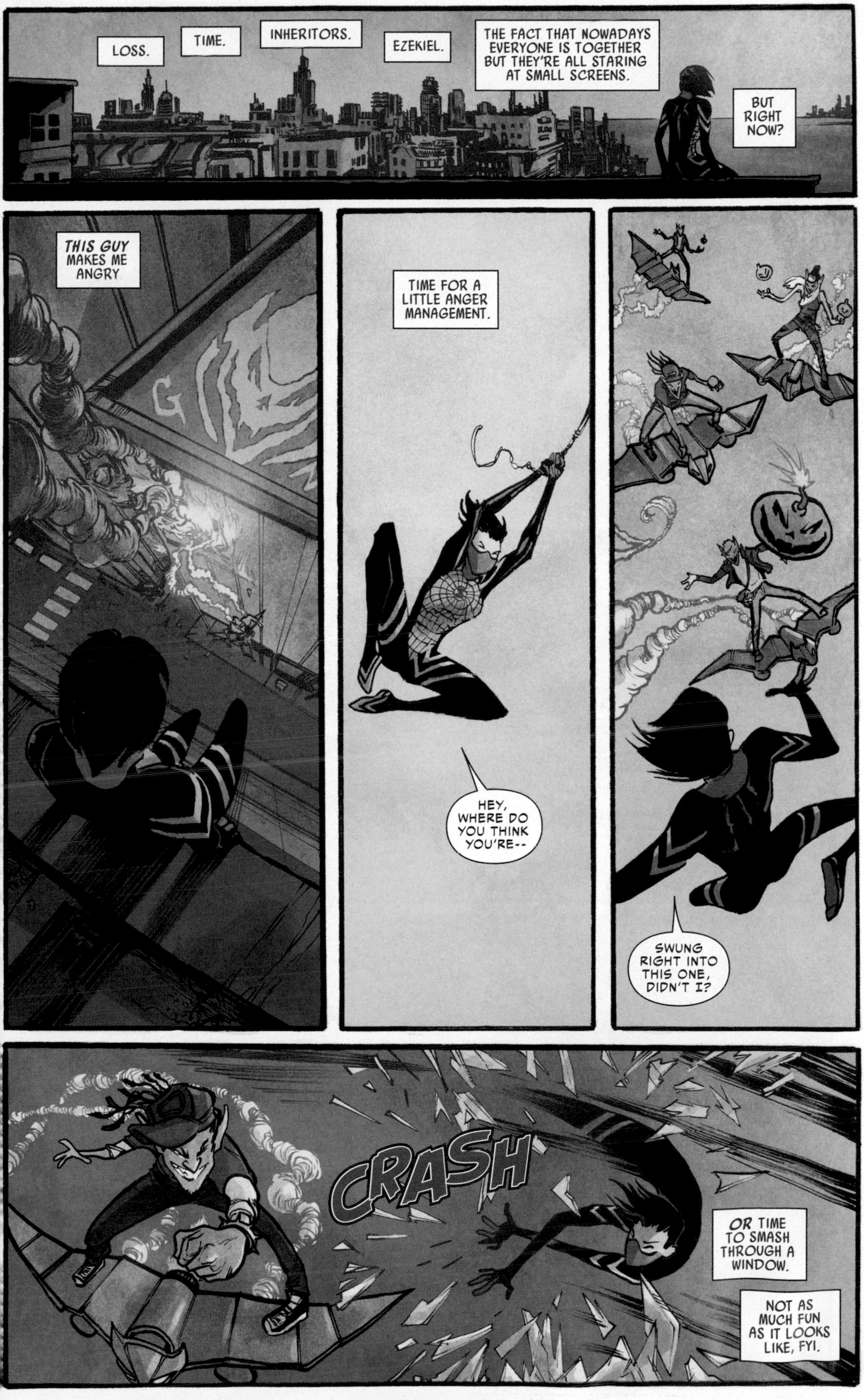
LOSS.
TIME.
INHERITORS.
EZEKIEL.
THE FACT THAT NOWADAYS EVERYONE IS TOGETHER BUT THEY'RE ALL STARING AT SMALL SCREENS.
BUT RIGHT NOW?
THIS GUY MAKES ME ANGRY
TIME FOR A LITTLE ANGER MANAGEMENT.
HEY, WHERE DO YOU THINK YOU'RE--
SWUNG RIGHT INTO THIS ONE, DIDN'T I?
CRASH
OR TIME TO SMASH THROUGH A WINDOW.
NOT AS MUCH FUN AS IT LOOKS LIKE, FYI.

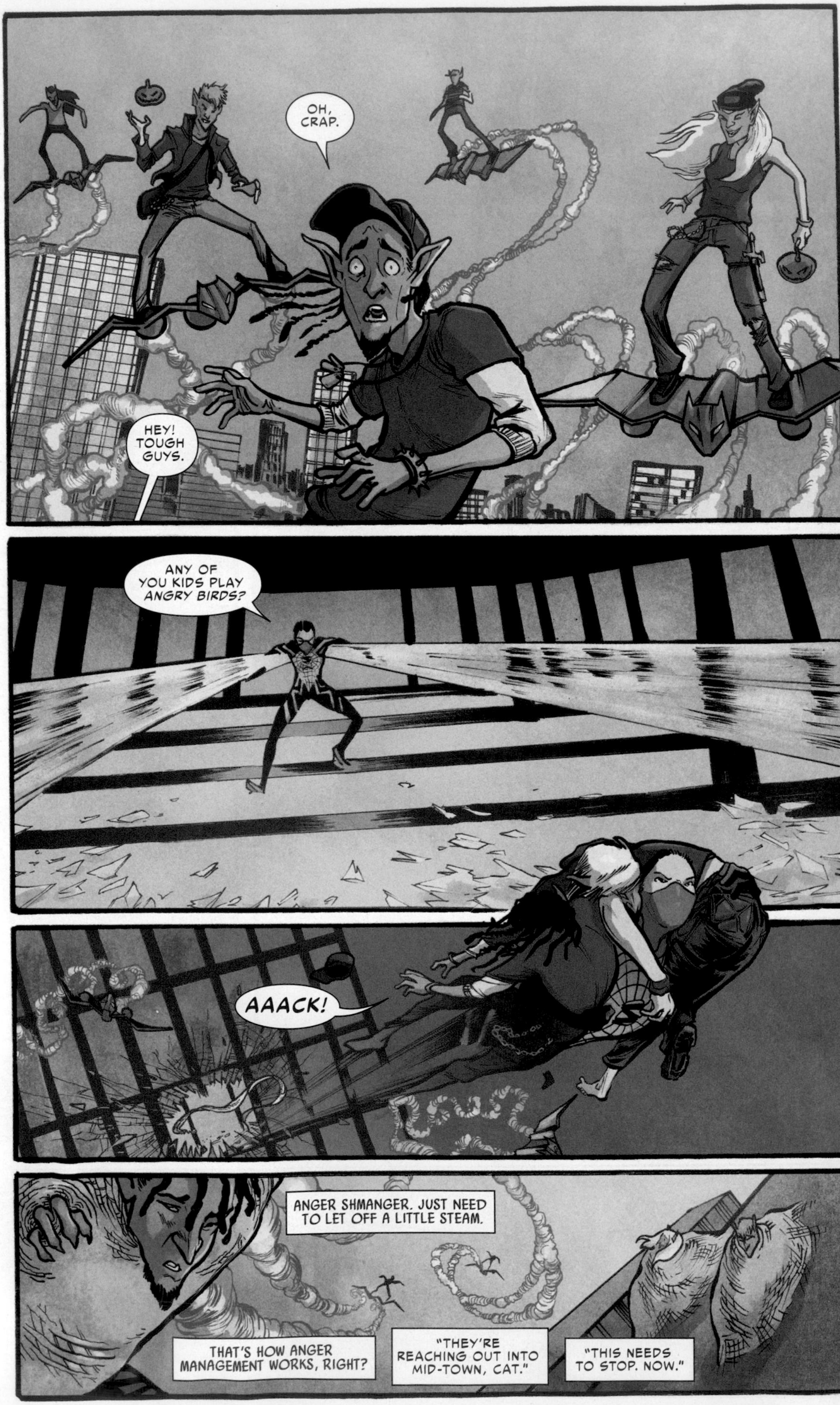
OH, CRAP.
HEY! TOUGH GUYS.
ANY OF YOU KIDS PLAY ANGRY BIRDS?
AAACK!
ANGER SHMANGER. JUST NEED TO LET OFF A LITTLE STEAM.
THAT'S HOW ANGER MANAGEMENT WORKS, RIGHT?
"THEY'RE REACHING OUT INTO MID-TOWN, CAT."
"THIS NEEDS TO STOP. NOW."

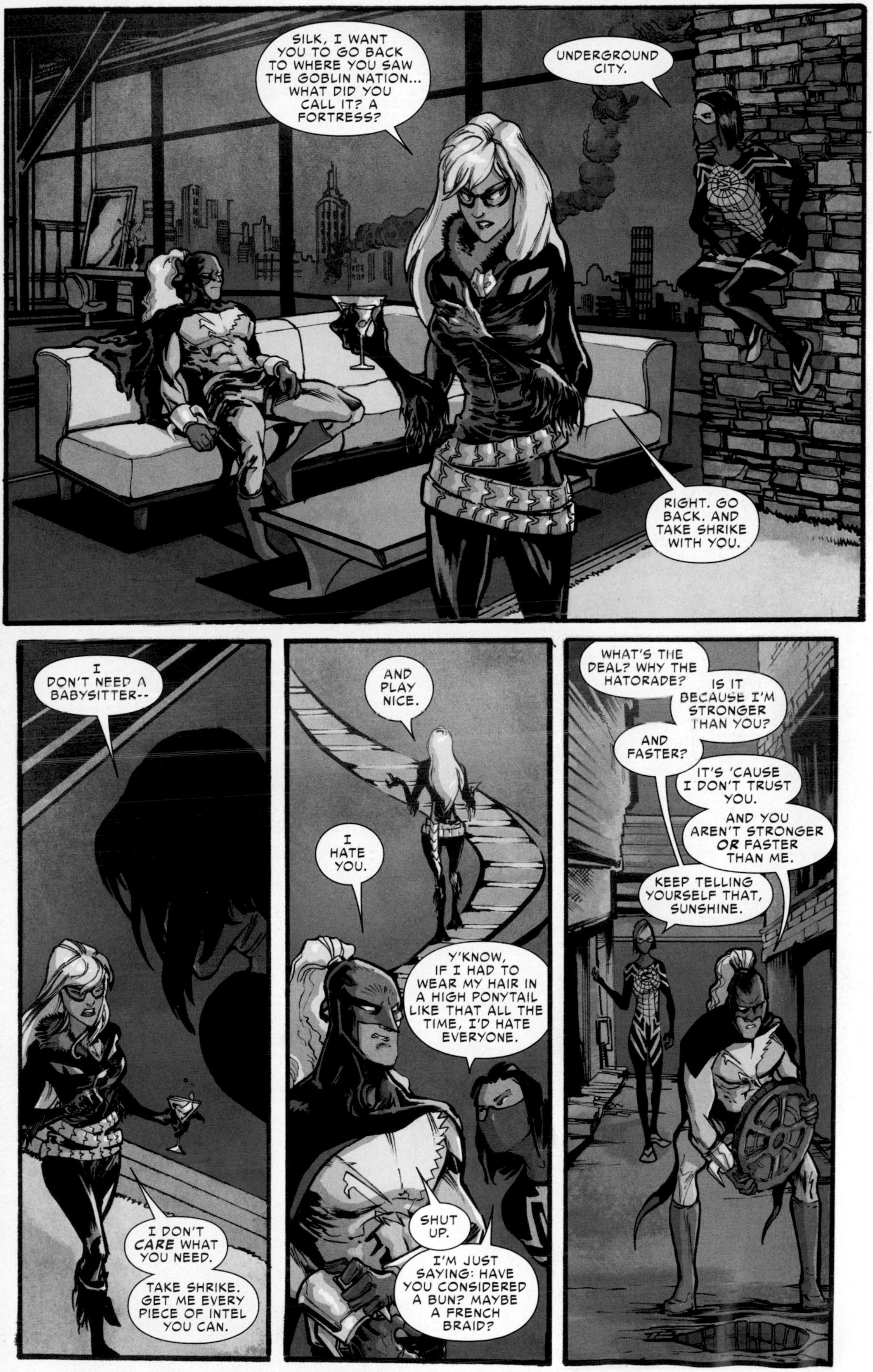
SILK, I WANT YOU TO GO BACK TO WHERE YOU SAW THE GOBLIN NATION... WHAT DID YOU CALL IT? A FORTRESS?
UNDERGROUND CITY.
RIGHT. GO BACK. AND TAKE SHRIKE WITH YOU.
I DON'T NEED A BABYSITTER--
I DON'T CARE WHAT YOU NEED.
TAKE SHRIKE. GET ME EVERY PIECE OF INTEL YOU CAN.
AND PLAY NICE.
I HATE YOU.
Y'KNOW, IF I HAD TO WEAR MY HAIR IN A HIGH PONYTAIL LIKE THAT ALL THE TIME, I'D HATE EVERYONE.
SHUT UP.
I'M JUST SAYING: HAVE YOU CONSIDERED A BUN? MAYBE A FRENCH BRAID?
WHAT'S THE DEAL? WHY THE HATORADE?
IS IT BECAUSE I'M STRONGER THAN YOU?
AND FASTER?
IT'S 'CAUSE I DON'T TRUST YOU.
AND YOU AREN'T STRONGER OR FASTER THAN ME.
KEEP TELLING YOURSELF THAT, SUNSHINE.

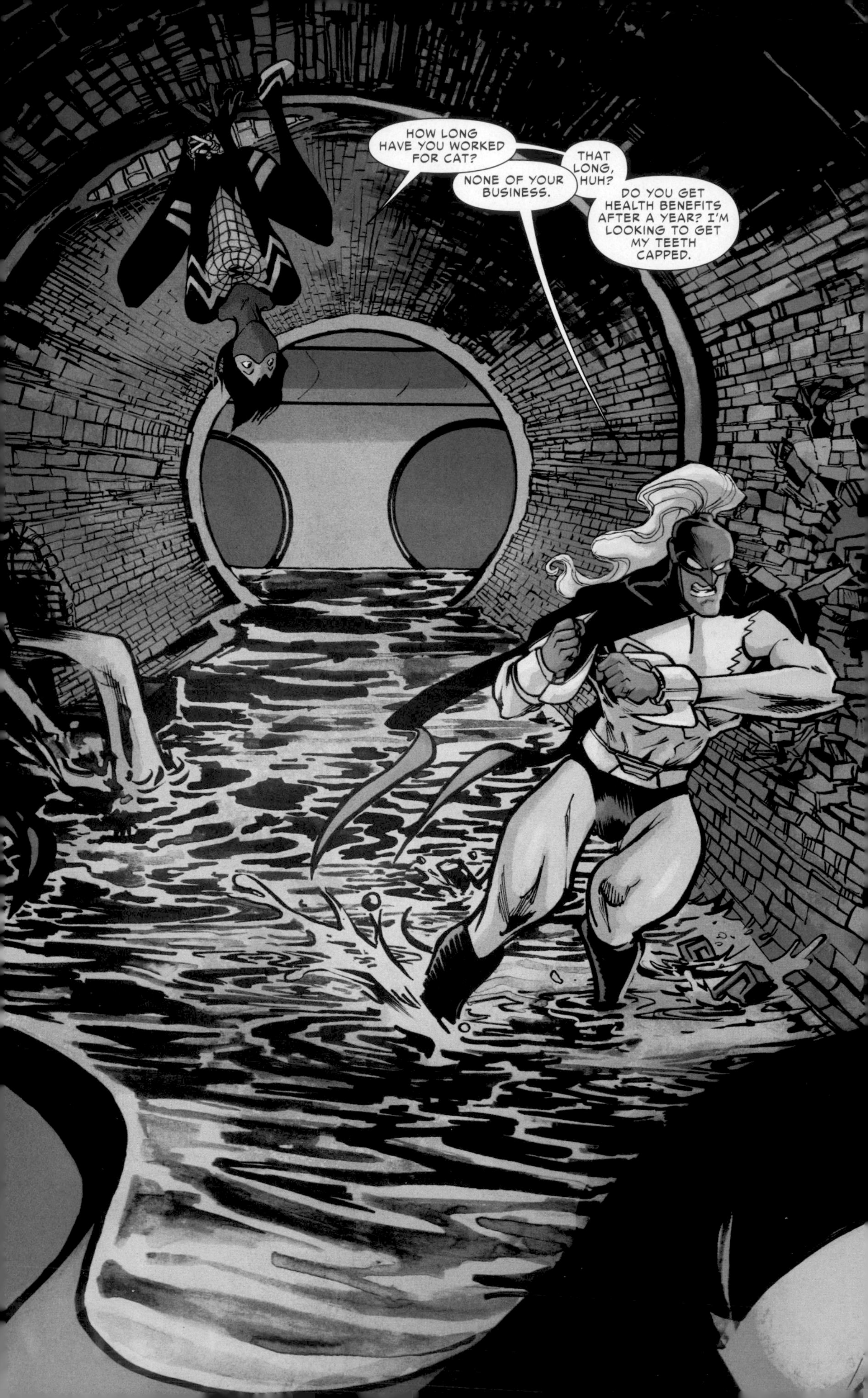
HOW LONG HAVE YOU WORKED FOR CAT?
NONE OF YOUR BUSINESS.
THAT LONG, HUH?
DO YOU GET HEALTH BENEFITS AFTER A YEAR? I'M LOOKING TO GET MY TEETH CAPPED.

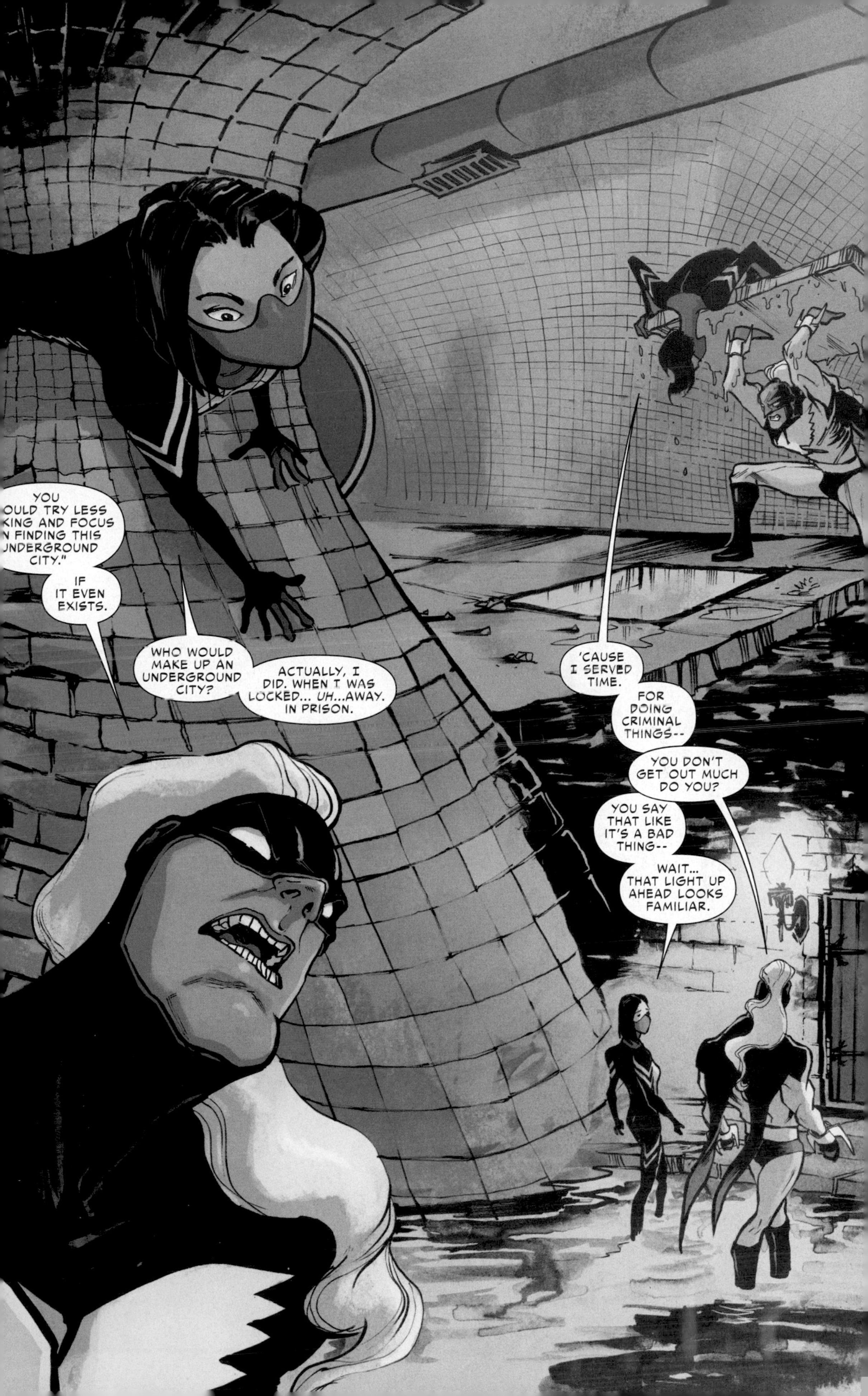
YOU OULD TRY LESS KING AND FOCUS N FINDING THIS NDERGROUND CITY."
IF IT EVEN EXISTS.
WHO WOULD MAKE UP AN UNDERGROUND CITY?
ACTUALLY, I DID. WHEN I WAS LOCKED... *UH*...AWAY. IN PRISON.
'CAUSE I SERVED TIME.
FOR DOING CRIMINAL THINGS--
YOU DON'T GET OUT MUCH DO YOU?
YOU SAY THAT LIKE IT'S A BAD THING--
WAIT... THAT LIGHT UP AHEAD LOOKS FAMILIAR.

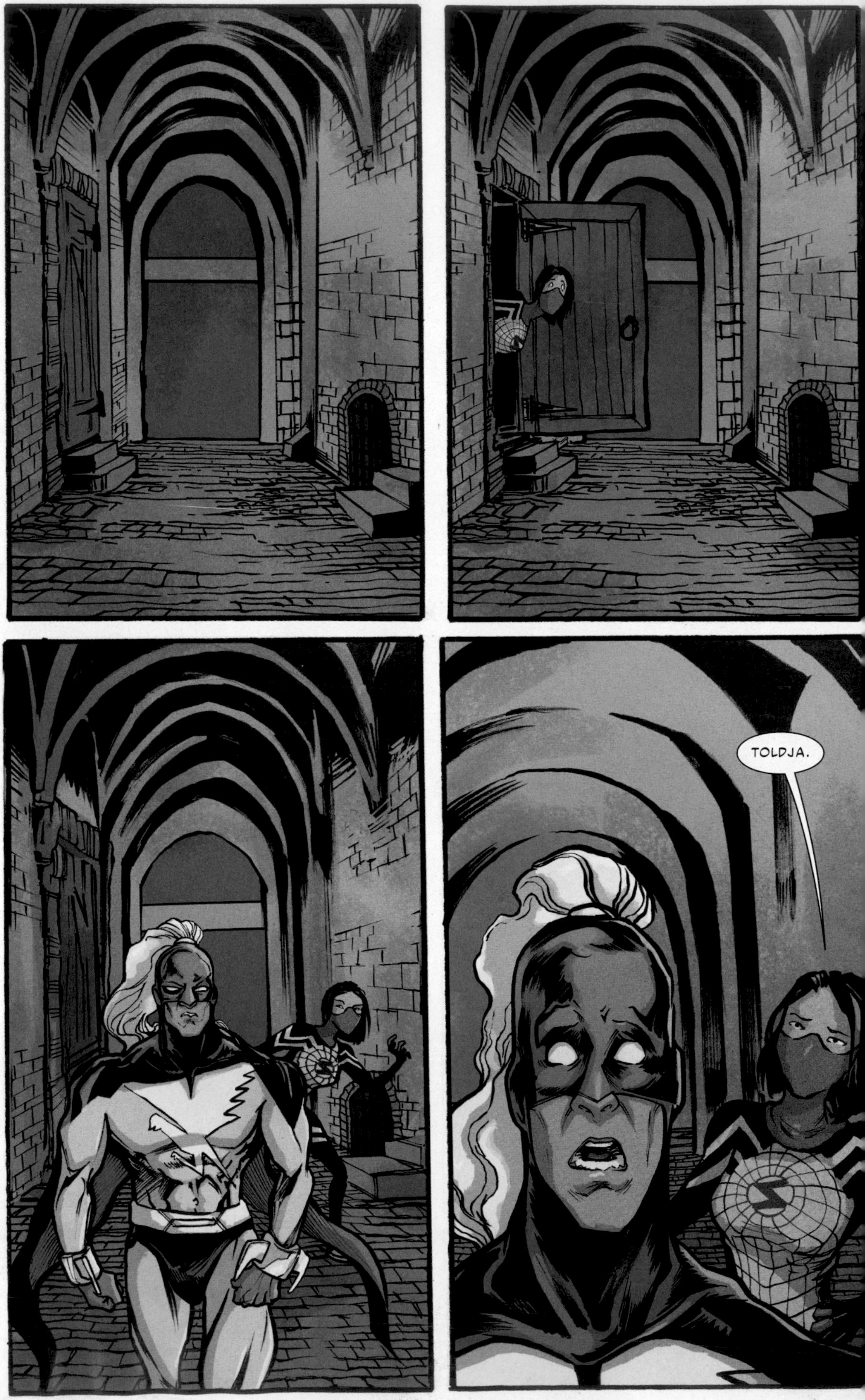
TOLDJA.

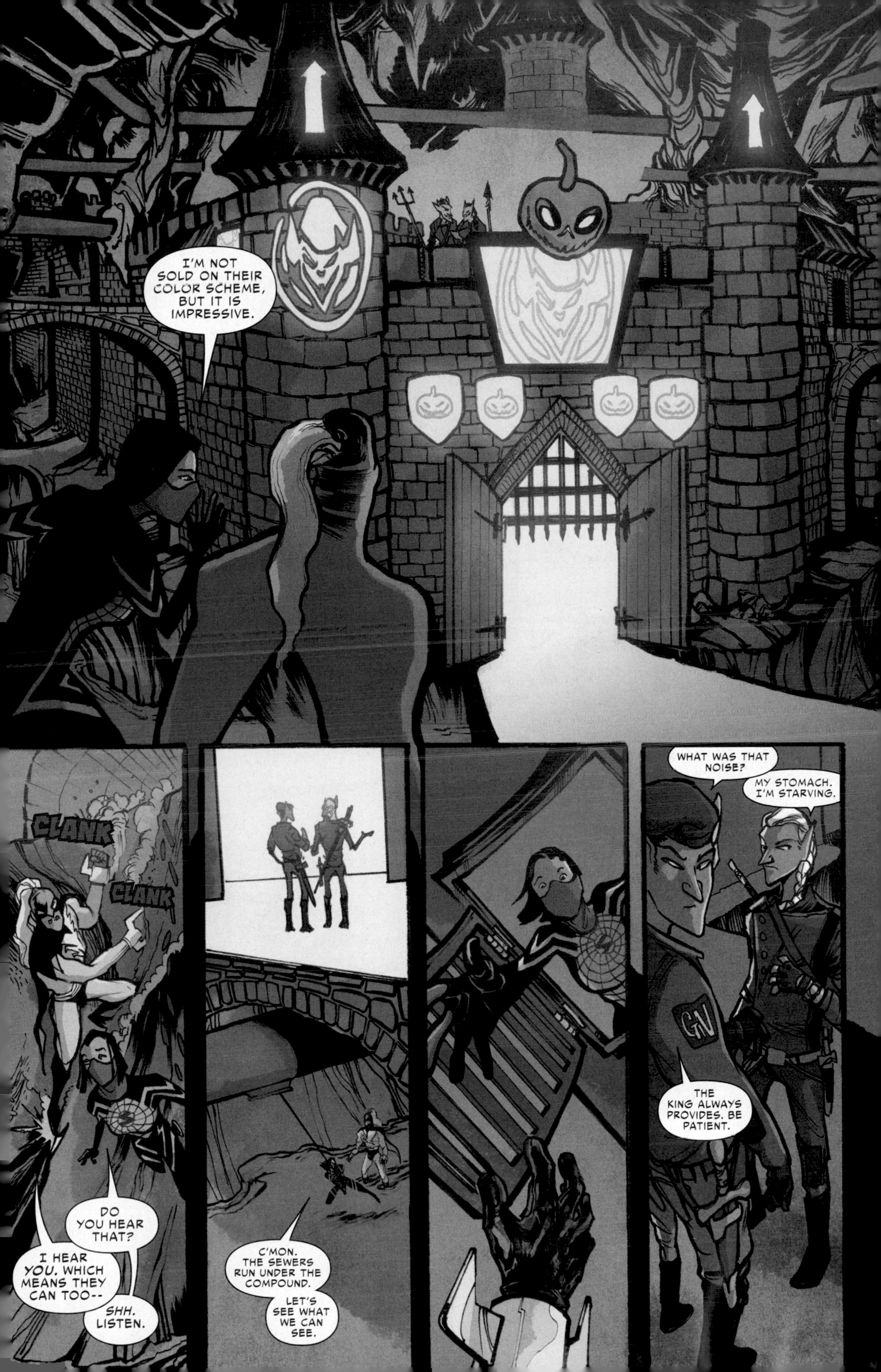

I'M NOT SOLD ON THEIR COLOR SCHEME, BUT IT IS IMPRESSIVE.
CLANK
CLANK
DO YOU HEAR THAT?
I HEAR YOU. WHICH MEANS THEY CAN TOO--
SHH. LISTEN.
C'MON. THE SEWERS RUN UNDER THE COMPOUND.
LET'S SEE WHAT WE CAN SEE.
WHAT WAS THAT NOISE?
MY STOMACH. I'M STARVING.
GN
THE KING ALWAYS PROVIDES. BE PATIENT.

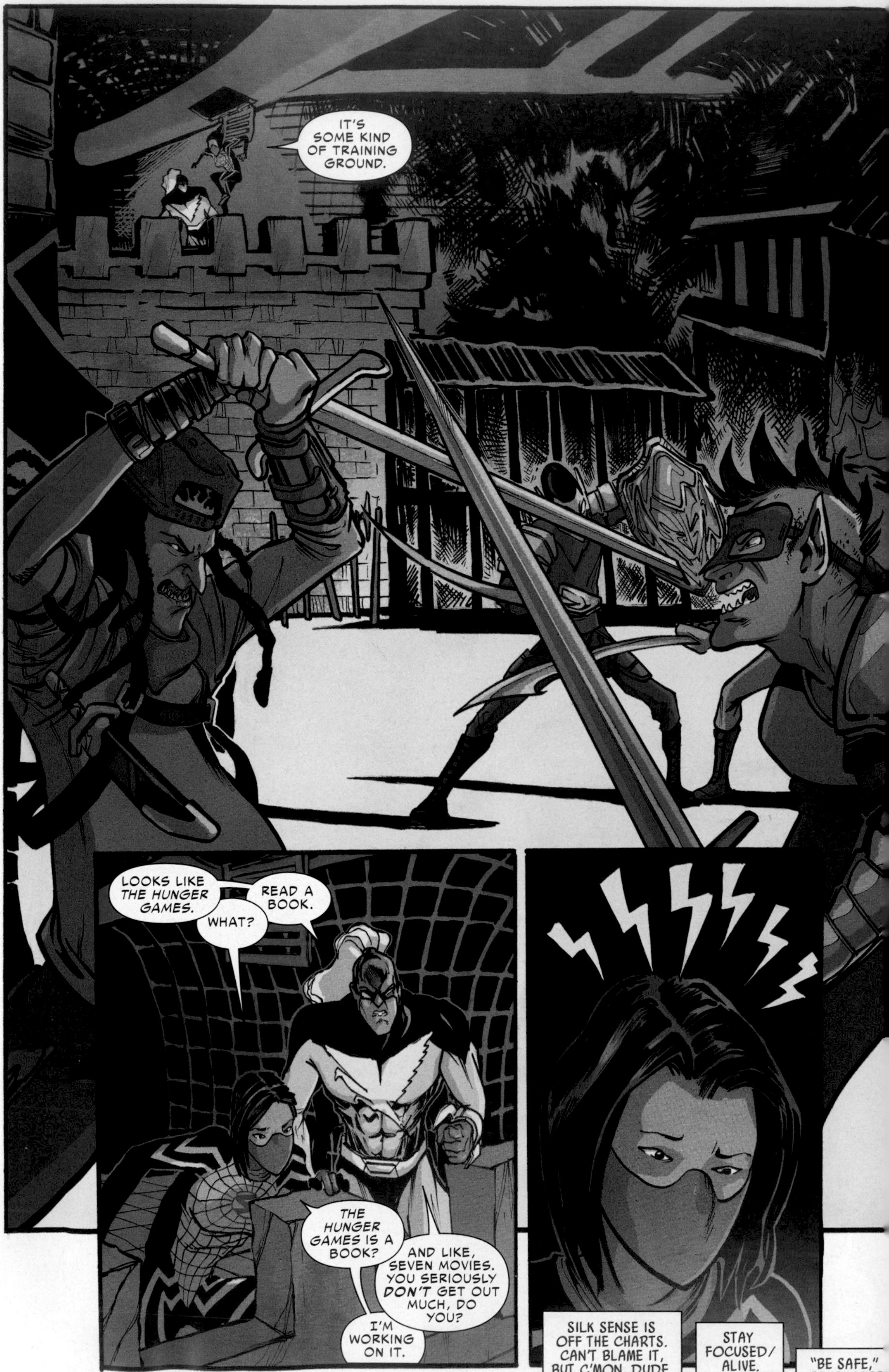
IT'S SOME KIND OF TRAINING GROUND.
LOOKS LIKE THE HUNGER GAMES.
READ A BOOK.
WHAT?
THE HUNGER GAMES IS A BOOK?
AND LIKE, SEVEN MOVIES. YOU SERIOUSLY DON'T GET OUT MUCH, DO YOU?
I'M WORKING ON IT.
SILK SENSE IS OFF THE CHARTS. CAN'T BLAME IT, BUT C'MON, DUDE. PACE YOURSELF.
STAY FOCUSED/ ALIVE.
"BE SAFE," REMEMBER?

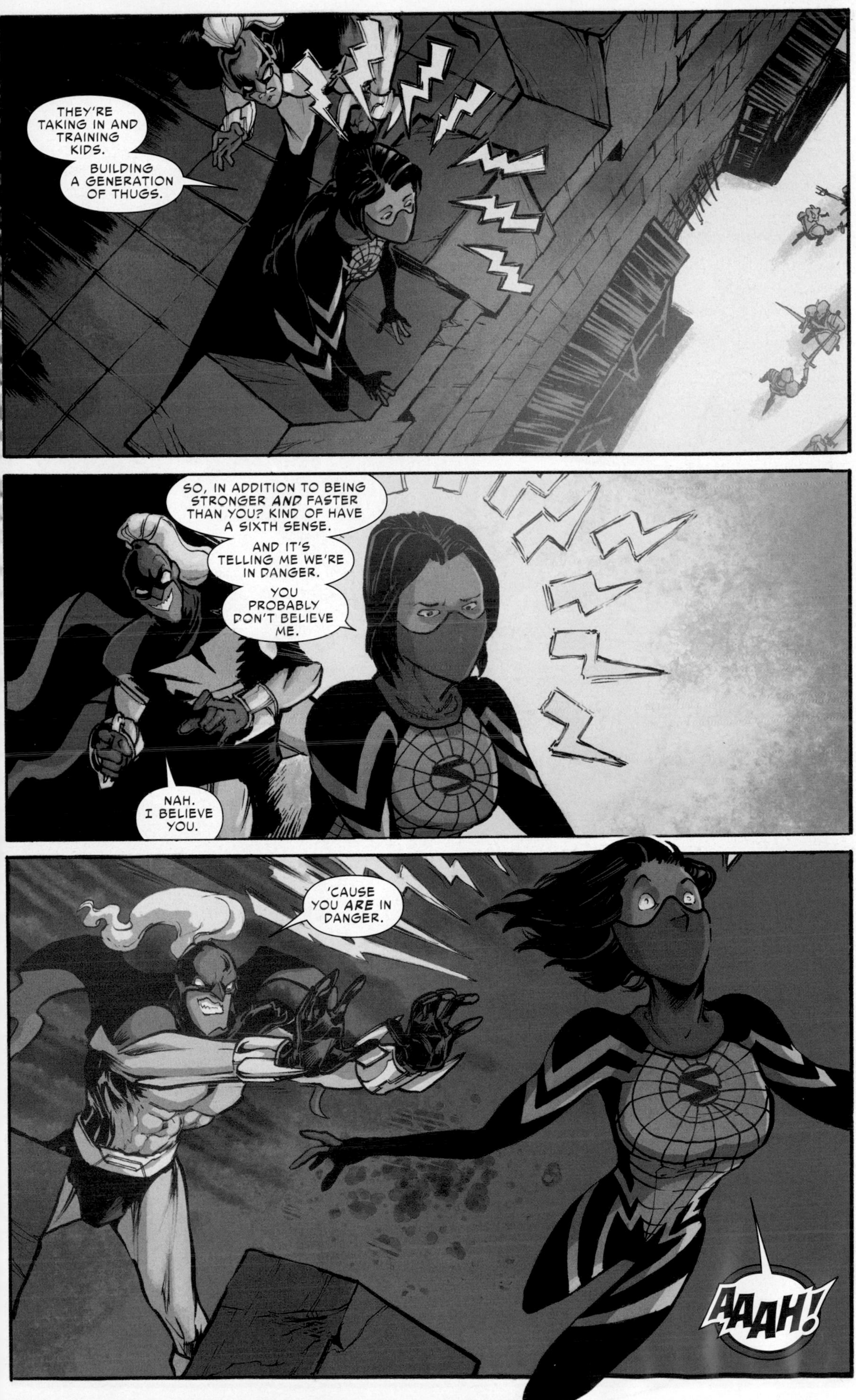
THEY'RE TAKING IN AND TRAINING KIDS.
BUILDING A GENERATION OF THUGS.
SO, IN ADDITION TO BEING STRONGER AND FASTER THAN YOU? KIND OF HAVE A SIXTH SENSE.
AND IT'S TELLING ME WE'RE IN DANGER.
YOU PROBABLY DON'T BELIEVE ME.
NAH. I BELIEVE YOU.
'CAUSE YOU ARE IN DANGER.
AAAH!

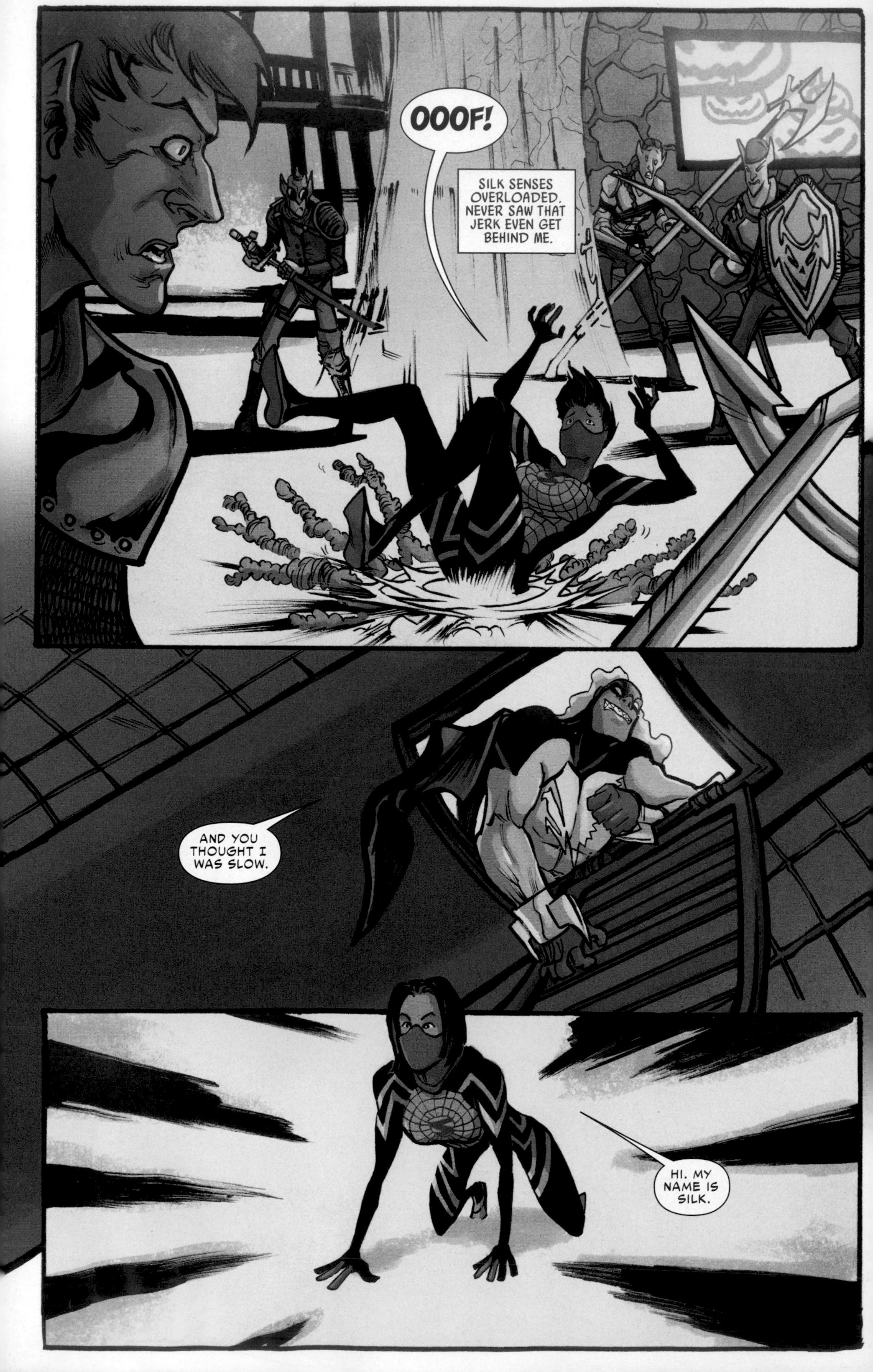
OOOF!
SILK SENSES OVERLOADED. NEVER SAW THAT JERK EVEN GET BEHIND ME.
AND YOU THOUGHT I WAS SLOW.
HI. MY NAME IS SILK.

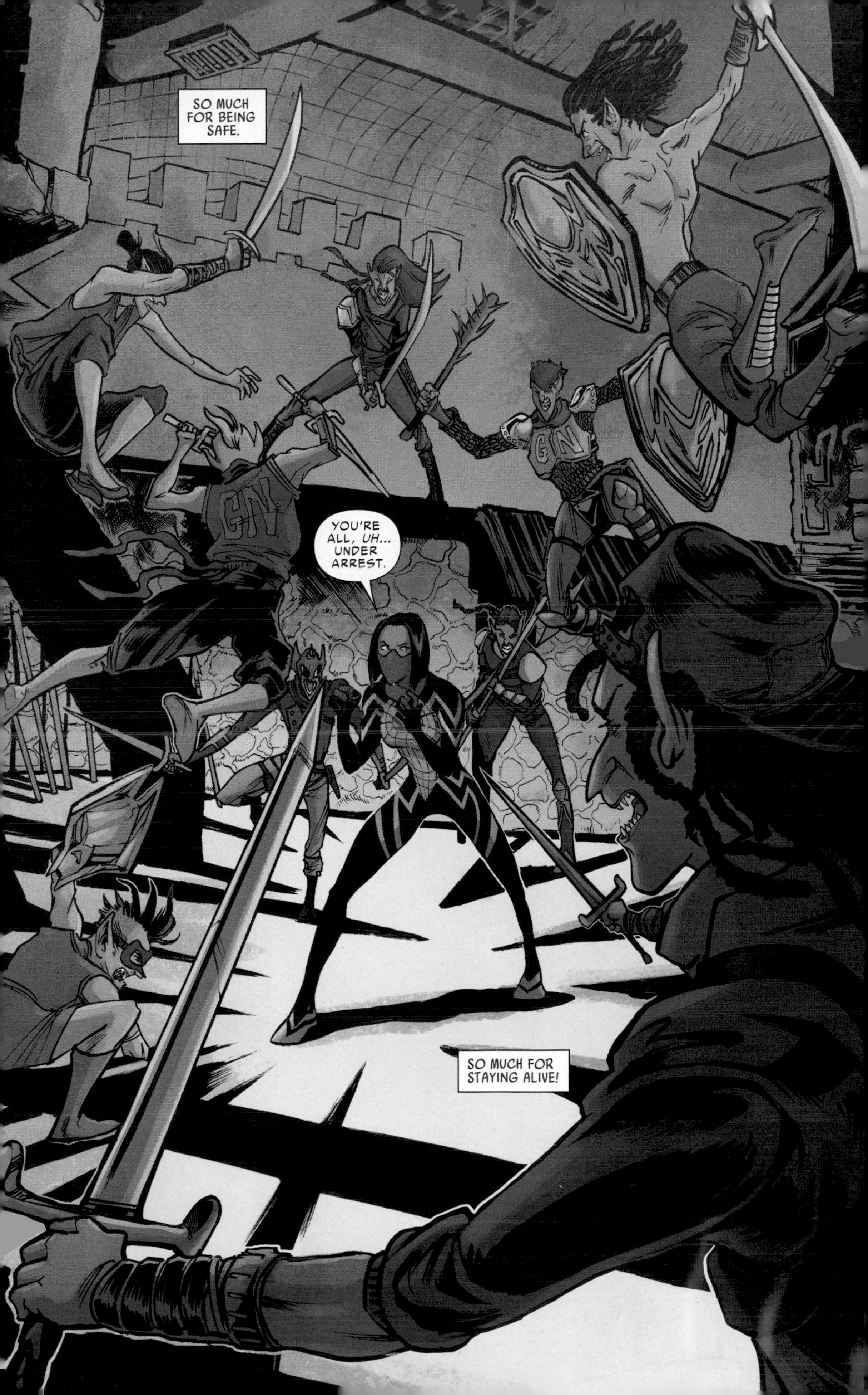
SO MUCH FOR BEING SAFE.
YOU'RE ALL, UH... UNDER ARREST.
SO MUCH FOR STAYING ALIVE!

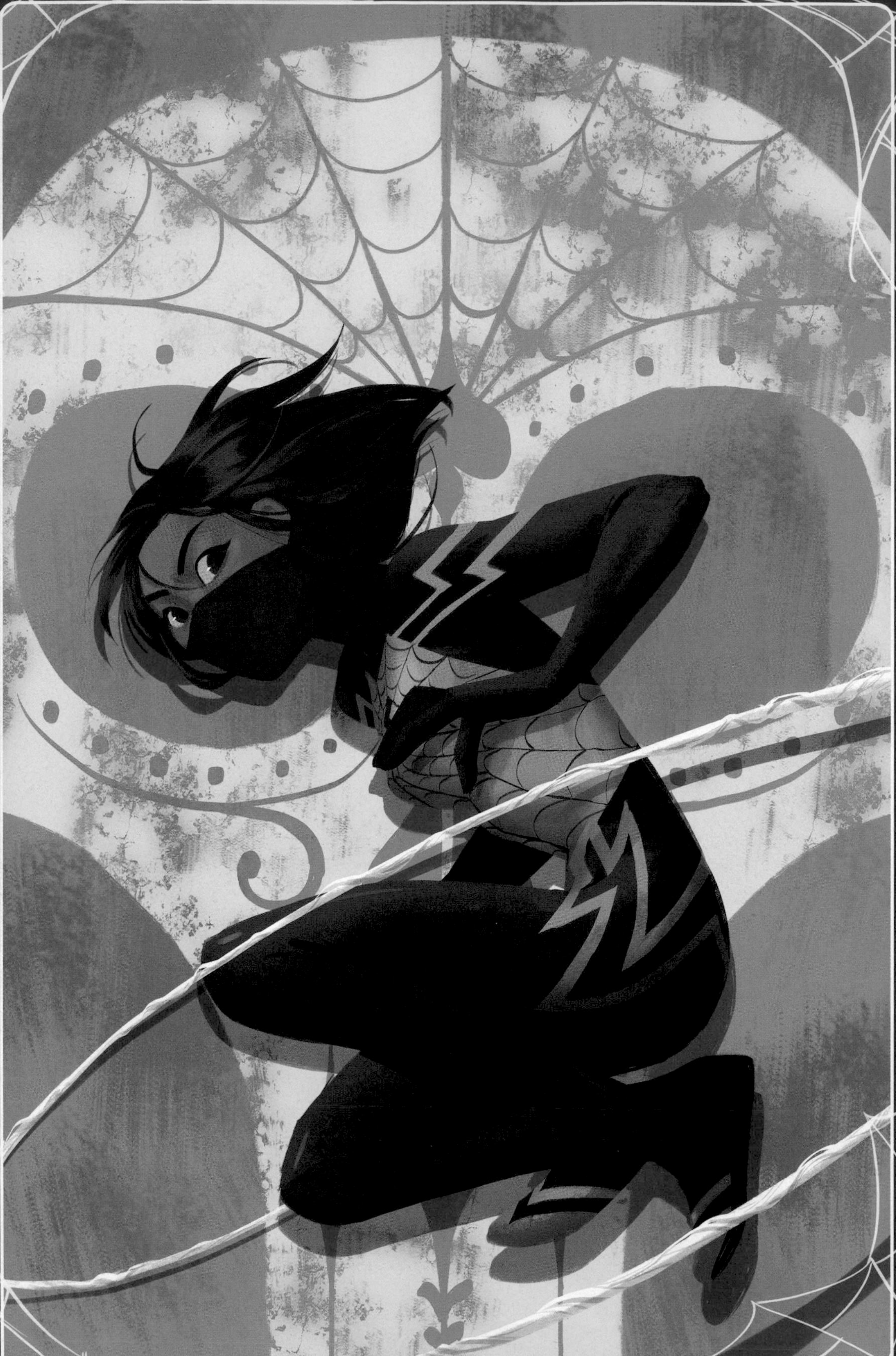

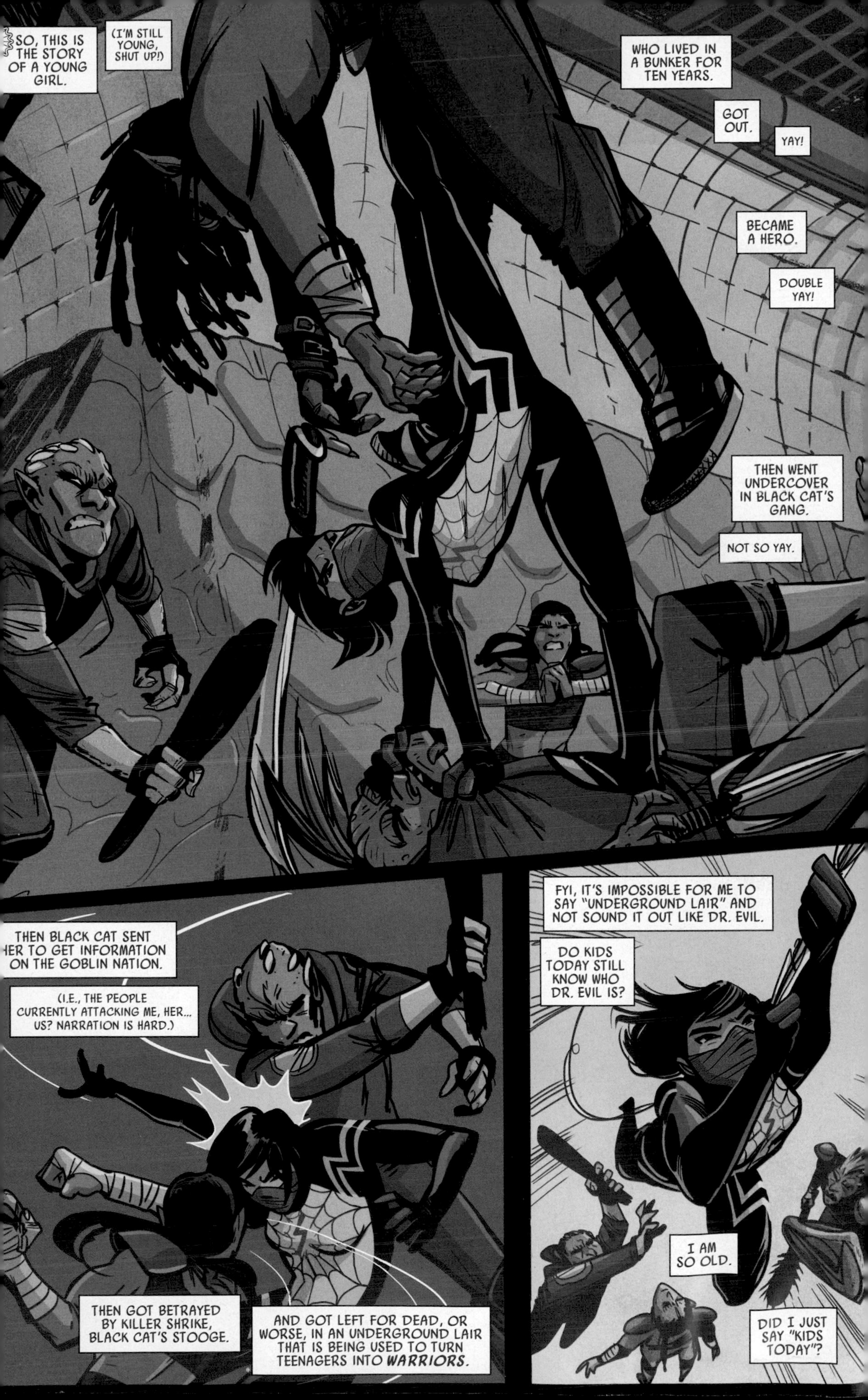

SO, THIS IS THE STORY OF A YOUNG GIRL.
(I'M STILL YOUNG, SHUT UP!)
WHO LIVED IN A BUNKER FOR TEN YEARS.
GOT OUT.
YAY!
BECAME A HERO.
DOUBLE YAY!
THEN WENT UNDERCOVER IN BLACK CAT'S GANG.
NOT SO YAY.
THEN BLACK CAT SENT HER TO GET INFORMATION ON THE GOBLIN NATION.
(I.E., THE PEOPLE CURRENTLY ATTACKING ME, HER... US? NARRATION IS HARD.)
THEN GOT BETRAYED BY KILLER SHRIKE, BLACK CAT'S STOOGE.
AND GOT LEFT FOR DEAD, OR WORSE, IN AN UNDERGROUND LAIR THAT IS BEING USED TO TURN TEENAGERS INTO *WARRIORS*.
FYI, IT'S IMPOSSIBLE FOR ME TO SAY "UNDERGROUND LAIR" AND NOT SOUND IT OUT LIKE DR. EVIL.
DO KIDS TODAY STILL KNOW WHO DR. EVIL IS?
I AM SO OLD.
DID I JUST SAY "KIDS TODAY"?

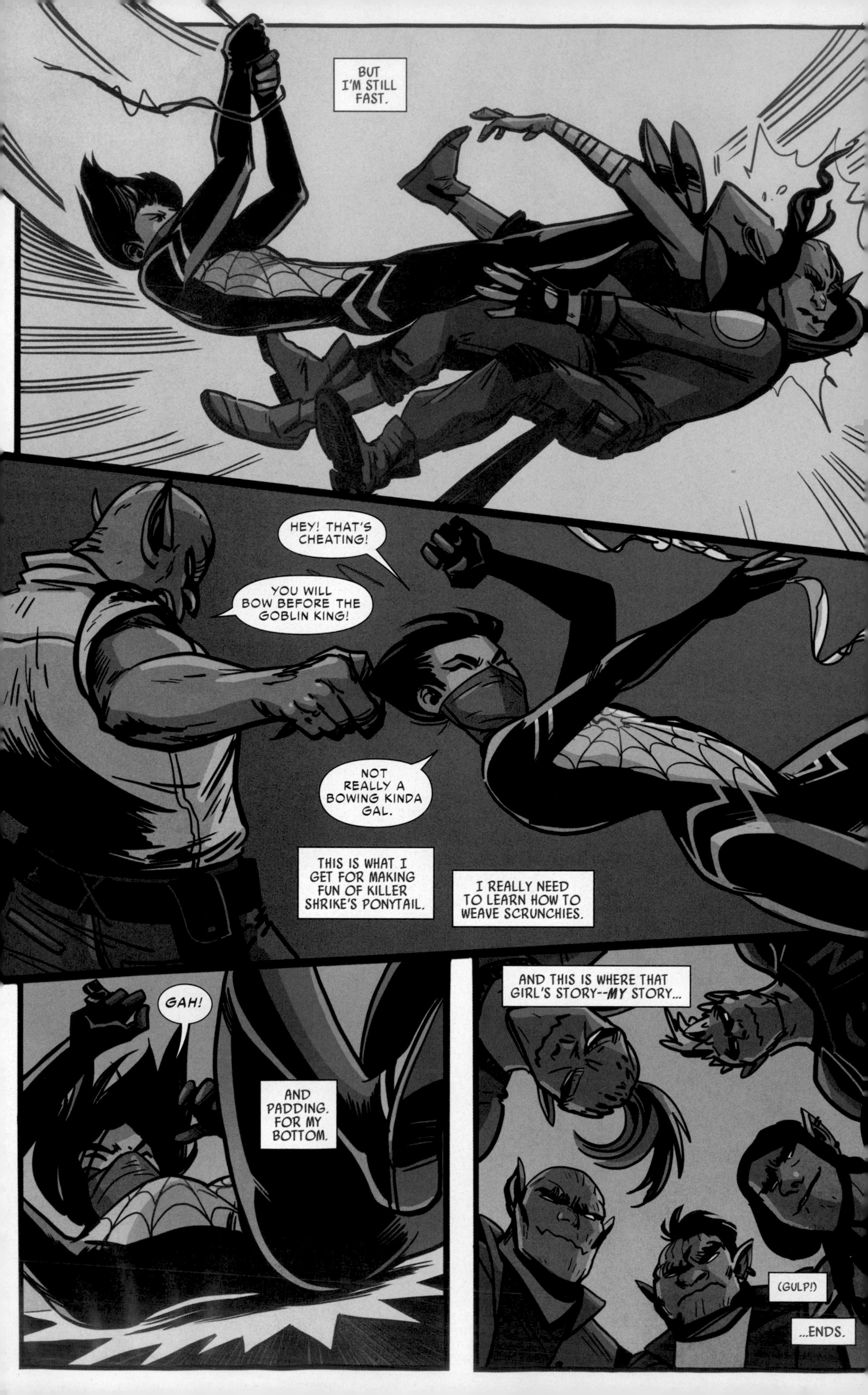

BUT I'M STILL FAST.
HEY! THAT'S CHEATING!
YOU WILL BOW BEFORE THE GOBLIN KING!
NOT REALLY A BOWING KINDA GAL.
THIS IS WHAT I GET FOR MAKING FUN OF KILLER SHRIKE'S PONYTAIL.
I REALLY NEED TO LEARN HOW TO WEAVE SCRUNCHIES.
GAH!
AND PADDING. FOR MY BOTTOM.
AND THIS IS WHERE THAT GIRL'S STORY--*MY* STORY...
(GULP!)
...ENDS.

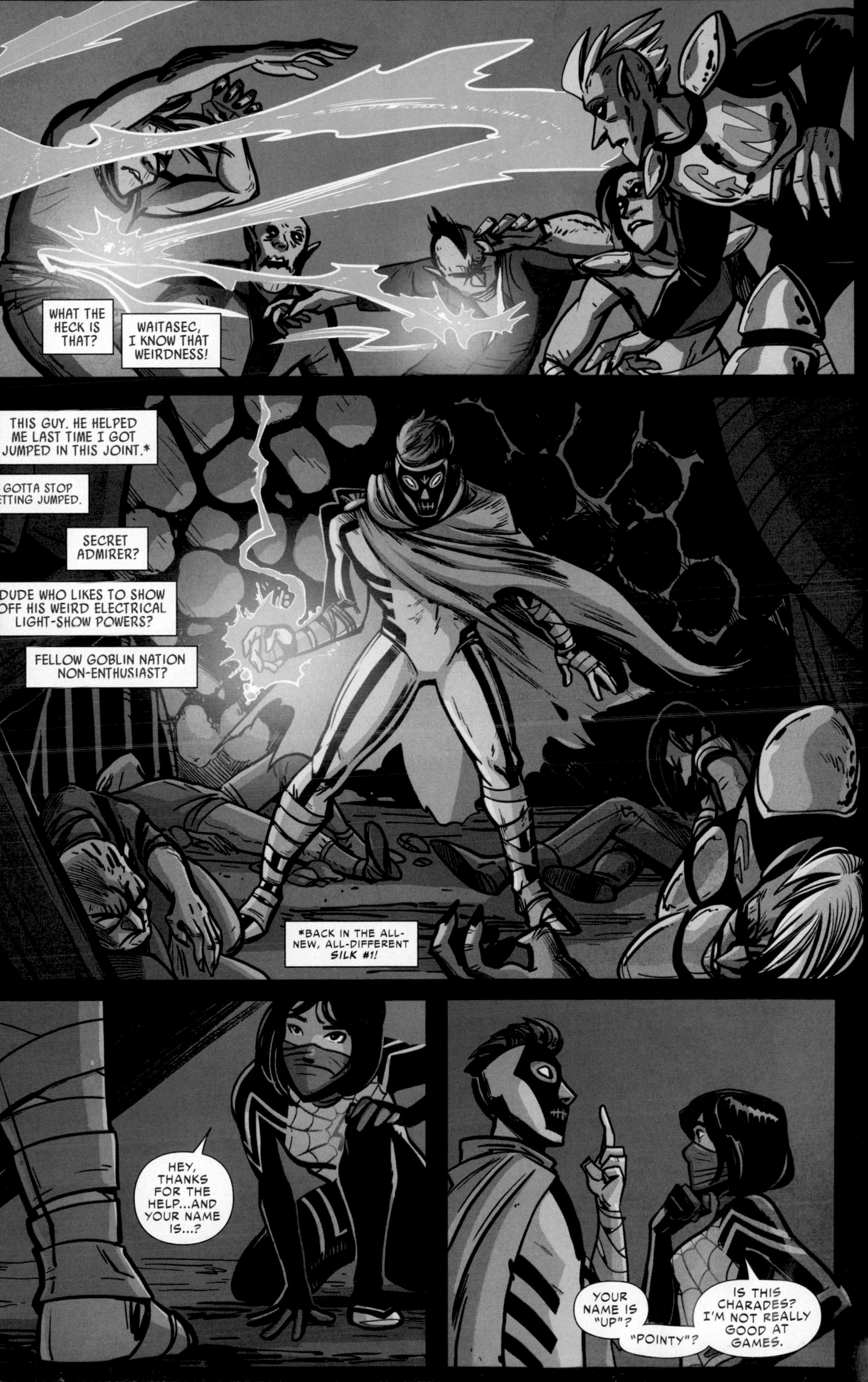
WHAT THE HECK IS THAT?
WAITASEC, I KNOW THAT WEIRDNESS!
THIS GUY. HE HELPED ME LAST TIME I GOT JUMPED IN THIS JOINT.*
GOTTA STOP ETTING JUMPED.
SECRET ADMIRER?
DUDE WHO LIKES TO SHOW OFF HIS WEIRD ELECTRICAL LIGHT-SHOW POWERS?
FELLOW GOBLIN NATION NON-ENTHUSIAST?
*BACK IN THE ALL-NEW, ALL-DIFFERENT SILK #1!
HEY, THANKS FOR THE HELP...AND YOUR NAME IS...?
YOUR NAME IS "UP"?
"POINTY"?
IS THIS CHARADES? I'M NOT REALLY GOOD AT GAMES.

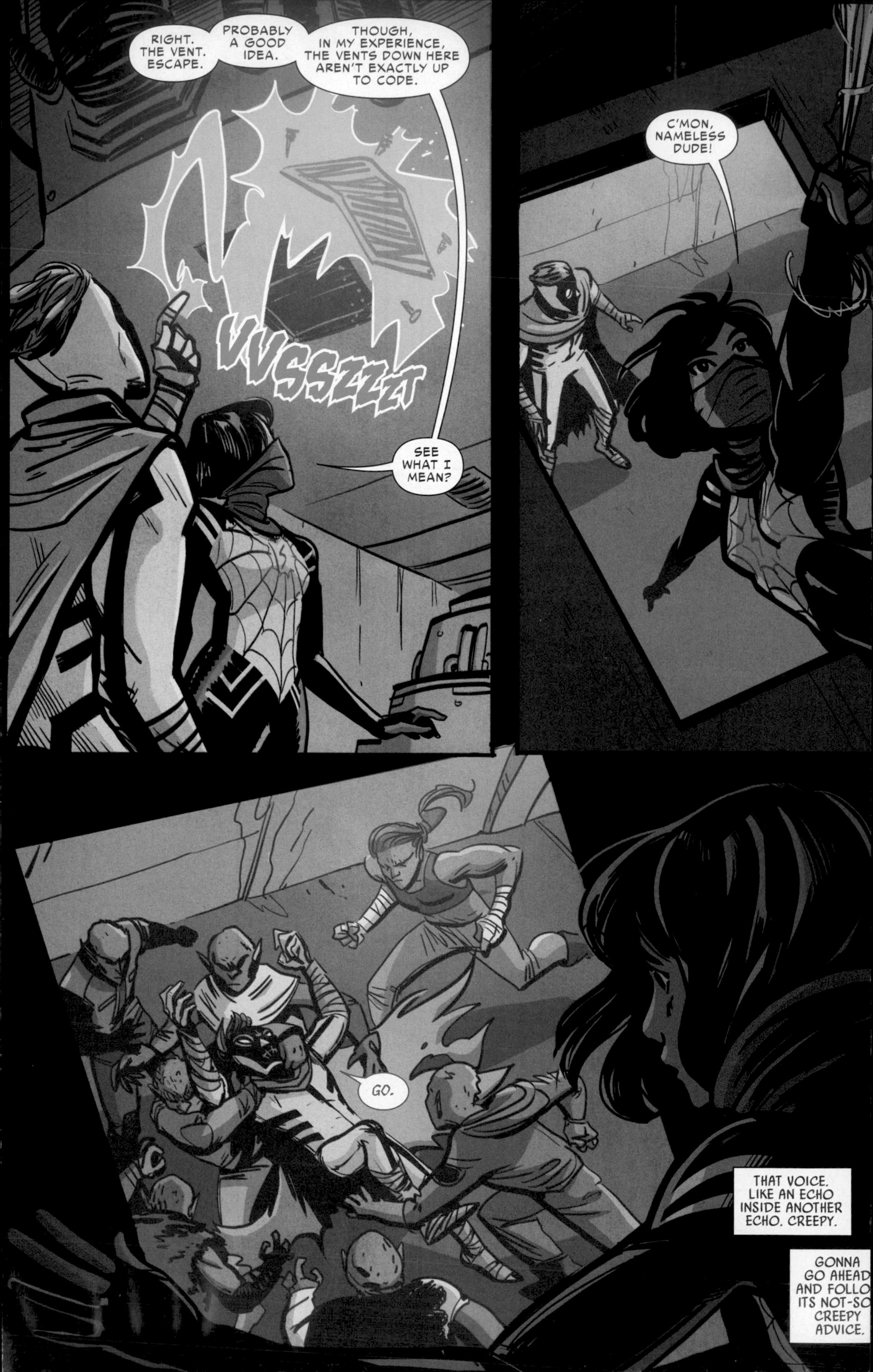
RIGHT. THE VENT. ESCAPE.
PROBABLY A GOOD IDEA.
THOUGH, IN MY EXPERIENCE, THE VENTS DOWN HERE AREN'T EXACTLY UP TO CODE.
VVSSZZZT
SEE WHAT I MEAN?
C'MON, NAMELESS DUDE!
GO.
THAT VOICE. LIKE AN ECHO INSIDE ANOTHER ECHO. CREEPY.
GONNA GO AHEAD AND FOLLO ITS NOT-SO CREEPY ADVICE.

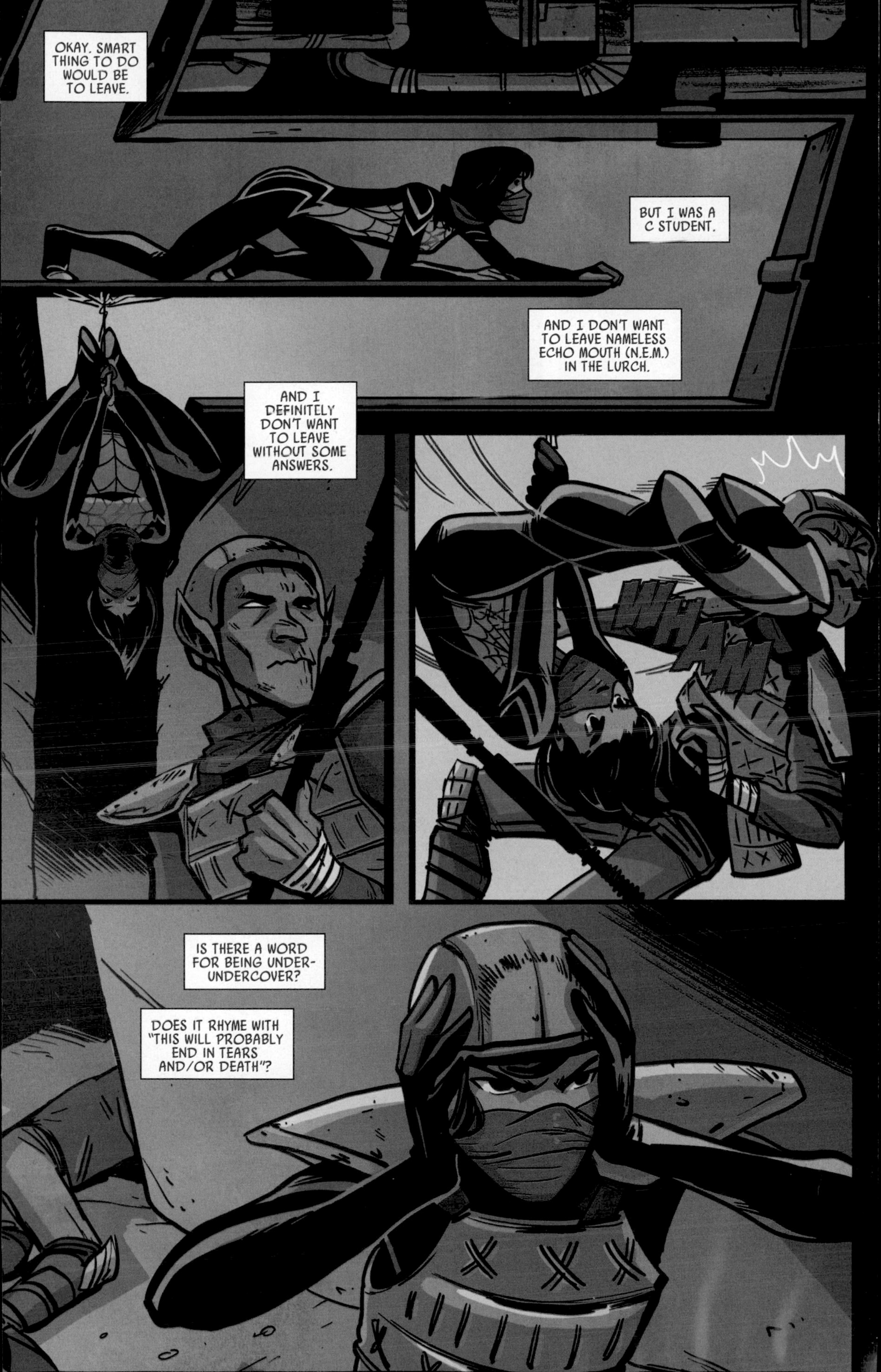

OKAY. SMART THING TO DO WOULD BE TO LEAVE.
BUT I WAS A C STUDENT.
AND I DON'T WANT TO LEAVE NAMELESS ECHO MOUTH (N.E.M.) IN THE LURCH.
AND I DEFINITELY DON'T WANT TO LEAVE WITHOUT SOME ANSWERS.
WHAM
IS THERE A WORD FOR BEING UNDER-UNDERCOVER?
DOES IT RHYME WITH "THIS WILL PROBABLY END IN TEARS AND/OR DEATH"?

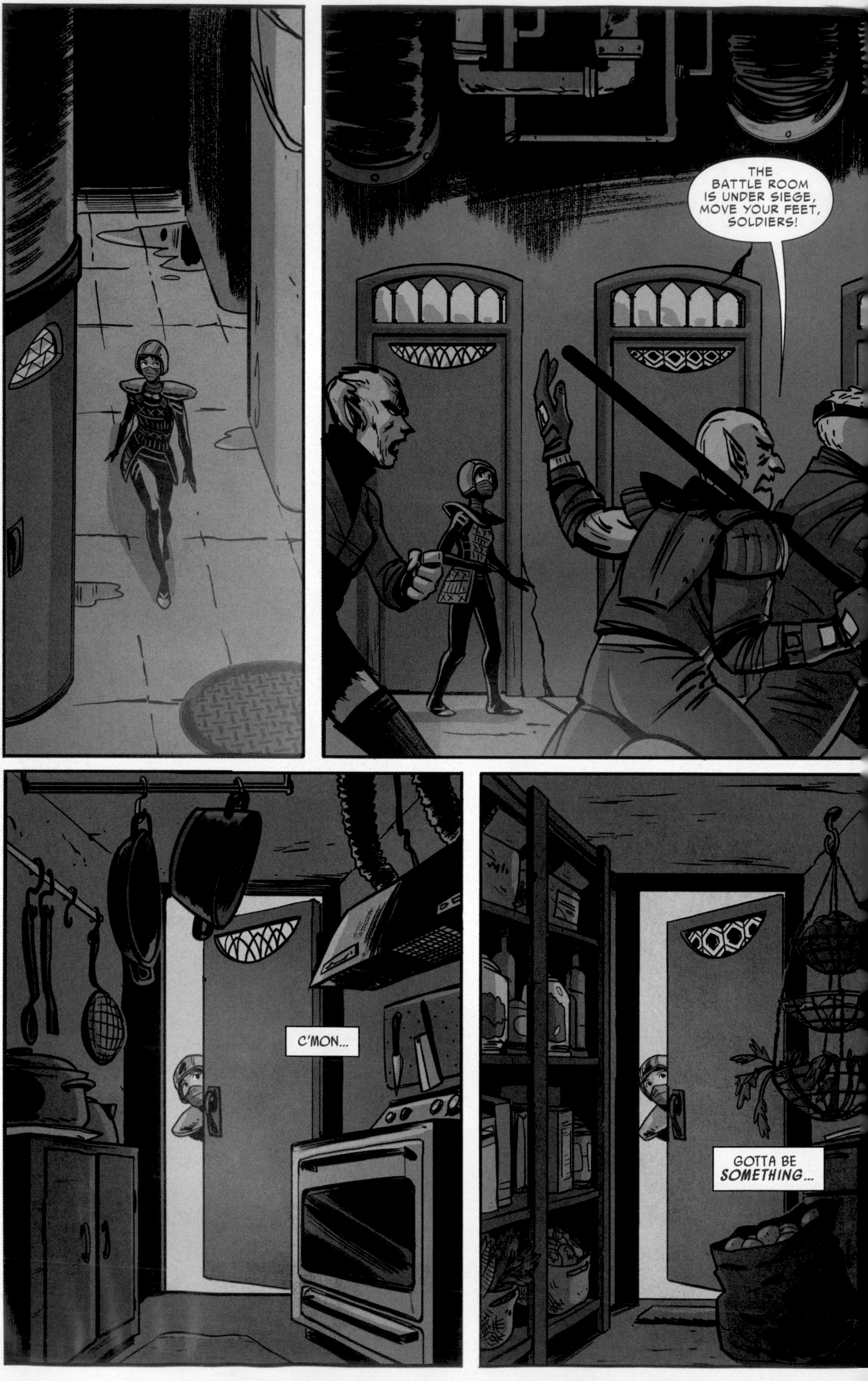
THE BATTLE ROOM IS UNDER SIEGE, MOVE YOUR FEET, SOLDIERS!
C'MON...
GOTTA BE *SOMETHING*...

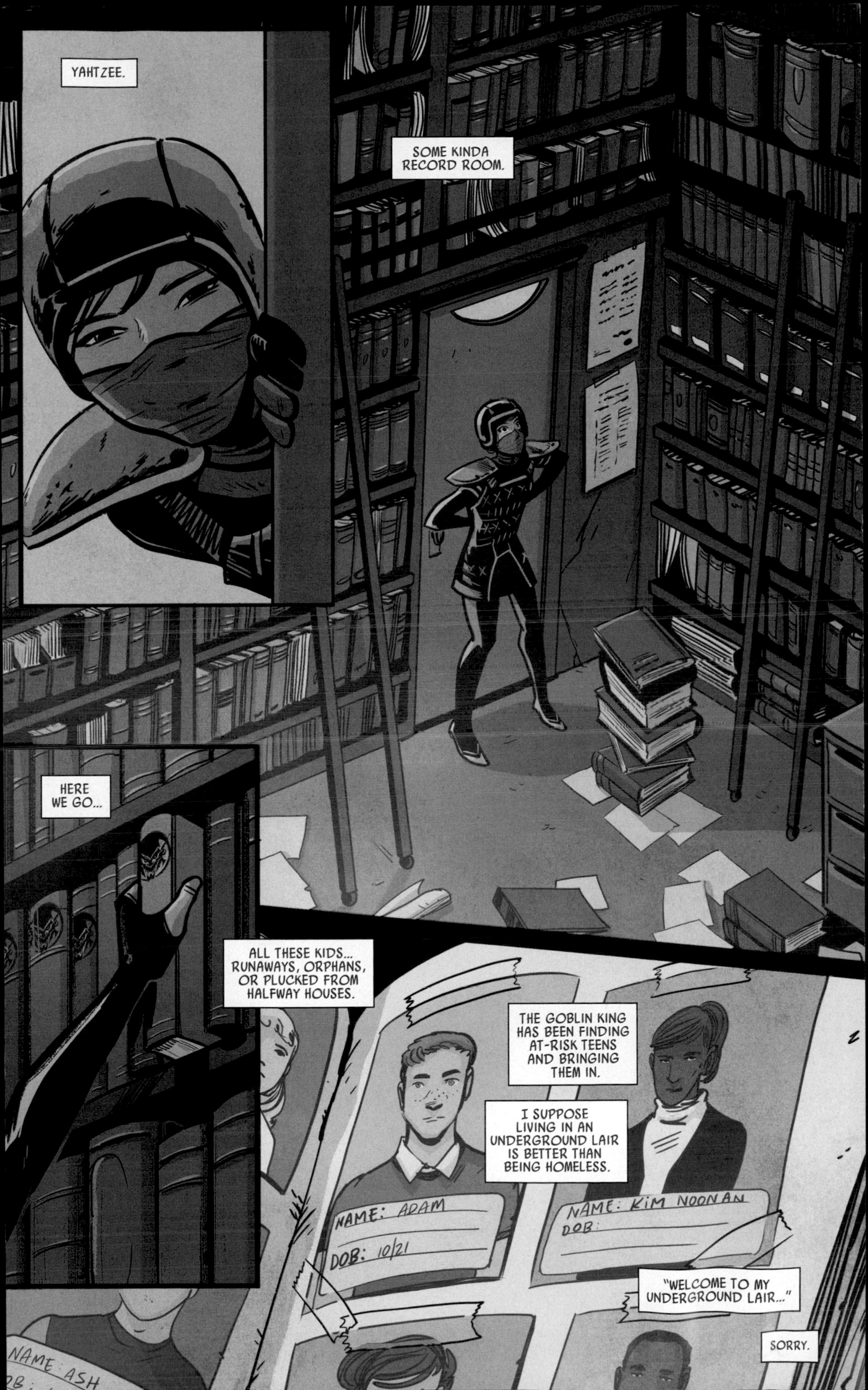

YAHTZEE.
SOME KINDA RECORD ROOM.
HERE WE GO...
ALL THESE KIDS... RUNAWAYS, ORPHANS, OR PLUCKED FROM HALFWAY HOUSES.
THE GOBLIN KING HAS BEEN FINDING AT-RISK TEENS AND BRINGING THEM IN.
I SUPPOSE LIVING IN AN UNDERGROUND LAIR IS BETTER THAN BEING HOMELESS.
NAME: ADAM
DOB: 10/21
NAME: KIM NOONAN
DOB:
"WELCOME TO MY UNDERGROUND LAIR..."
SORRY.
NAME: ASH

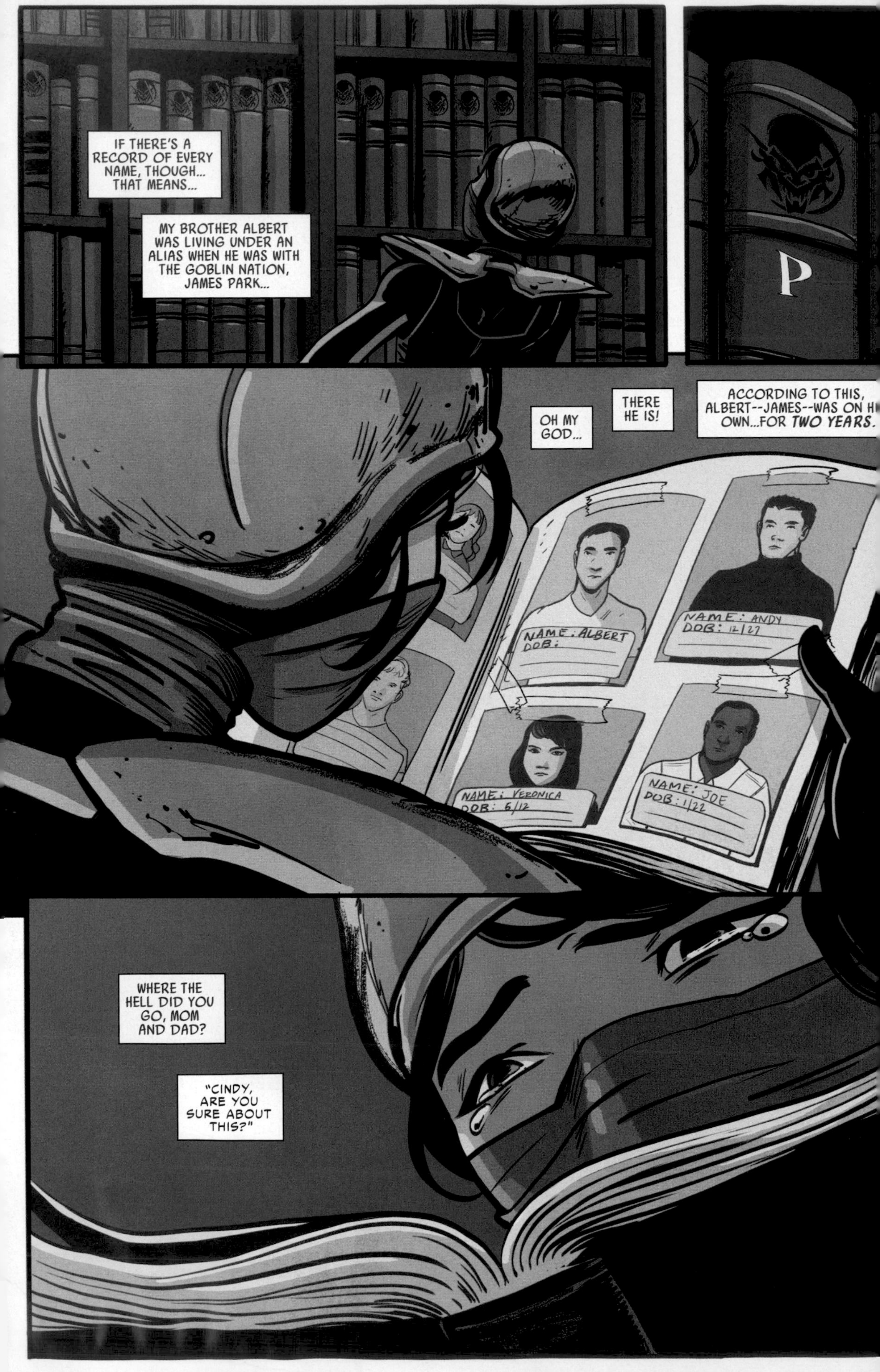
IF THERE'S A RECORD OF EVERY NAME, THOUGH... THAT MEANS...
MY BROTHER ALBERT WAS LIVING UNDER AN ALIAS WHEN HE WAS WITH THE GOBLIN NATION, JAMES PARK...
P
OH MY GOD...
THERE HE IS!
ACCORDING TO THIS, ALBERT--JAMES--WAS ON H OWN...FOR TWO YEARS.
NAME: ALBERT DOB:
NAME: ANDY DOB: 12/27
NAME: VERONICA DOB: 6/12
NAME: JOE DOB: 1/22
WHERE THE HELL DID YOU GO, MOM AND DAD?
"CINDY, ARE YOU SURE ABOUT THIS?"

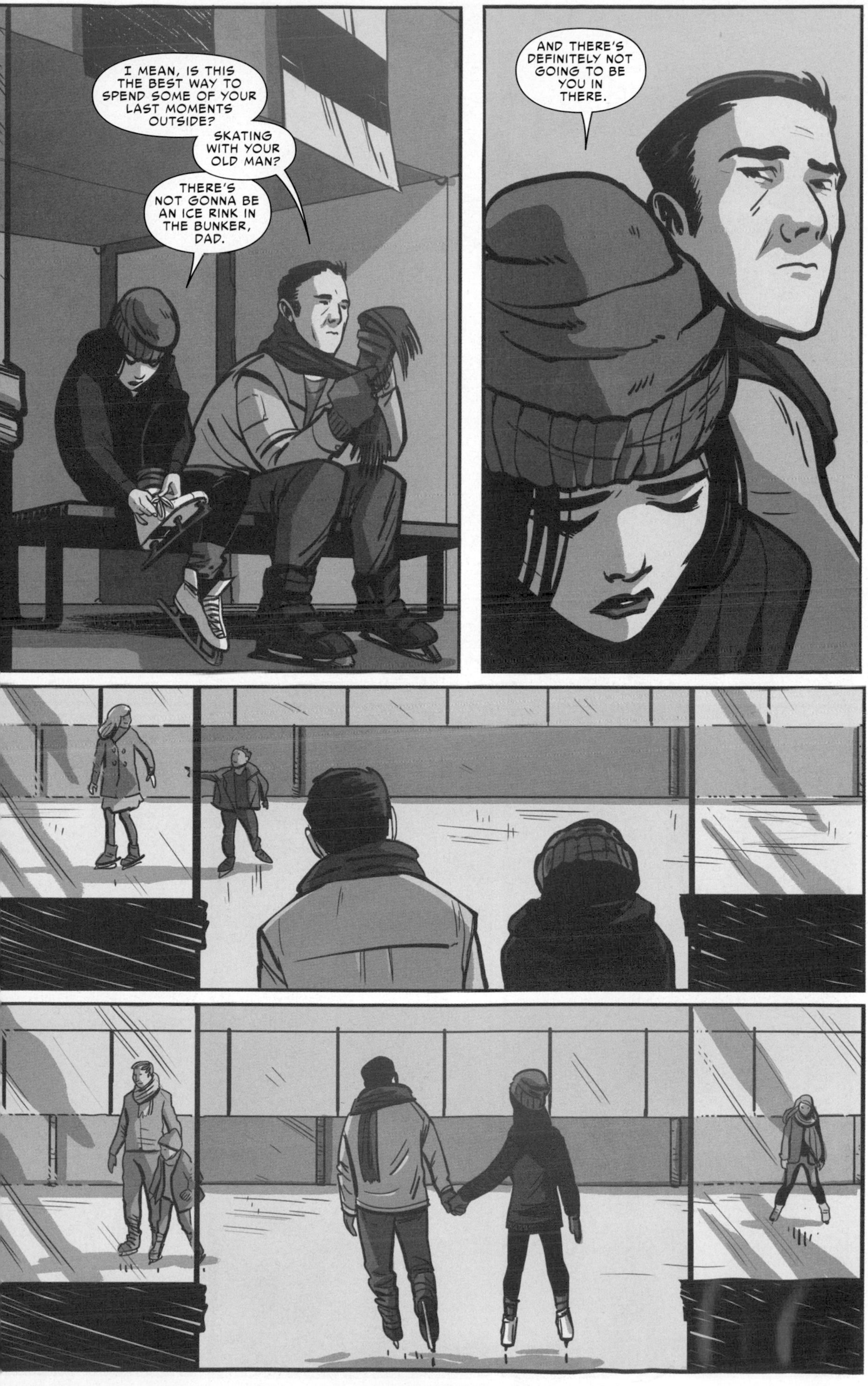
I MEAN, IS THIS THE BEST WAY TO SPEND SOME OF YOUR LAST MOMENTS OUTSIDE?
SKATING WITH YOUR OLD MAN?
THERE'S NOT GONNA BE AN ICE RINK IN THE BUNKER, DAD.
AND THERE'S DEFINITELY NOT GOING TO BE YOU IN THERE.

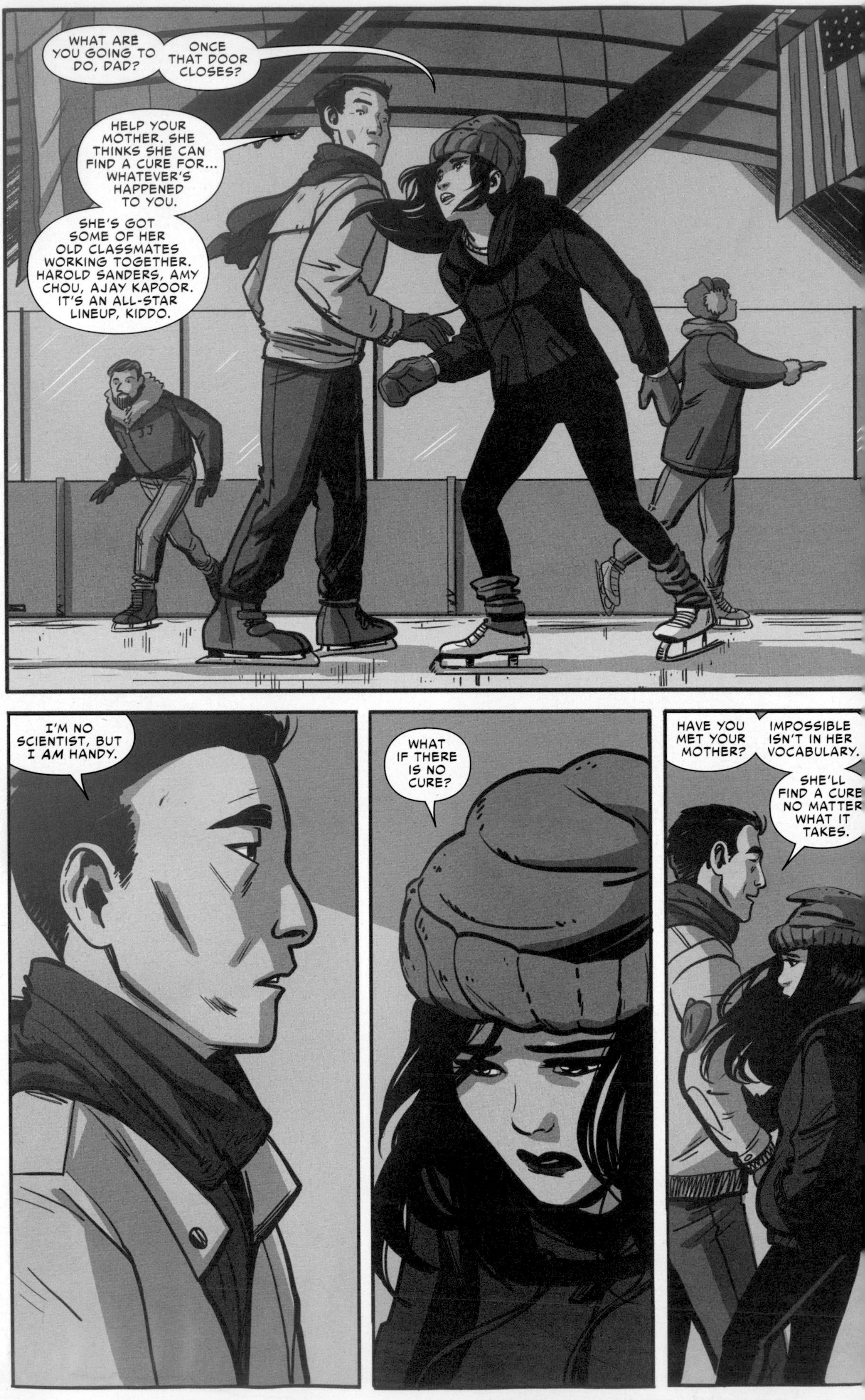
WHAT ARE YOU GOING TO DO, DAD?
ONCE THAT DOOR CLOSES?
HELP YOUR MOTHER. SHE THINKS SHE CAN FIND A CURE FOR... WHATEVER'S HAPPENED TO YOU.
SHE'S GOT SOME OF HER OLD CLASSMATES WORKING TOGETHER. HAROLD SANDERS, AMY CHOU, AJAY KAPOOR. IT'S AN ALL-STAR LINEUP, KIDDO.
I'M NO SCIENTIST, BUT I *AM* HANDY.
WHAT IF THERE IS NO CURE?
HAVE YOU MET YOUR MOTHER?
IMPOSSIBLE ISN'T IN HER VOCABULARY.
SHE'LL FIND A CURE NO MATTER WHAT IT TAKES.

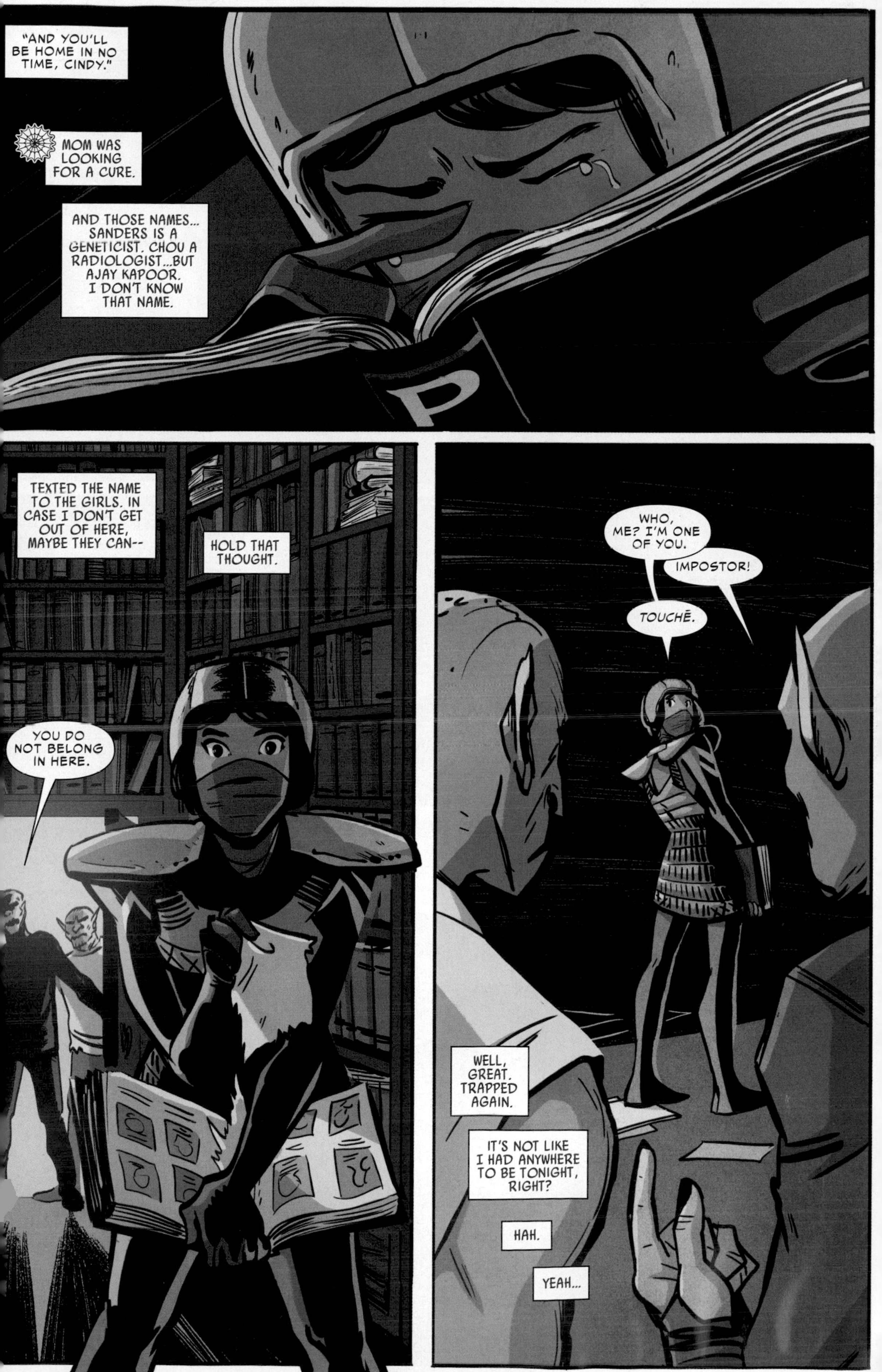
"AND YOU'LL BE HOME IN NO TIME, CINDY."
MOM WAS LOOKING FOR A CURE.
AND THOSE NAMES... SANDERS IS A GENETICIST. CHOU A RADIOLOGIST...BUT AJAY KAPOOR. I DON'T KNOW THAT NAME.
TEXTED THE NAME TO THE GIRLS. IN CASE I DON'T GET OUT OF HERE, MAYBE THEY CAN--
HOLD THAT THOUGHT.
YOU DO NOT BELONG IN HERE.
WHO, ME? I'M ONE OF YOU.
IMPOSTOR!
TOUCHÉ.
WELL, GREAT. TRAPPED AGAIN.
IT'S NOT LIKE I HAD ANYWHERE TO BE TONIGHT, RIGHT?
HAH.
YEAH...

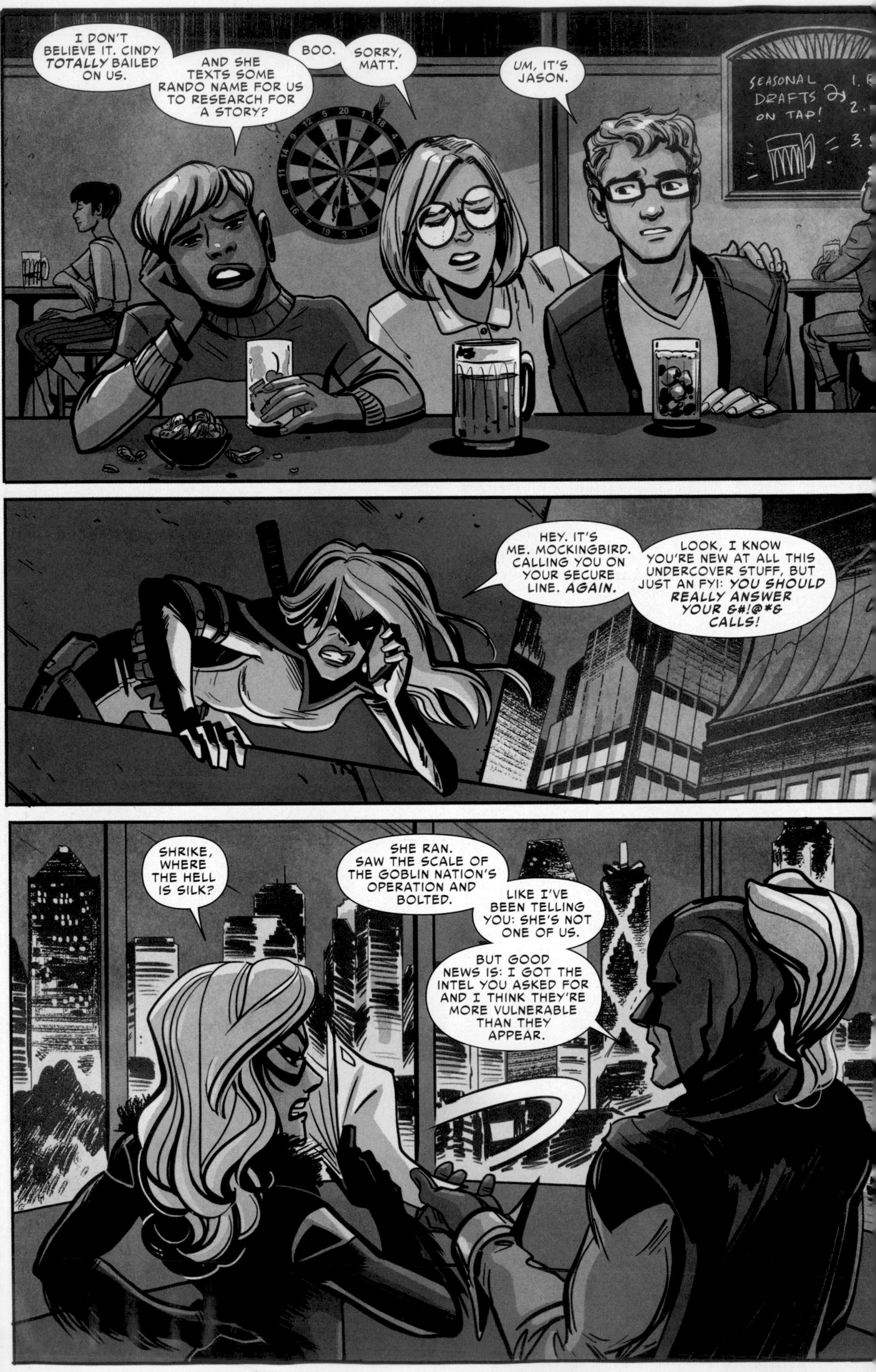
I DON'T BELIEVE IT. CINDY TOTALLY BAILED ON US.
AND SHE TEXTS SOME RANDO NAME FOR US TO RESEARCH FOR A STORY?
BOO.
SORRY, MATT.
UM, IT'S JASON.
SEASONAL DRAFTS ON TAP!
HEY. IT'S ME. MOCKINGBIRD. CALLING YOU ON YOUR SECURE LINE. AGAIN.
LOOK, I KNOW YOU'RE NEW AT ALL THIS UNDERCOVER STUFF, BUT JUST AN FYI: YOU SHOULD REALLY ANSWER YOUR &#!@*& CALLS!
SHRIKE, WHERE THE HELL IS SILK?
SHE RAN. SAW THE SCALE OF THE GOBLIN NATION'S OPERATION AND BOLTED.
LIKE I'VE BEEN TELLING YOU: SHE'S NOT ONE OF US.
BUT GOOD NEWS IS: I GOT THE INTEL YOU ASKED FOR AND I THINK THEY'RE MORE VULNERABLE THAN THEY APPEAR.

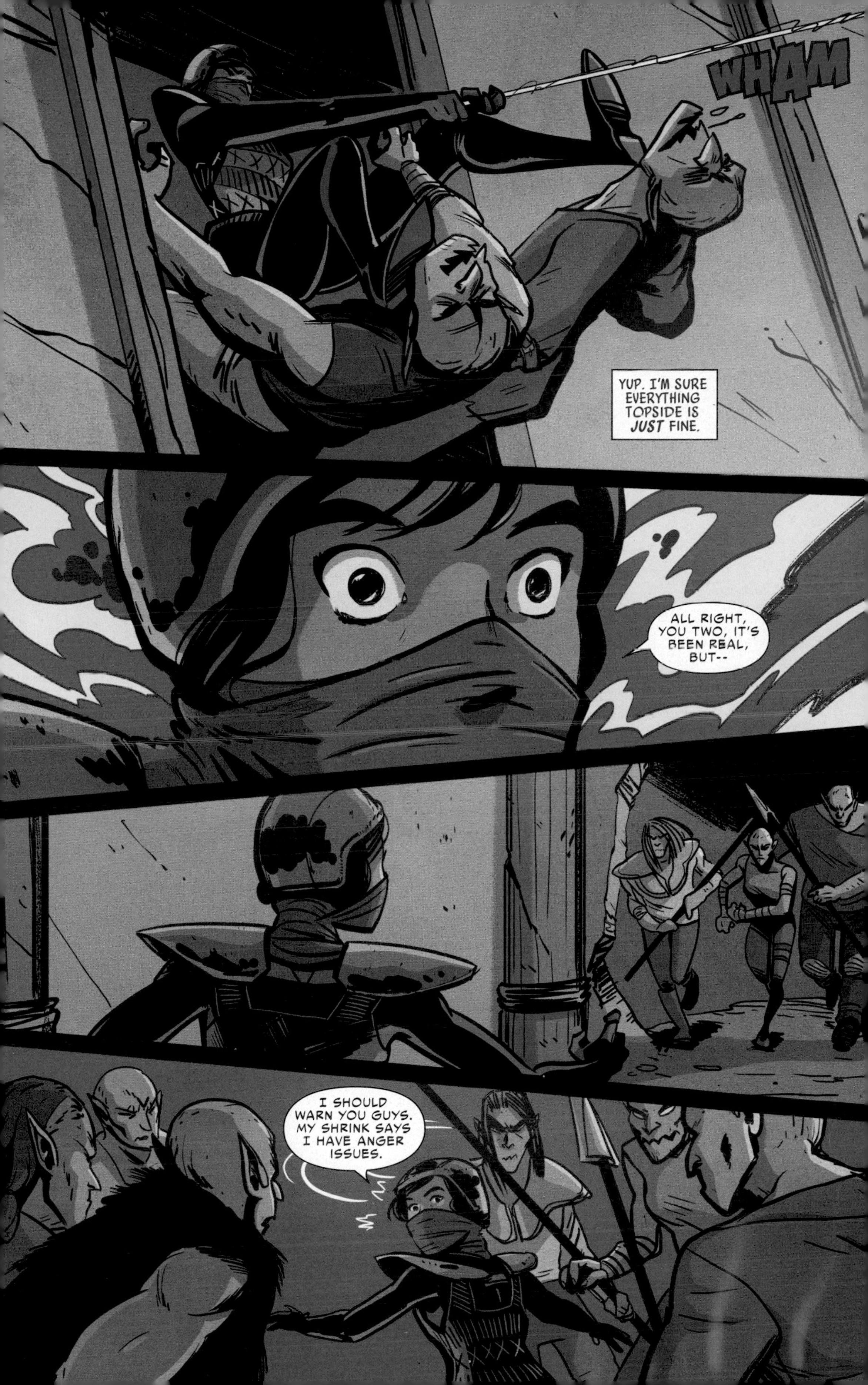
WHAM
YUP. I'M SURE EVERYTHING TOPSIDE IS *JUST* FINE.
ALL RIGHT, YOU TWO, IT'S BEEN REAL, BUT--
I SHOULD WARN YOU GUYS. MY SHRINK SAYS I HAVE ANGER ISSUES.

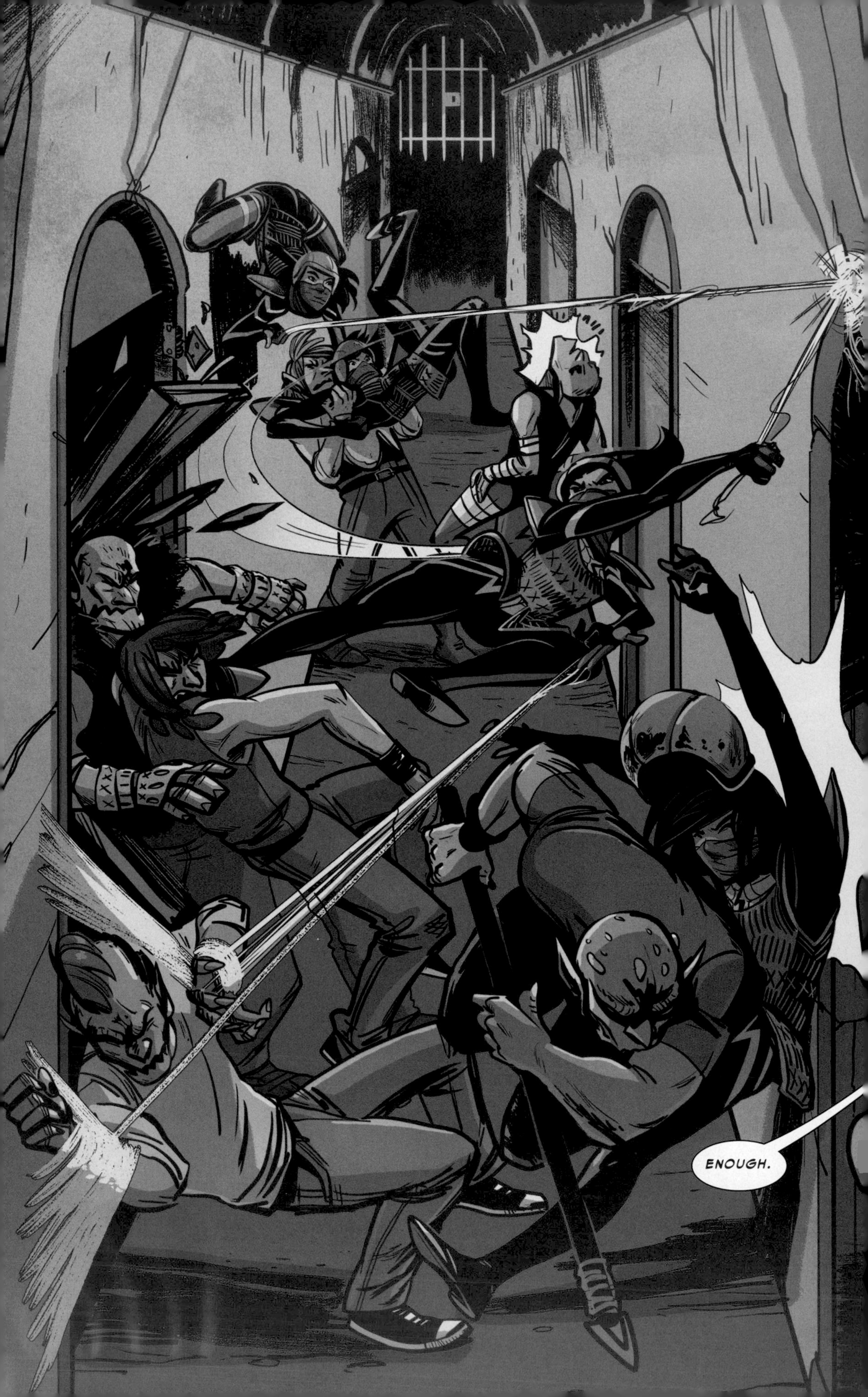
ENOUGH.

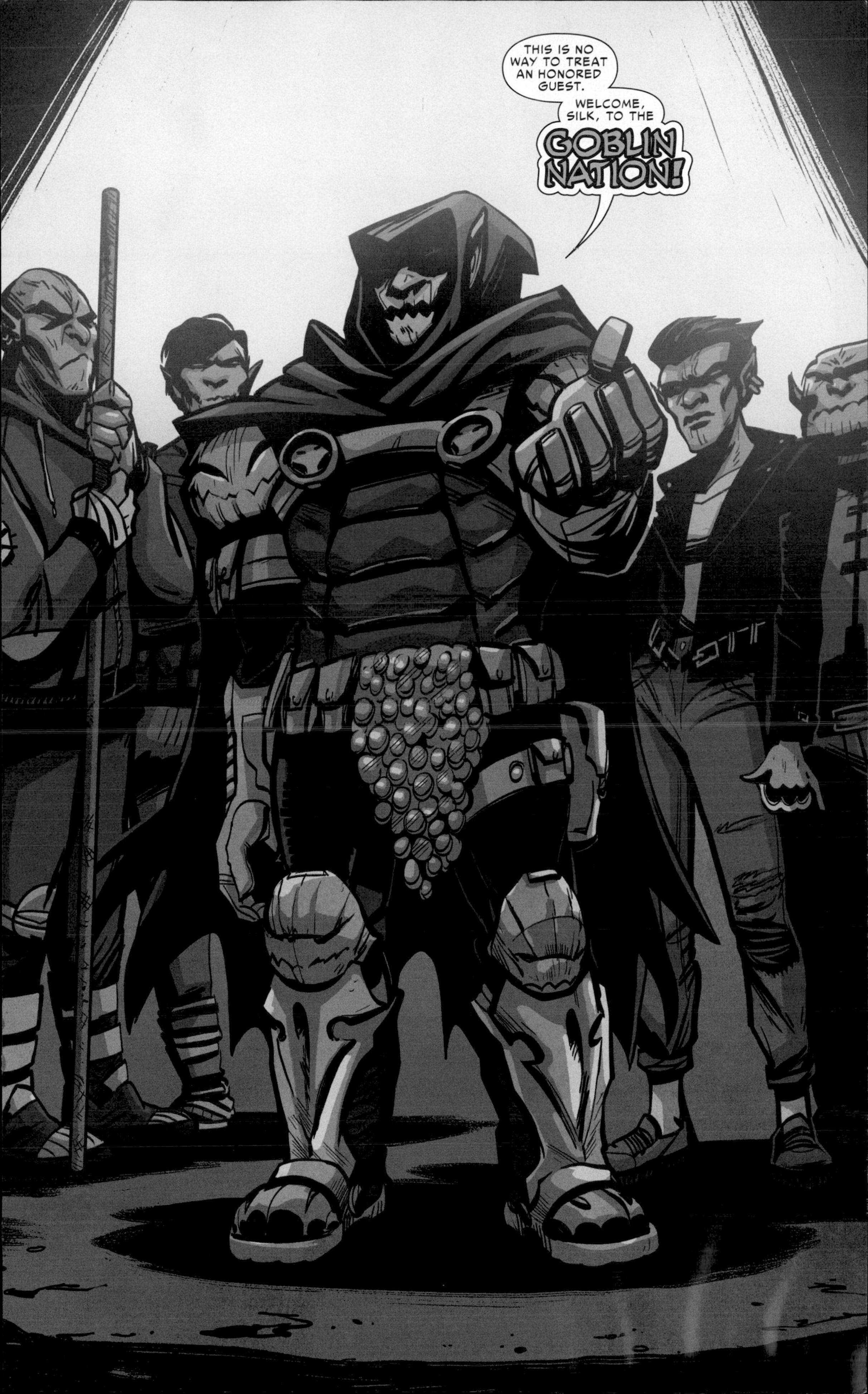
THIS IS NO WAY TO TREAT AN HONORED GUEST.
WELCOME, SILK, TO THE
GOBLIN NATION!

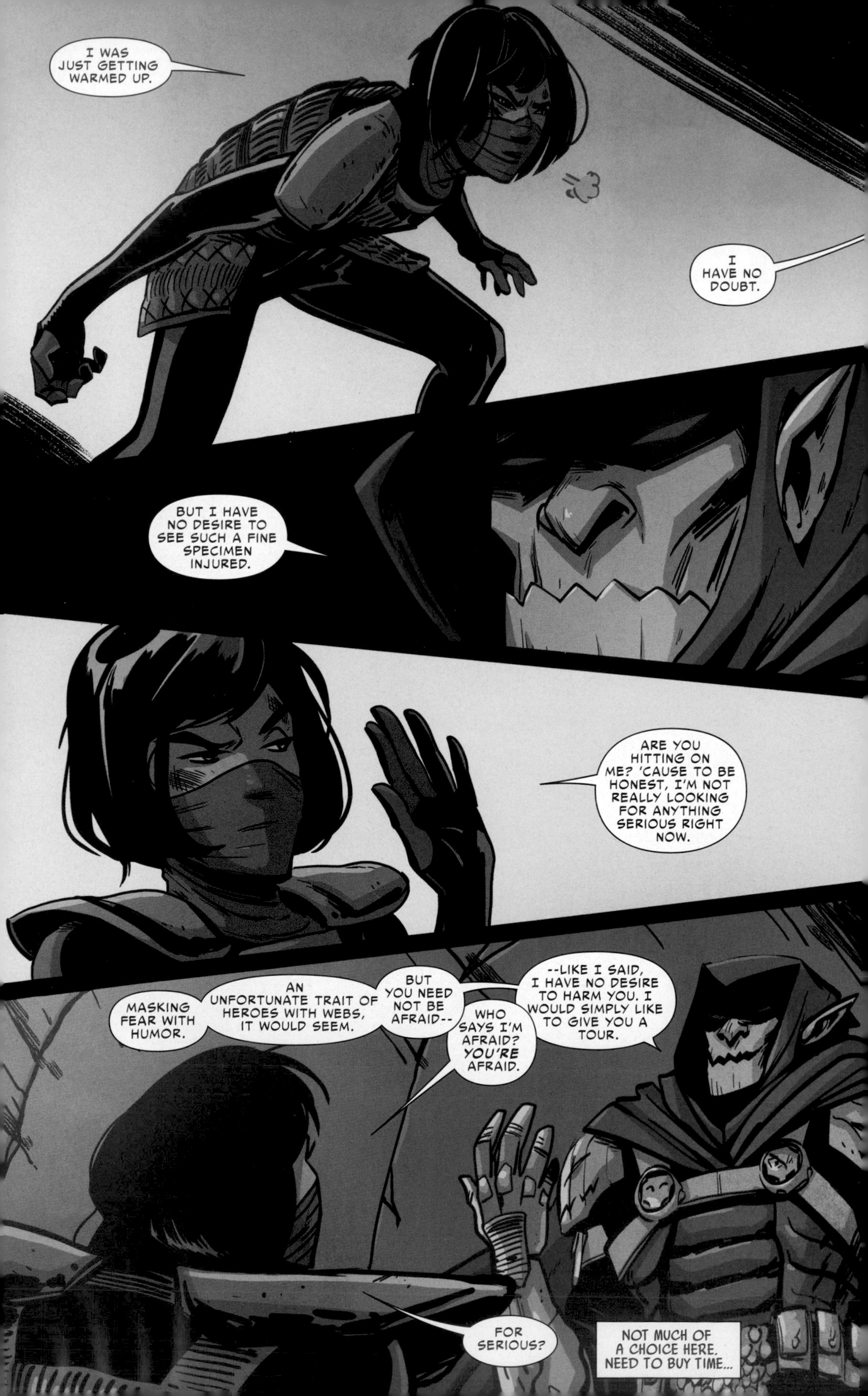
I WAS JUST GETTING WARMED UP.
I HAVE NO DOUBT.
BUT I HAVE NO DESIRE TO SEE SUCH A FINE SPECIMEN INJURED.
ARE YOU HITTING ON ME? 'CAUSE TO BE HONEST, I'M NOT REALLY LOOKING FOR ANYTHING SERIOUS RIGHT NOW.
MASKING FEAR WITH HUMOR.
AN UNFORTUNATE TRAIT OF HEROES WITH WEBS, IT WOULD SEEM.
BUT YOU NEED NOT BE AFRAID--
--LIKE I SAID, I HAVE NO DESIRE TO HARM YOU. I WOULD SIMPLY LIKE TO GIVE YOU A TOUR.
WHO SAYS I'M AFRAID? YOU'RE AFRAID.
FOR SERIOUS?
NOT MUCH OF A CHOICE HERE. NEED TO BUY TIME...

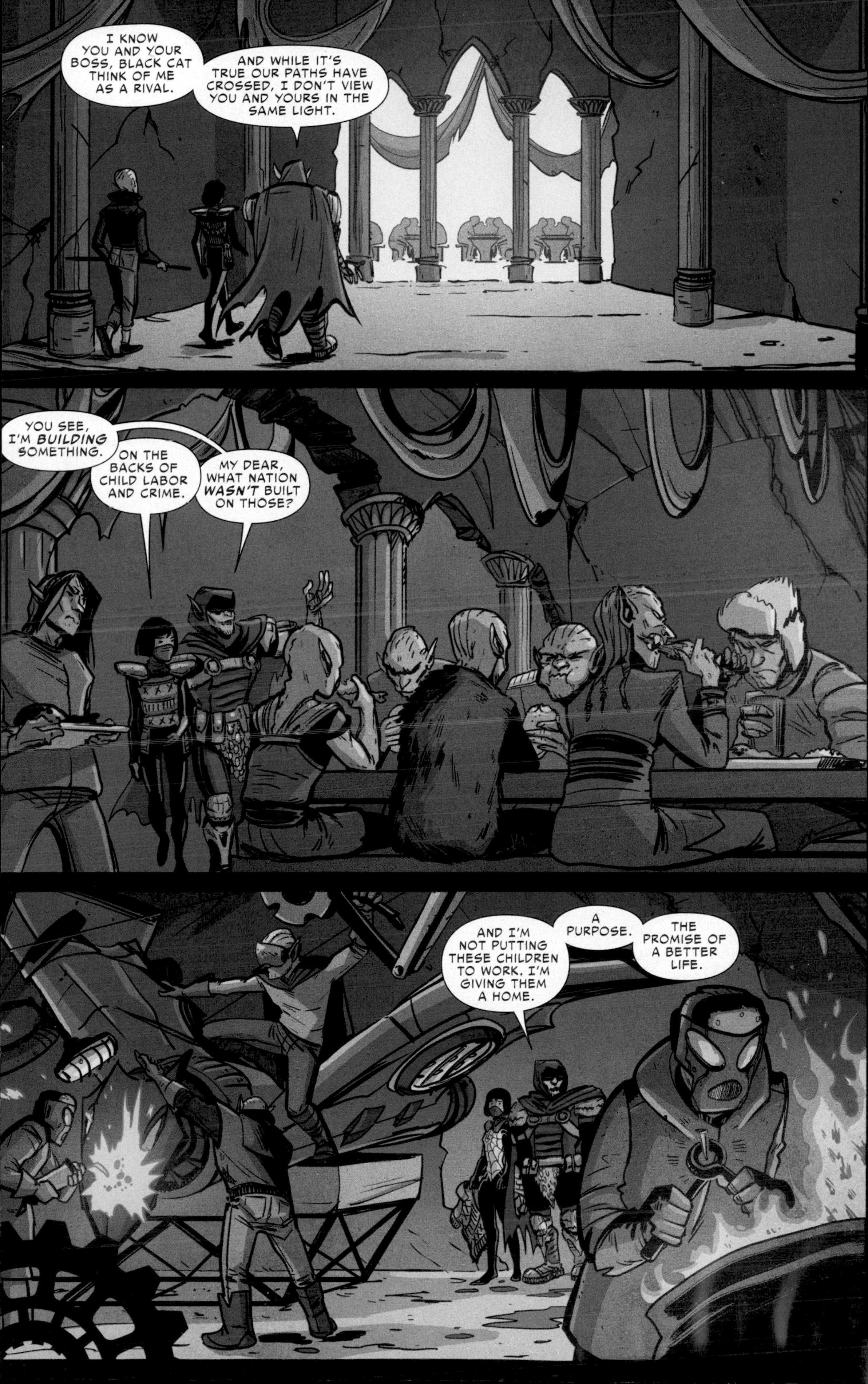
I KNOW YOU AND YOUR BOSS, BLACK CAT THINK OF ME AS A RIVAL.
AND WHILE IT'S TRUE OUR PATHS HAVE CROSSED, I DON'T VIEW YOU AND YOURS IN THE SAME LIGHT.
YOU SEE, I'M *BUILDING* SOMETHING.
ON THE BACKS OF CHILD LABOR AND CRIME.
MY DEAR, WHAT NATION *WASN'T* BUILT ON THOSE?
AND I'M NOT PUTTING THESE CHILDREN TO WORK. I'M GIVING THEM A HOME.
A PURPOSE.
THE PROMISE OF A BETTER LIFE.

SO YOU SEE, THIS IS NOT SOME MERE GANG.

IT IS A NEW WAY OF LIVING.

AND OUR *NATION* IS GROWING.

SOON, IT WILL BE ABOVE GROUND AND ABOVE BOARD.

LEGIT, HUH?

NOTHING CAN STOP US.

ANYTHING THAT STANDS IN OUR WAY... ...WILL BE DESTROYED.

WHICH IS WHY YOU SHOULD *JOIN* ME.

WAIT.

YOU'RE OFFERING ME A *JOB*?

NO, MY DEAR, I'M OFFERING YOU A CHANCE TO LIVE.

FIRST OF ALL: CALLING ME "MY DEAR"? NOT COOL. CONDESCENDING AT BEST. SEXIST AT WORST.

SECOND OF ALL: UNLESS YOU GUYS HAVE COMPREHENSIVE DENTAL PLAN: MY ANSWER IS NO.

HELL, NO.

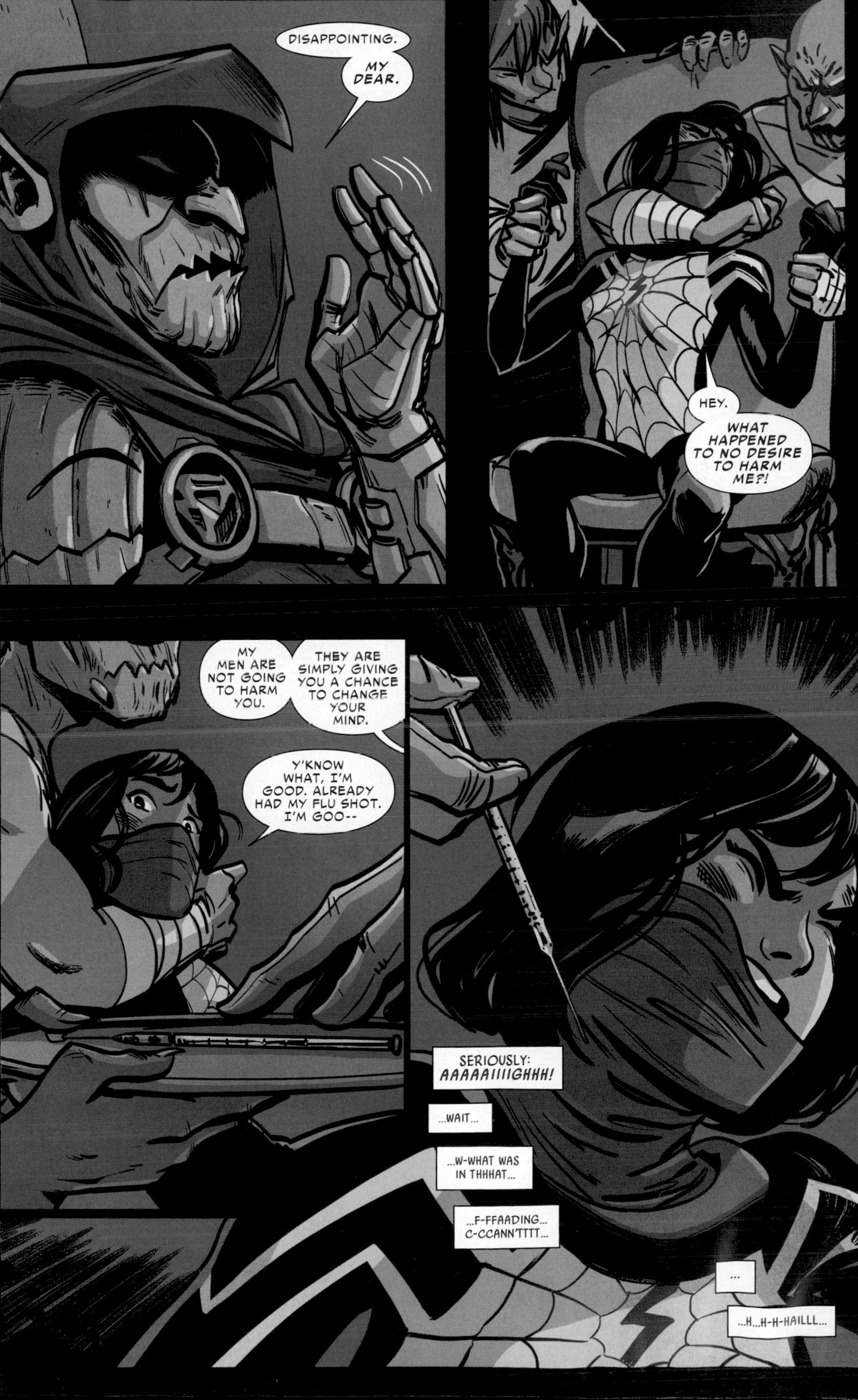

DISAPPOINTING.
MY DEAR.
HEY.
WHAT HAPPENED TO NO DESIRE TO HARM ME?!
MY MEN ARE NOT GOING TO HARM YOU.
THEY ARE SIMPLY GIVING YOU A CHANCE TO CHANGE YOUR MIND.
Y'KNOW WHAT, I'M GOOD. ALREADY HAD MY FLU SHOT. I'M GOO--
SERIOUSLY: AAAAAIIIIGHHH!
...WAIT...
...W-WHAT WAS IN THHHAT...
...F-FFAADING... C-CCANN'TTTT...
...
...H...H-H-HAILLL...

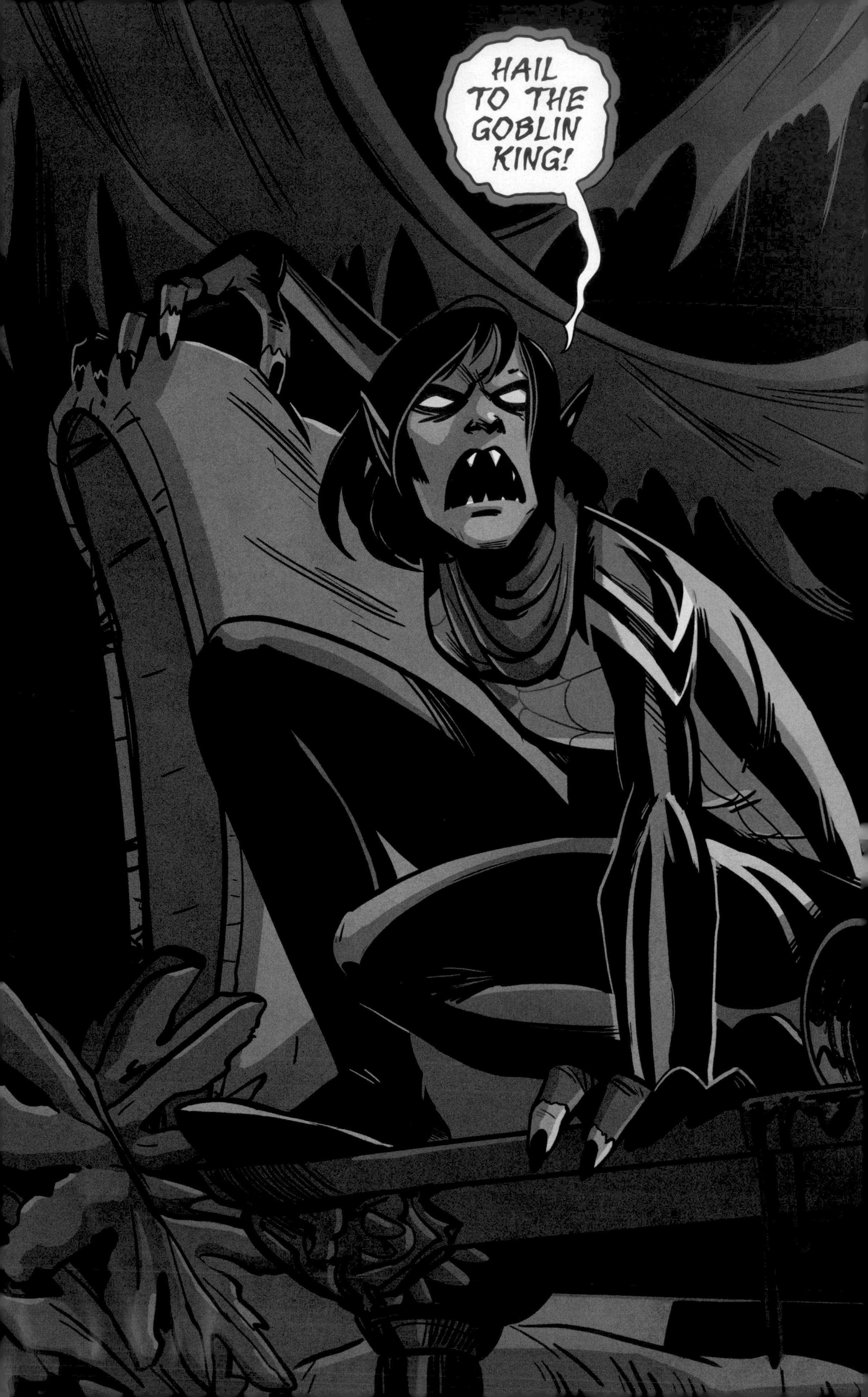
HAIL TO THE GOBLIN KING!

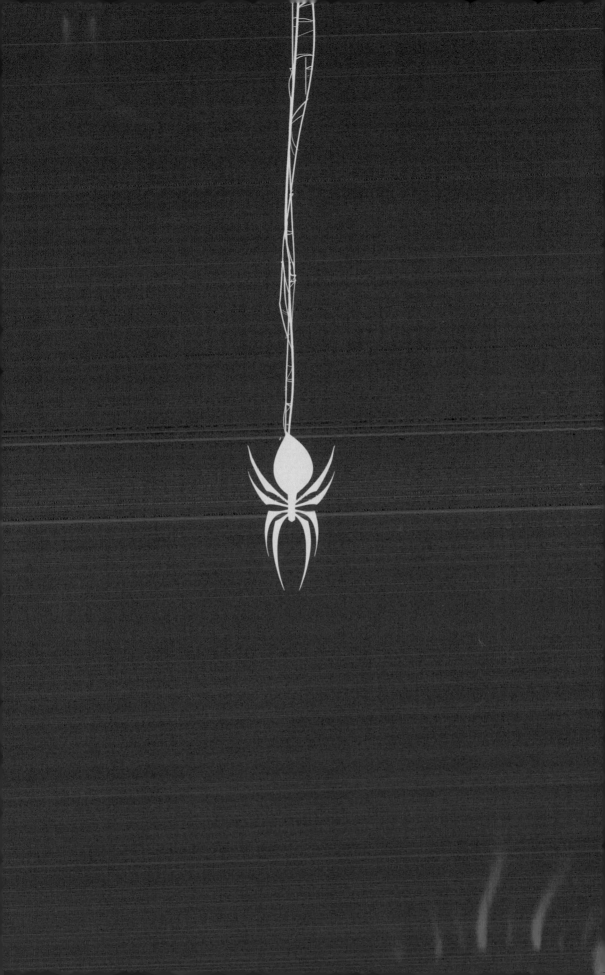

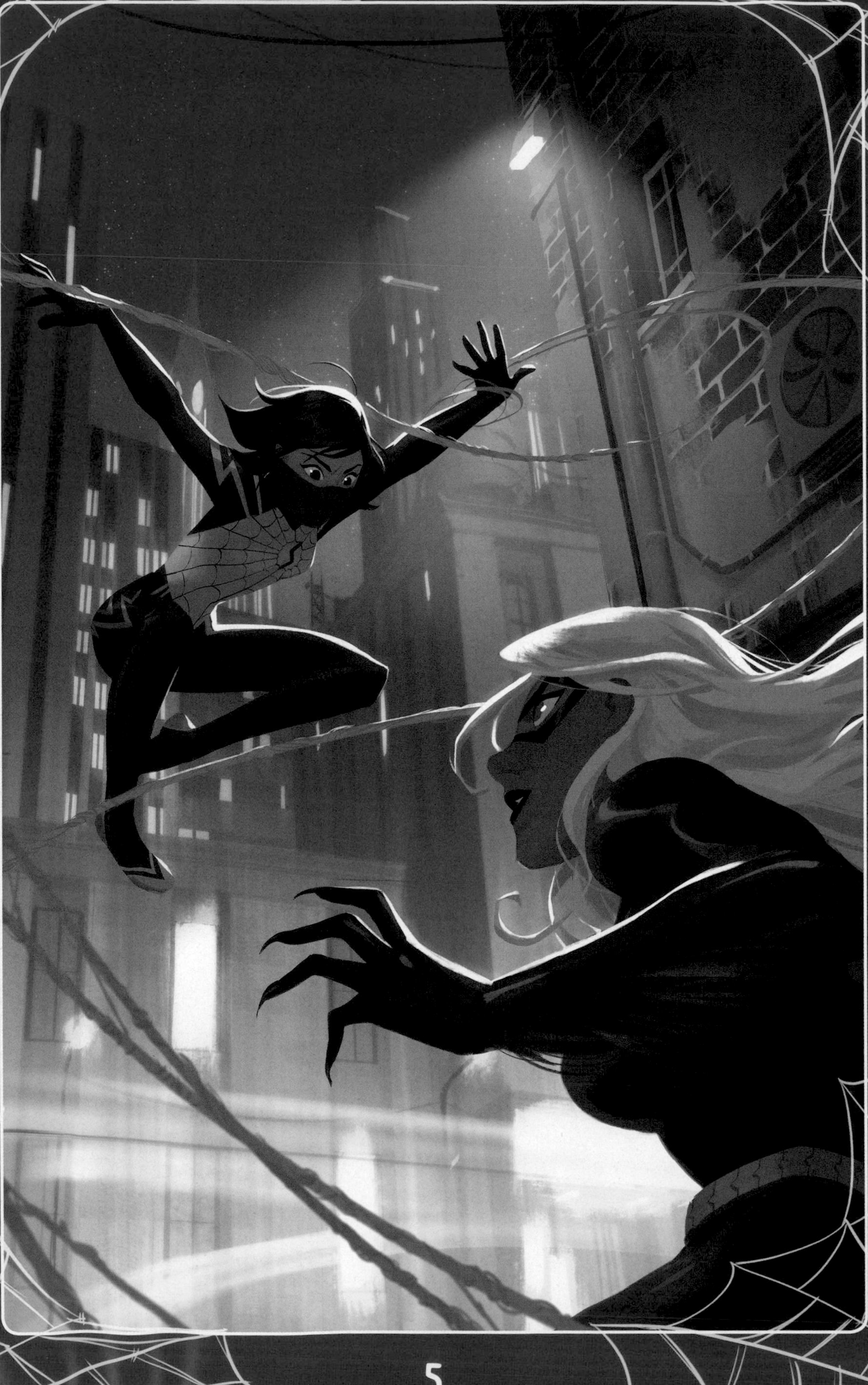

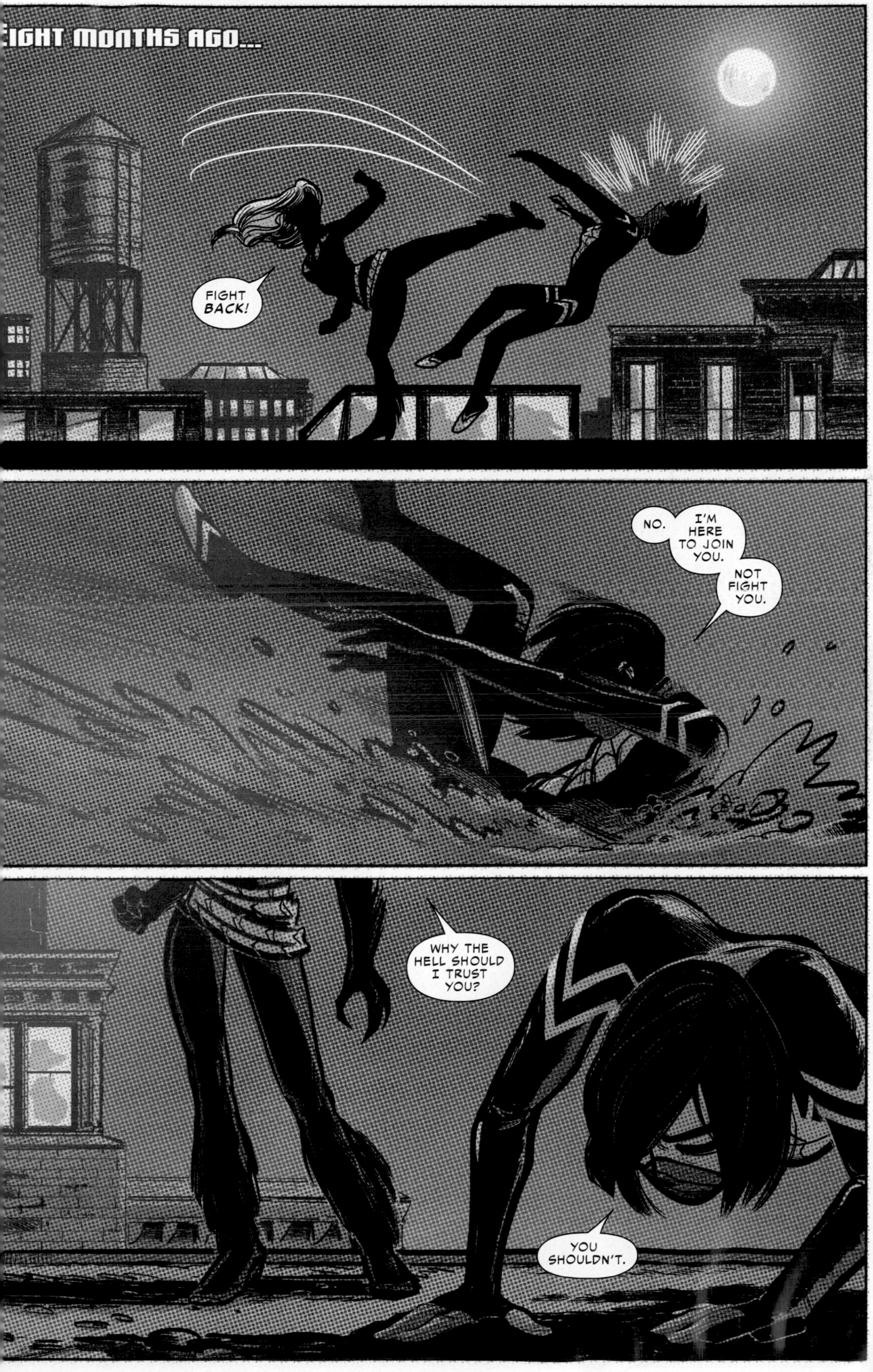
EIGHT MONTHS AGO...
FIGHT BACK!
NO.
I'M HERE TO JOIN YOU.
NOT FIGHT YOU.
WHY THE HELL SHOULD I TRUST YOU?
YOU SHOULDN'T.

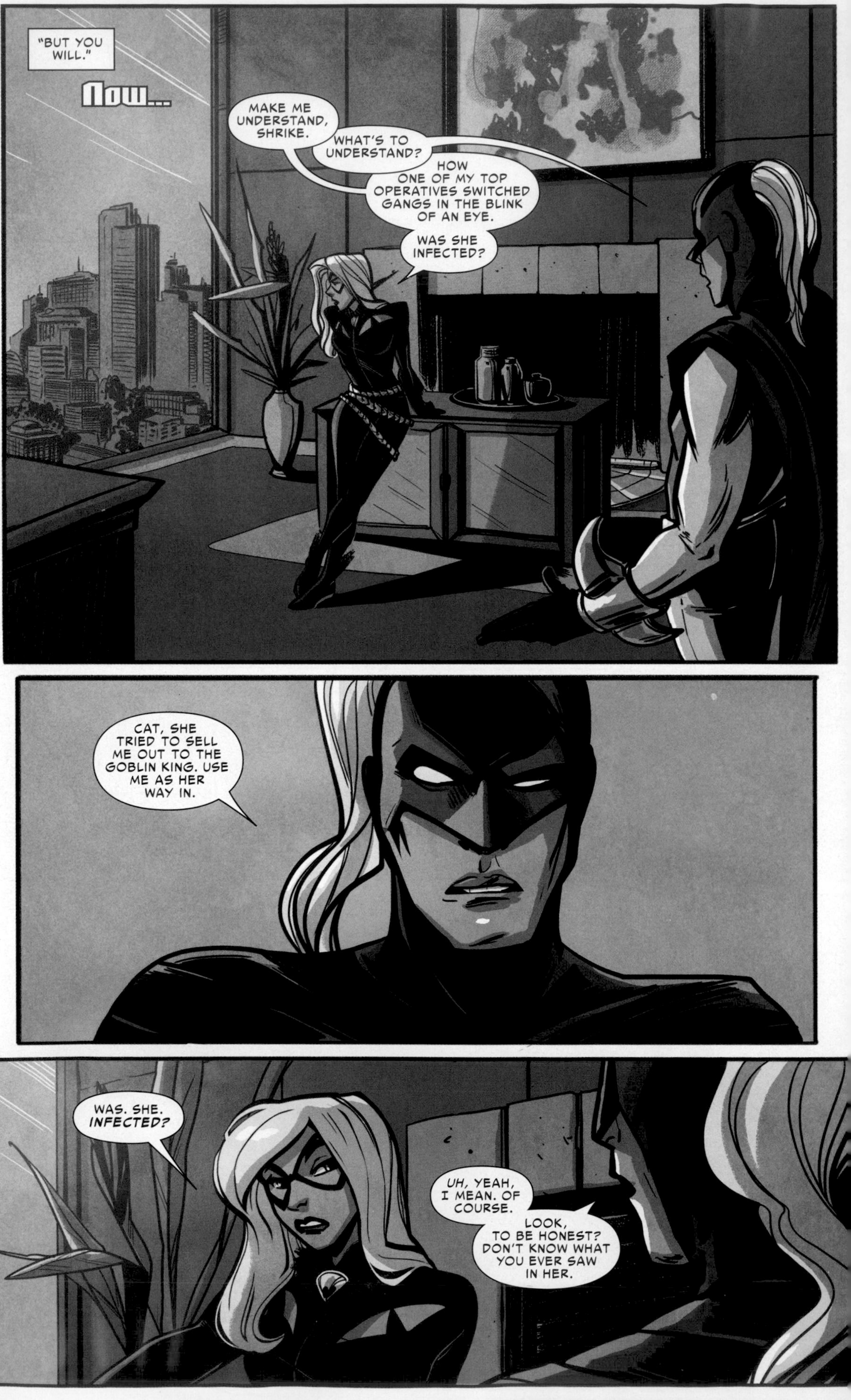
"BUT YOU WILL."
NOW...
MAKE ME UNDERSTAND, SHRIKE.
WHAT'S TO UNDERSTAND?
HOW ONE OF MY TOP OPERATIVES SWITCHED GANGS IN THE BLINK OF AN EYE.
WAS SHE INFECTED?
CAT, SHE TRIED TO SELL ME OUT TO THE GOBLIN KING. USE ME AS HER WAY IN.
WAS. SHE. *INFECTED?*
UH, YEAH, I MEAN. OF COURSE.
LOOK, TO BE HONEST? DON'T KNOW WHAT YOU EVER SAW IN HER.

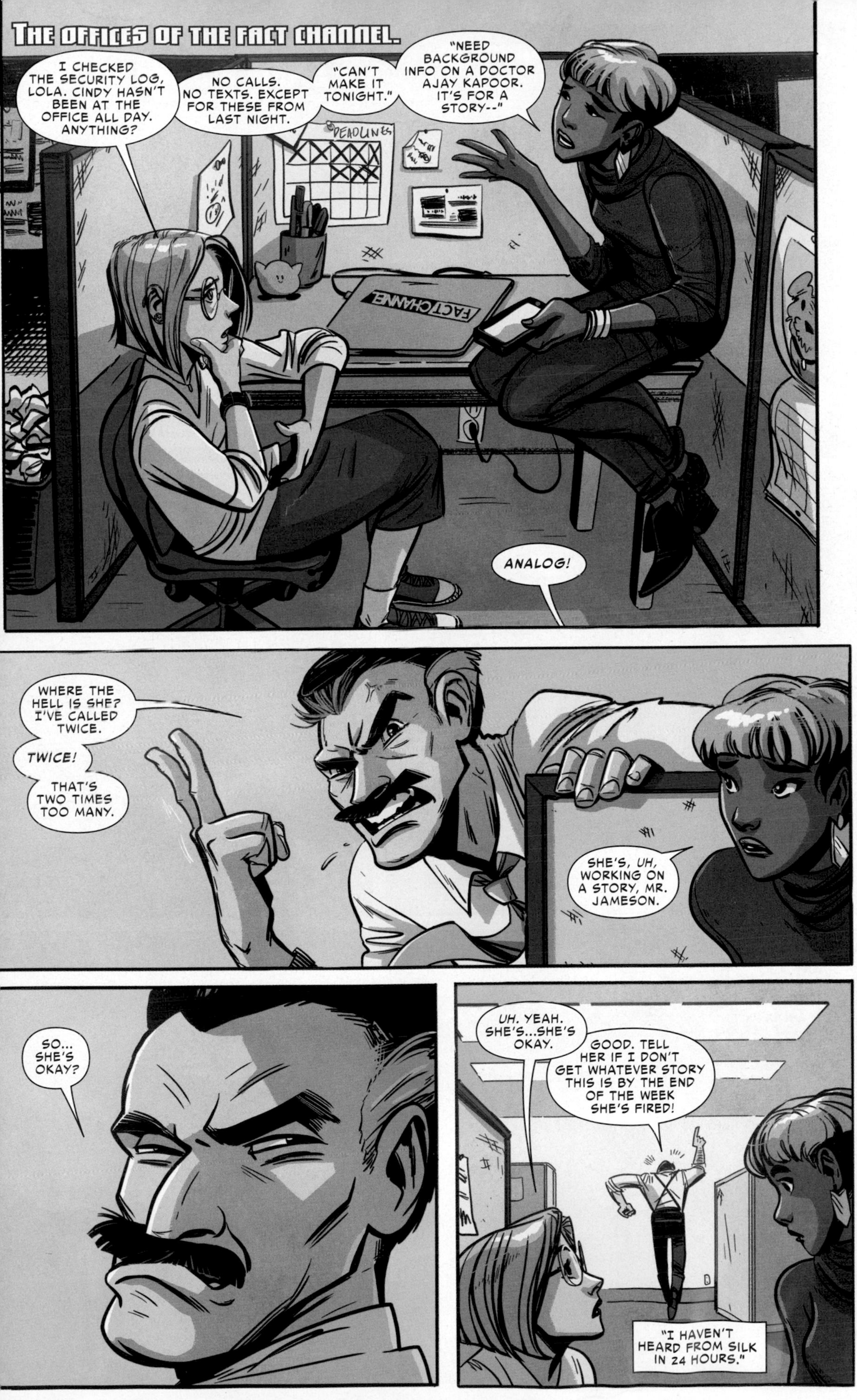
THE OFFICES OF THE FACT CHANNEL.
I CHECKED THE SECURITY LOG, LOLA. CINDY HASN'T BEEN AT THE OFFICE ALL DAY. ANYTHING?
NO CALLS. NO TEXTS. EXCEPT FOR THESE FROM LAST NIGHT.
"CAN'T MAKE IT TONIGHT."
"NEED BACKGROUND INFO ON A DOCTOR AJAY KAPOOR. IT'S FOR A STORY--"
DEADLINES
FACT CHANNEL
ANALOG!
WHERE THE HELL IS SHE? I'VE CALLED TWICE.
TWICE!
THAT'S TWO TIMES TOO MANY.
SHE'S, UH, WORKING ON A STORY, MR. JAMESON.
SO... SHE'S OKAY?
UH. YEAH. SHE'S...SHE'S OKAY.
GOOD. TELL HER IF I DON'T GET WHATEVER STORY THIS IS BY THE END OF THE WEEK SHE'S FIRED!
"I HAVEN'T HEARD FROM SILK IN 24 HOURS."

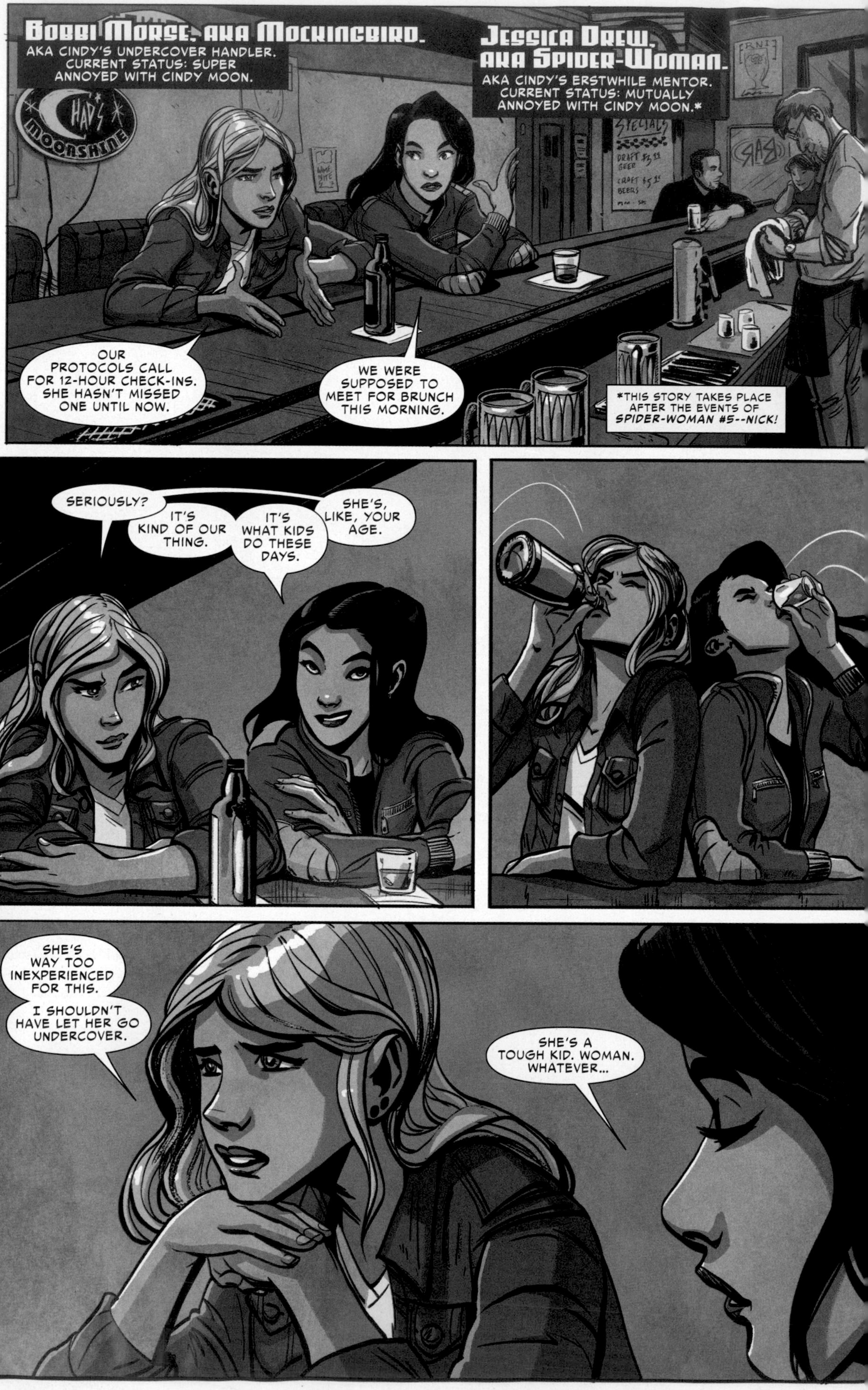

BOBBI MORSE, AKA MOCKINGBIRD.
AKA CINDY'S UNDERCOVER HANDLER. CURRENT STATUS: SUPER ANNOYED WITH CINDY MOON.
JESSICA DREW, AKA SPIDER-WOMAN.
AKA CINDY'S ERSTWHILE MENTOR. CURRENT STATUS: MUTUALLY ANNOYED WITH CINDY MOON.*
CHAD'S MOONSHINE
OUR PROTOCOLS CALL FOR 12-HOUR CHECK-INS. SHE HASN'T MISSED ONE UNTIL NOW.
WE WERE SUPPOSED TO MEET FOR BRUNCH THIS MORNING.
*THIS STORY TAKES PLACE AFTER THE EVENTS OF SPIDER-WOMAN #5--NICK!
SERIOUSLY?
IT'S KIND OF OUR THING.
IT'S WHAT KIDS DO THESE DAYS.
SHE'S, LIKE, YOUR AGE.
SHE'S WAY TOO INEXPERIENCED FOR THIS.
I SHOULDN'T HAVE LET HER GO UNDERCOVER.
SHE'S A TOUGH KID. WOMAN. WHATEVER...

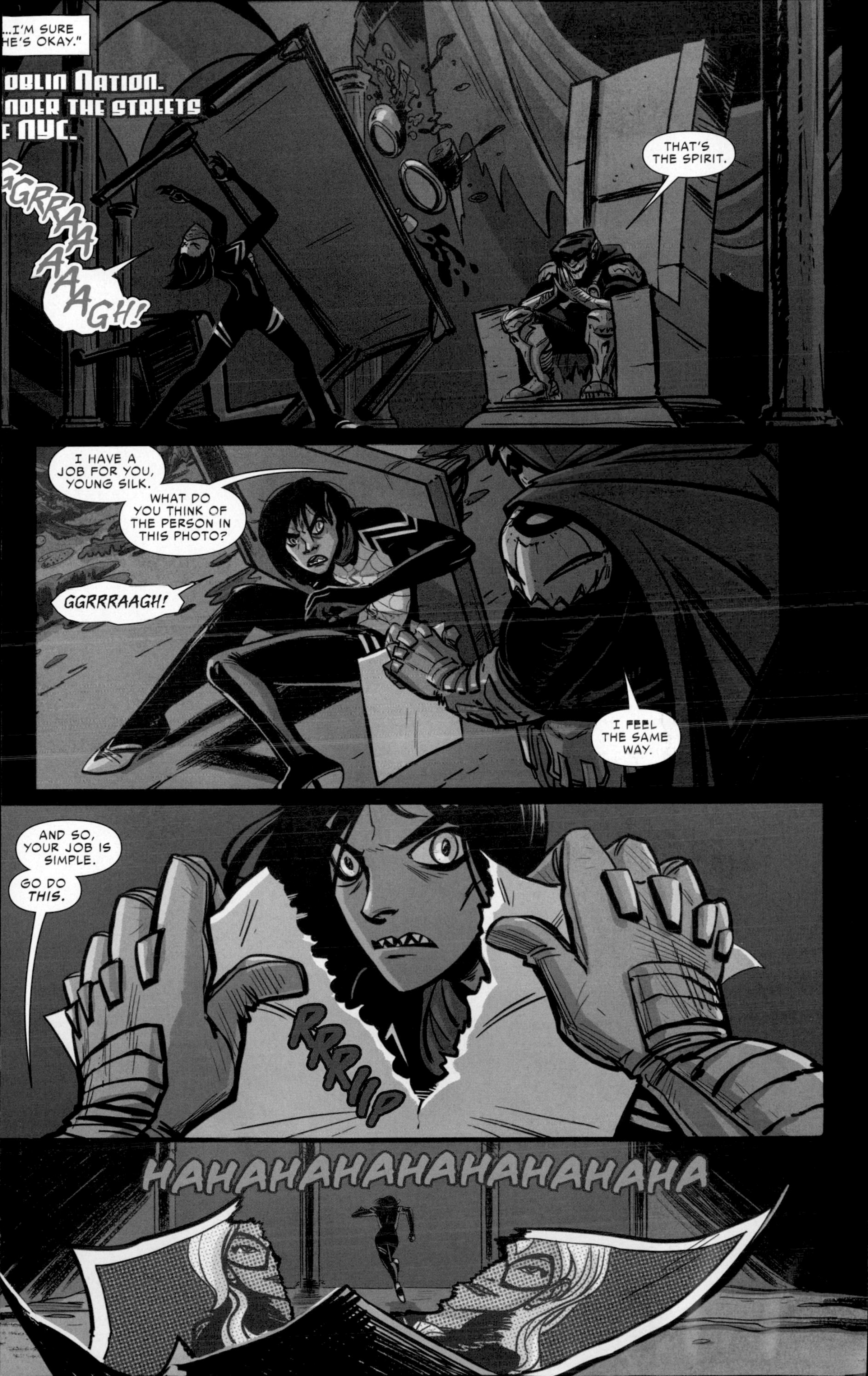

...I'M SURE HE'S OKAY."
OBLIN NATION. NDER THE STREETS F NYC.
GGRRAAAAAAGH!
THAT'S THE SPIRIT.
I HAVE A JOB FOR YOU, YOUNG SILK.
WHAT DO YOU THINK OF THE PERSON IN THIS PHOTO?
GGRRRAAGH!
I FEEL THE SAME WAY.
AND SO, YOUR JOB IS SIMPLE.
GO DO THIS.
RRRIIP
HAHAHAHAHAHAHAHAHAHA

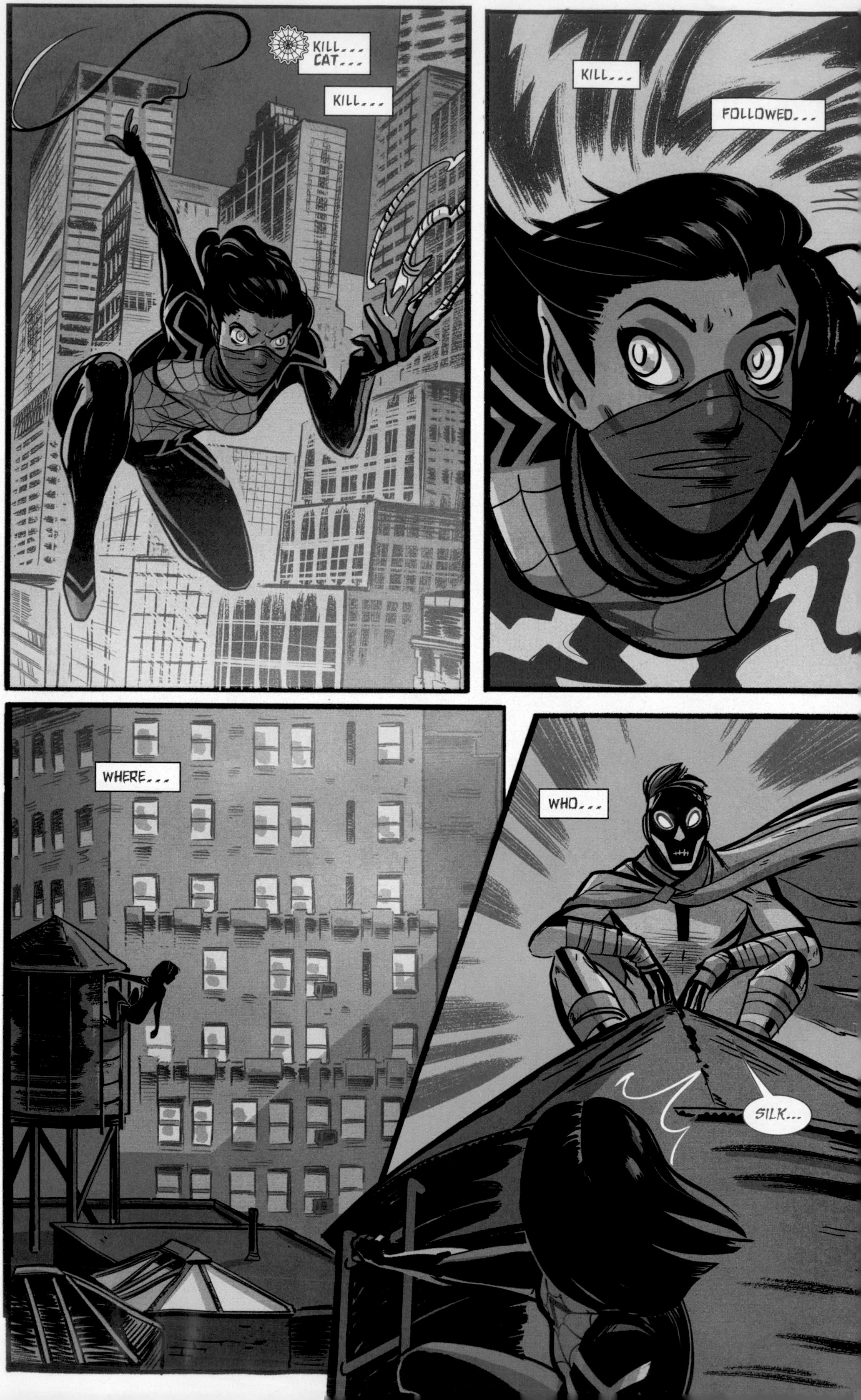
KILL...
CAT...
KILL...
KILL...
FOLLOWED...
WHERE...
WHO...
SILK...

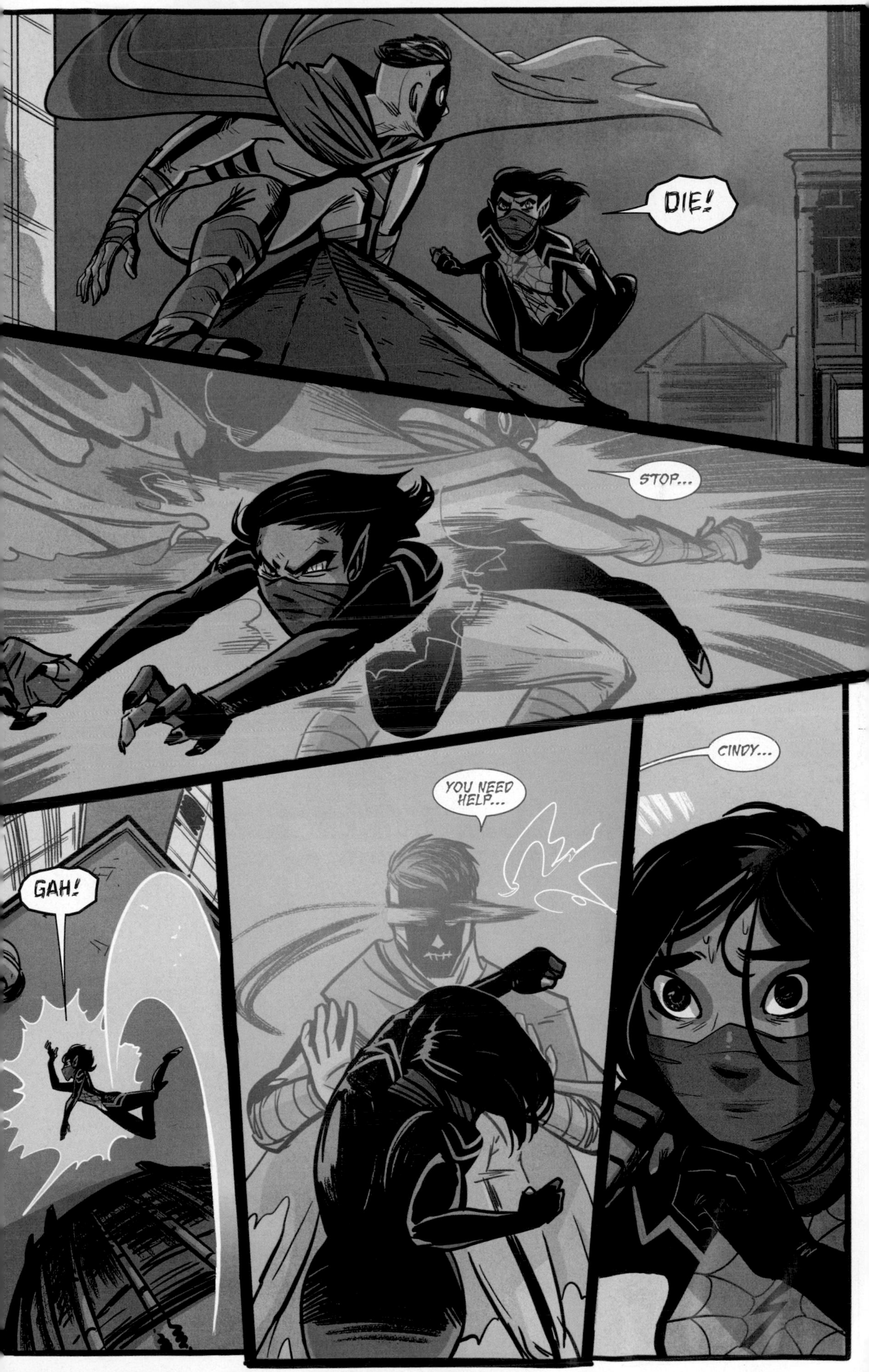
DIE!
STOP...
GAH!
YOU NEED HELP...
CINDY...

LEAVE.
ME.

FFFFFFSHHHH

ALONE.

I'M
SORRY...

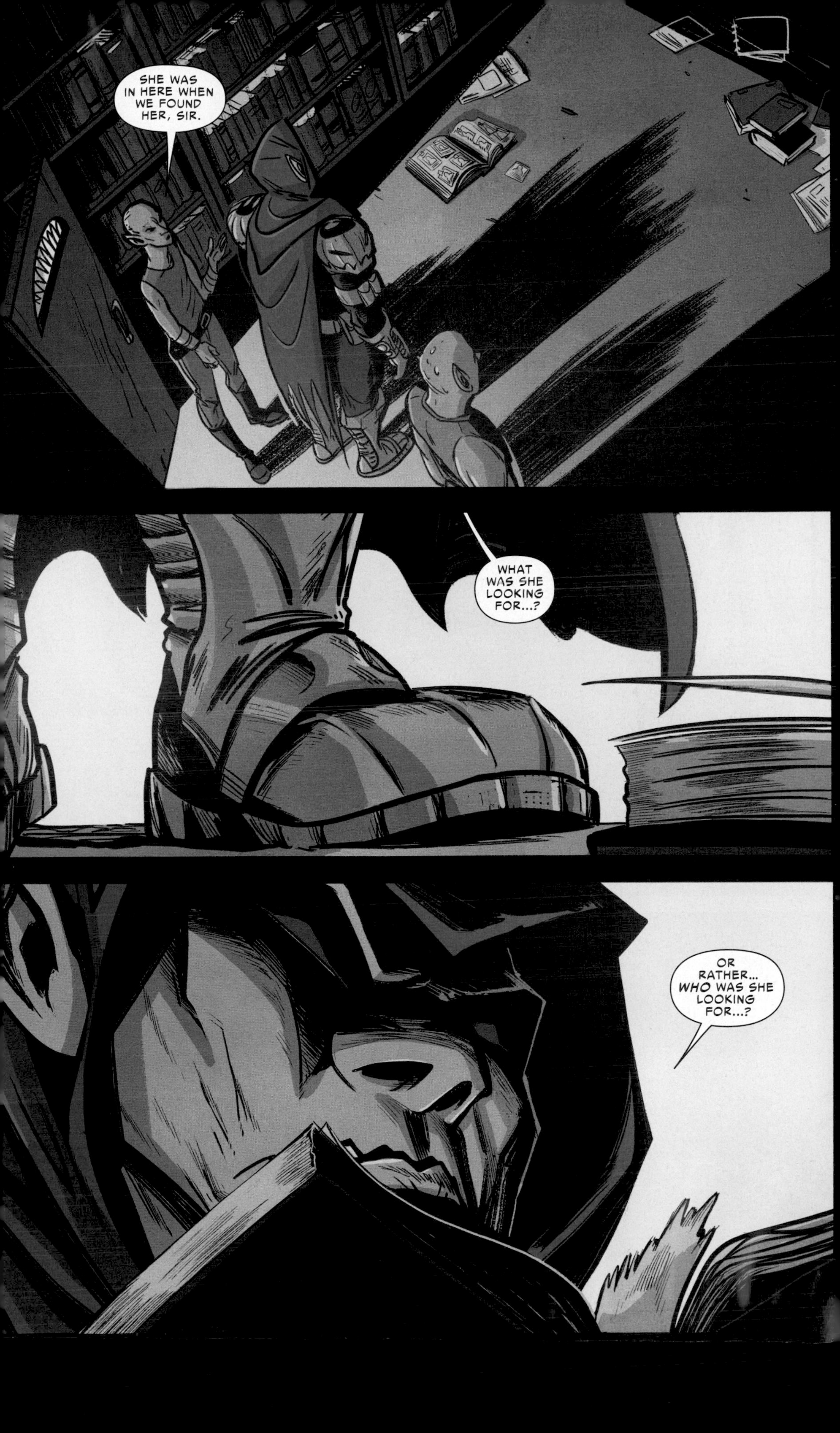
SHE WAS IN HERE WHEN WE FOUND HER, SIR.
WHAT WAS SHE LOOKING FOR...?
OR RATHER... WHO WAS SHE LOOKING FOR...?

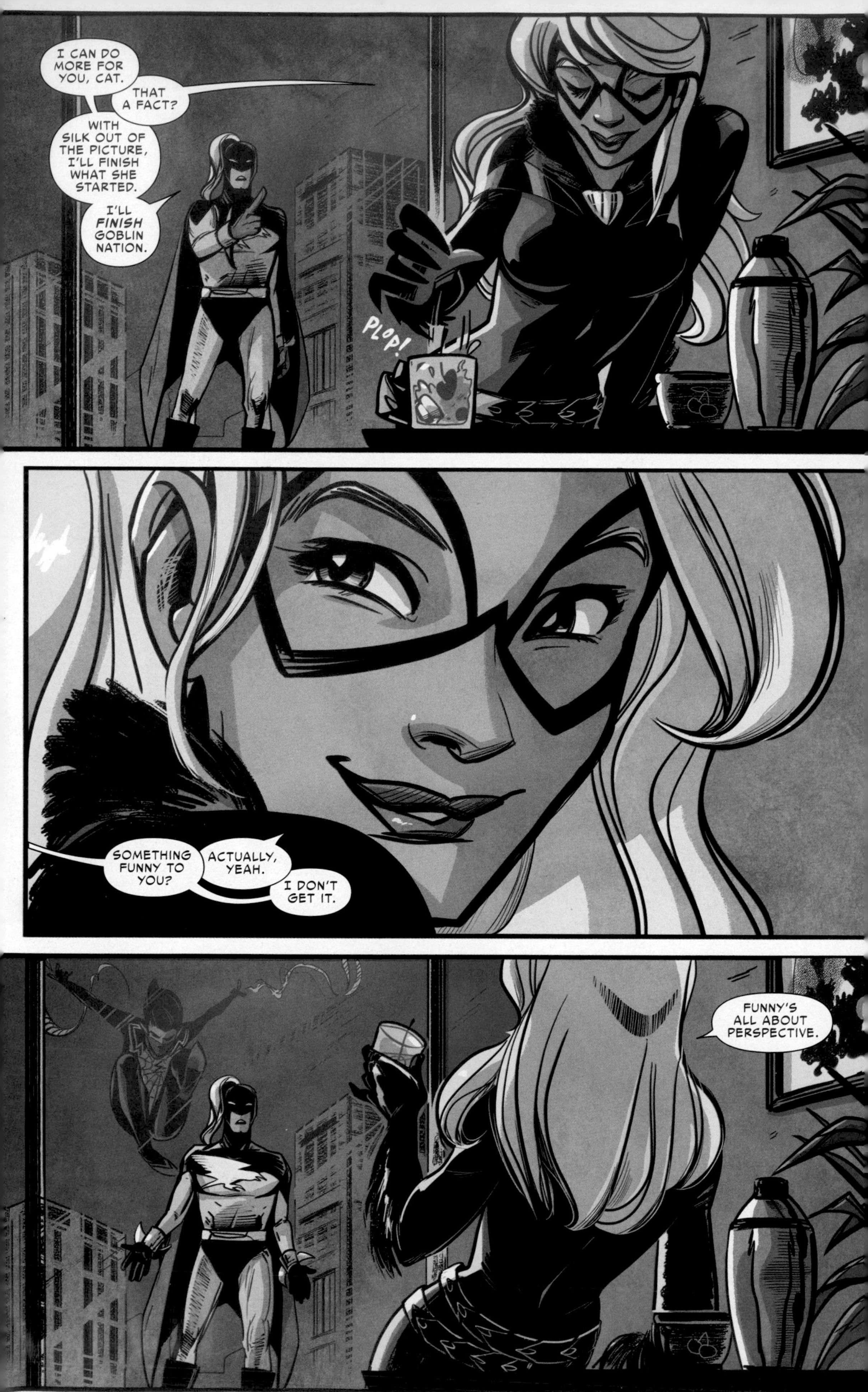
I CAN DO MORE FOR YOU, CAT.
THAT A FACT?
WITH SILK OUT OF THE PICTURE, I'LL FINISH WHAT SHE STARTED.
I'LL *FINISH* GOBLIN NATION.
PLOP!
SOMETHING FUNNY TO YOU?
ACTUALLY, YEAH.
I DON'T GET IT.
FUNNY'S ALL ABOUT PERSPECTIVE.

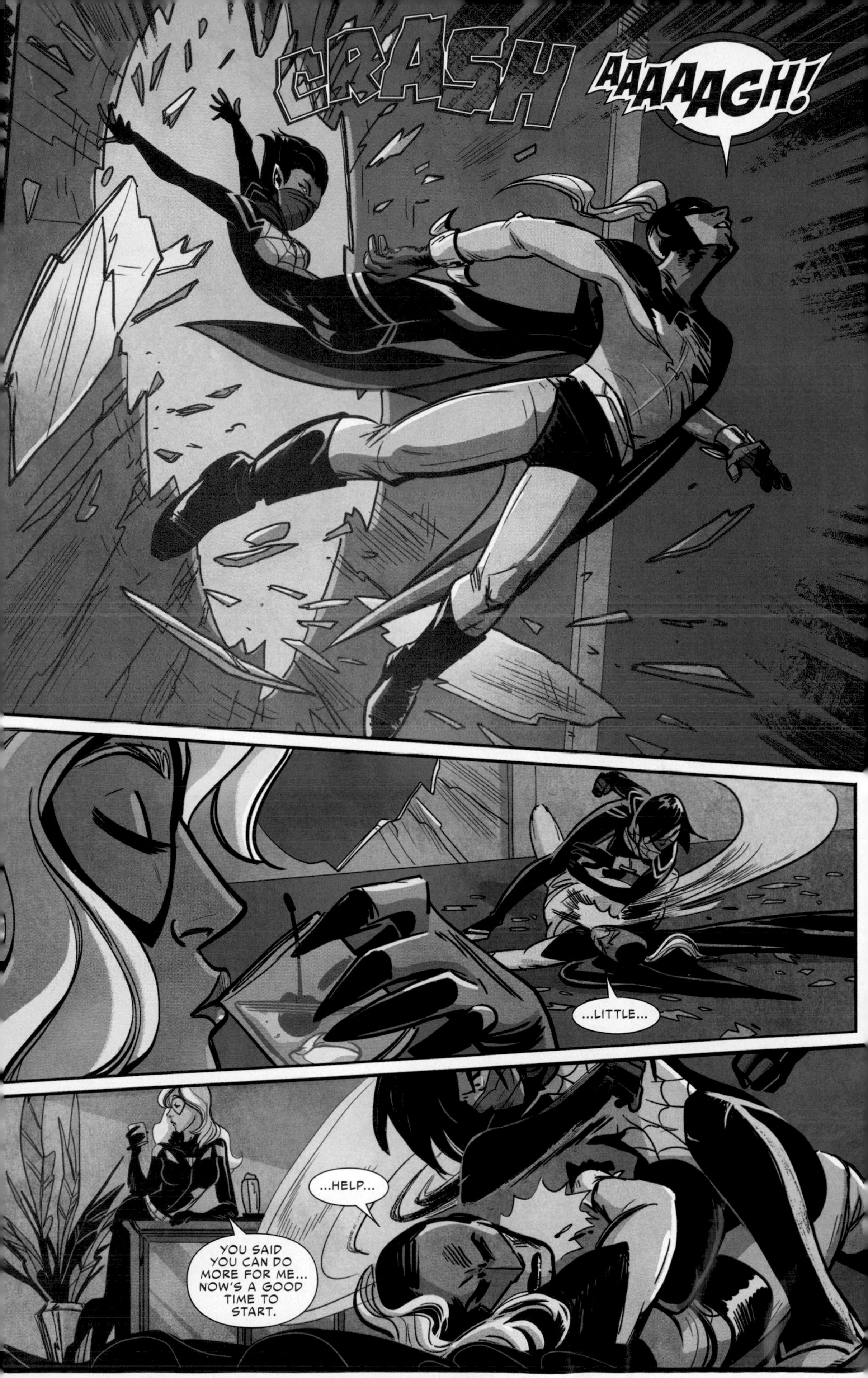
CRASH
AAAAAGH!
...LITTLE...
...HELP...
YOU SAID YOU CAN DO MORE FOR ME... NOW'S A GOOD TIME TO START.

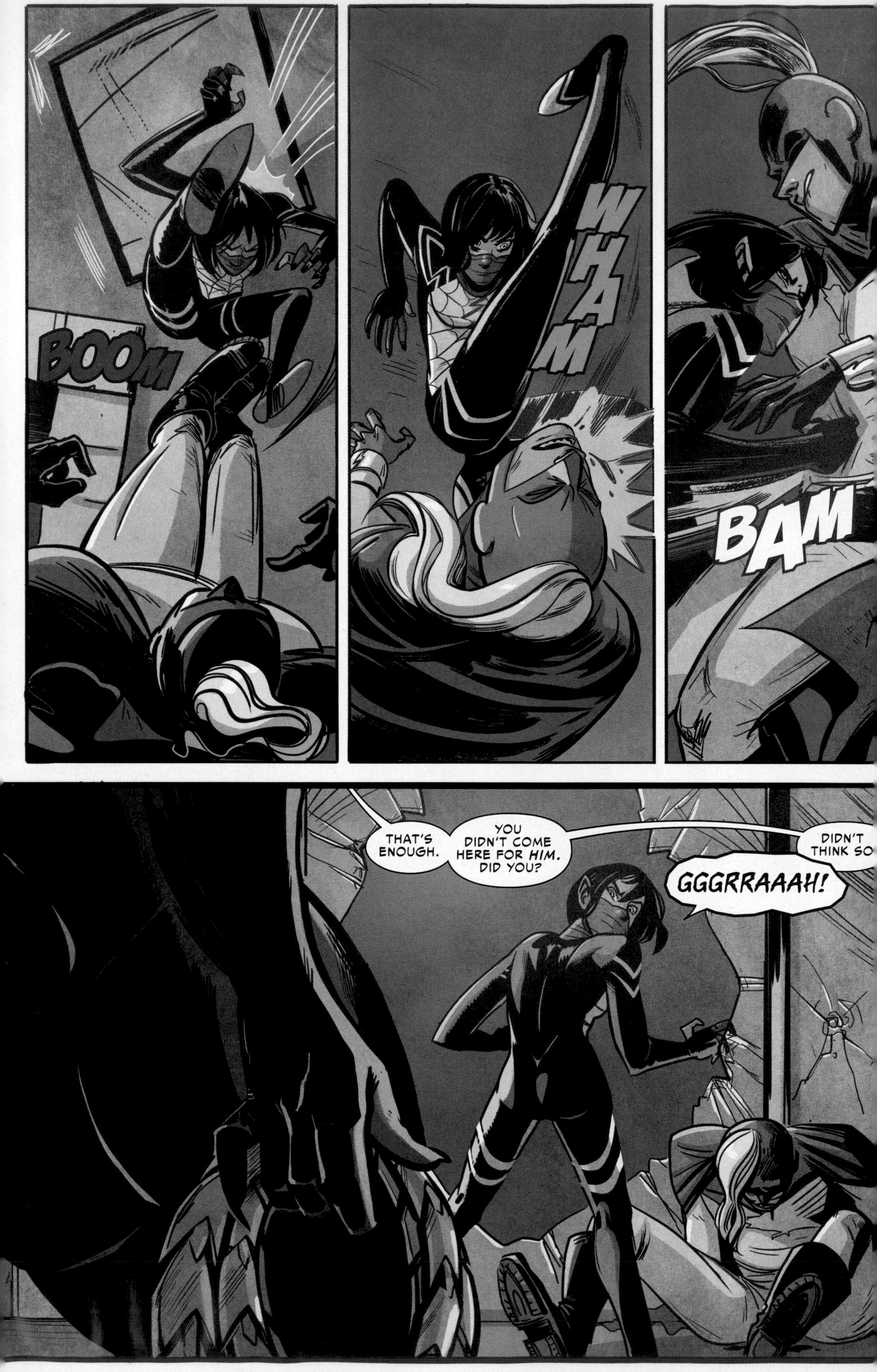
BOOM
WHAM
BAM
THAT'S ENOUGH.
YOU DIDN'T COME HERE FOR *HIM*. DID YOU?
DIDN'T THINK SO
GGGRRAAAH!

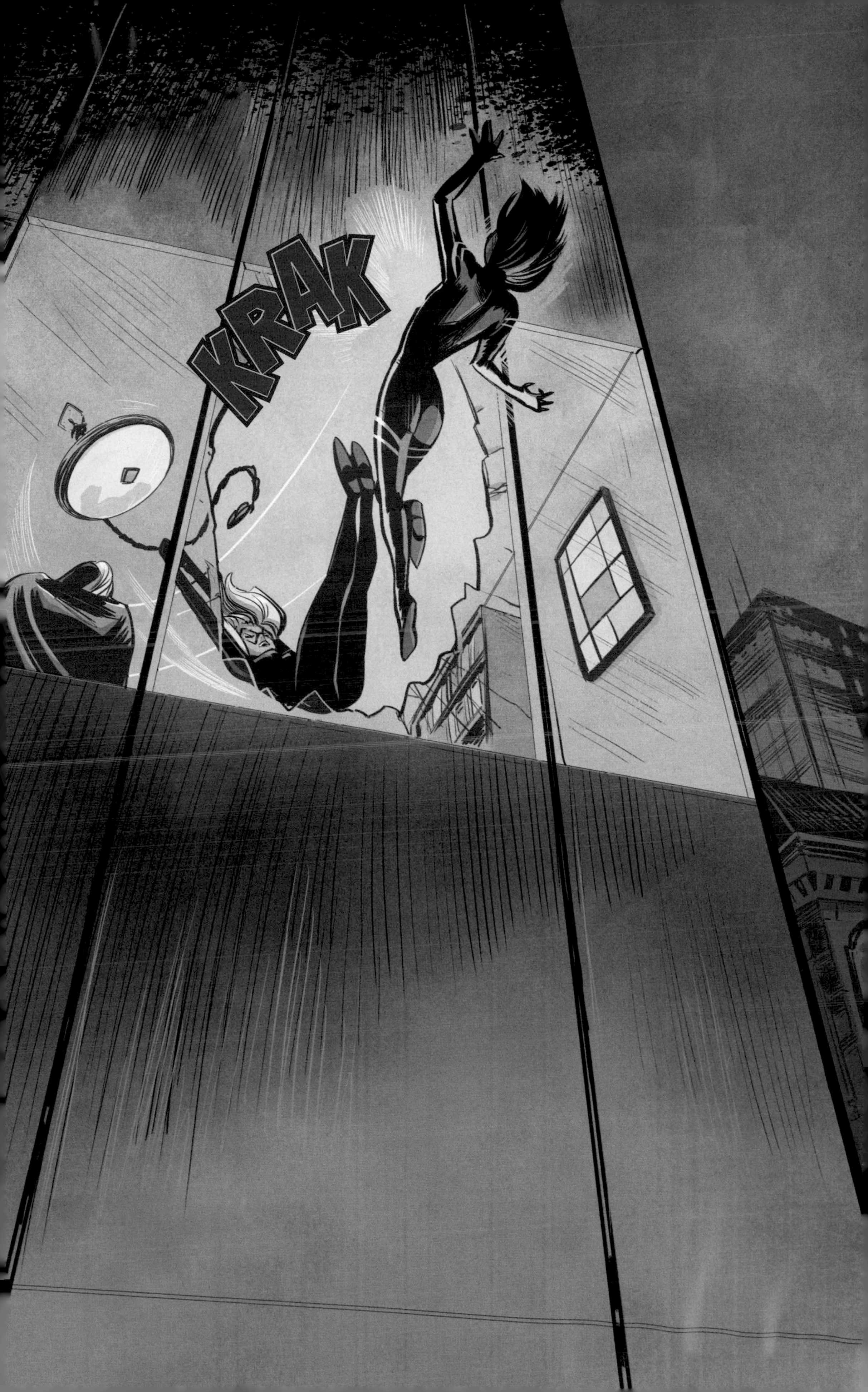
KRAK

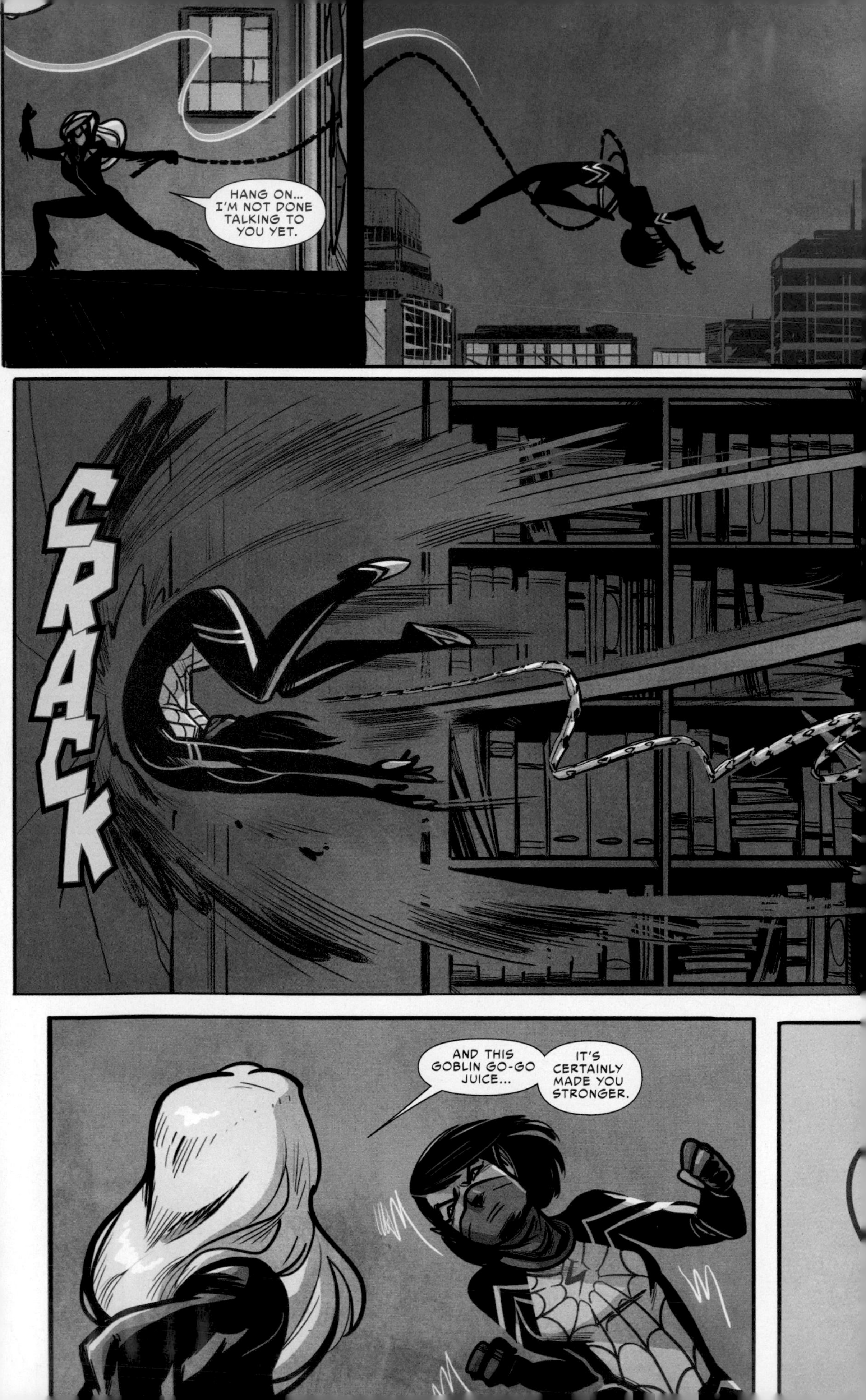
HANG ON... I'M NOT DONE TALKING TO YOU YET.
CRACK
AND THIS GOBLIN GO-GO JUICE...
IT'S CERTAINLY MADE YOU STRONGER.

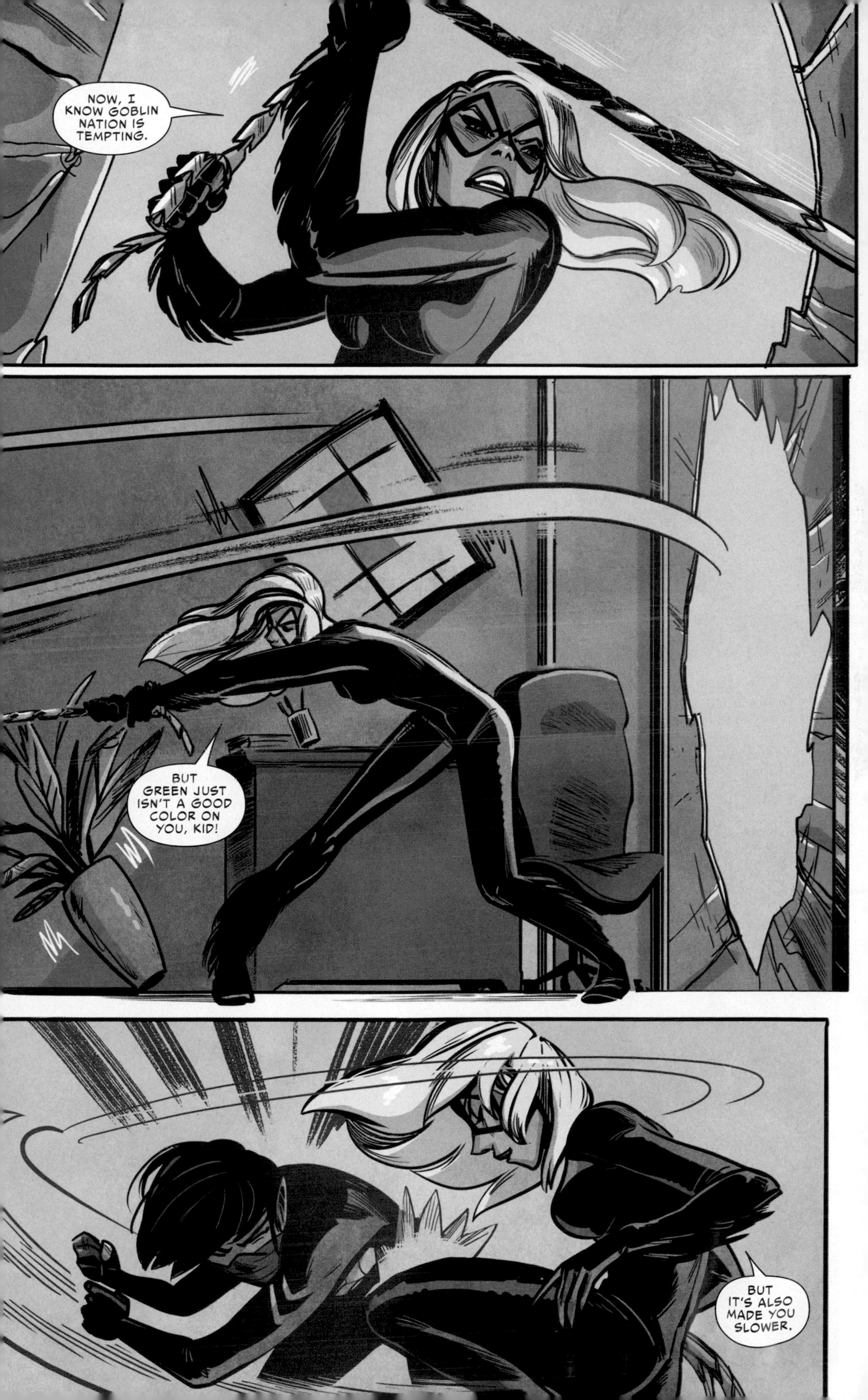
NOW, I KNOW GOBLIN NATION IS TEMPTING.
BUT GREEN JUST ISN'T A GOOD COLOR ON YOU, KID!
BUT IT'S ALSO MADE YOU SLOWER.

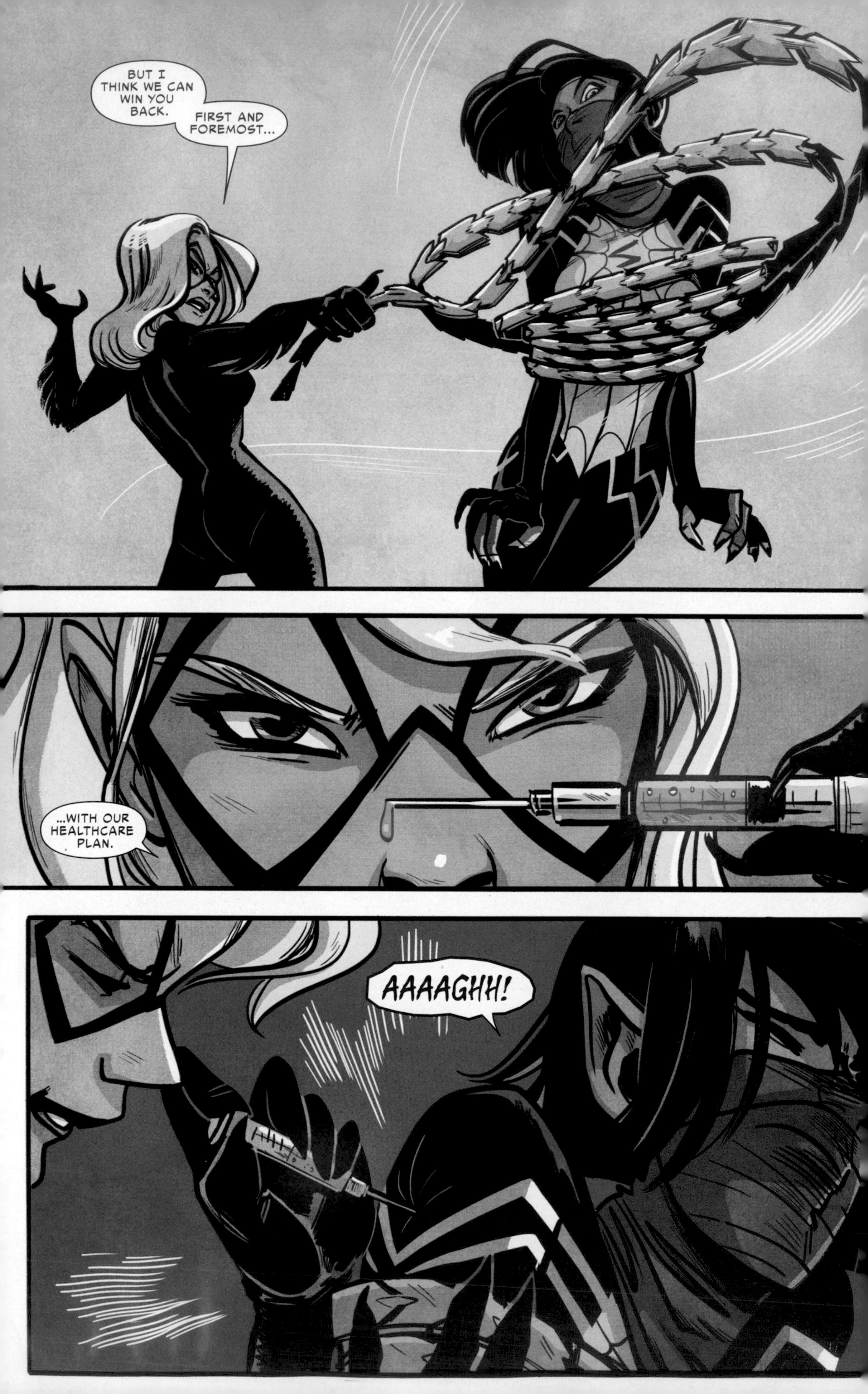
BUT I THINK WE CAN WIN YOU BACK.
FIRST AND FOREMOST...
...WITH OUR HEALTHCARE PLAN.
AAAAGHH!

THERE. THAT'S BETTER, ISN'T IT?

...THIS... THIS WAS YOUR PLAN?

THAT'S RIGHT.

HEAD... SWIMMING...

THAT SERUM... DUG INTO MY BRAIN.

UNLEASHED ALL MY ANGER.

SO MUCH ANGER...

SO MUCH...

WAIT...WHAT IS HAPPENING--

GGAAAHH!!

ALL THE TECH WE'VE BEEN STEALING...

...HELPED ME CREATE AN *ANTIDOTE* FOR THE IMITATION-BRAND GOBLIN FORMULA PHIL URICH AND HIS PATHETIC GOBLIN NATION IS PEDDLING!

HAND OVER THE SAFETY DEPOSIT BOX. NOW.

JUST KNOW MY BOSS WANTS IT.

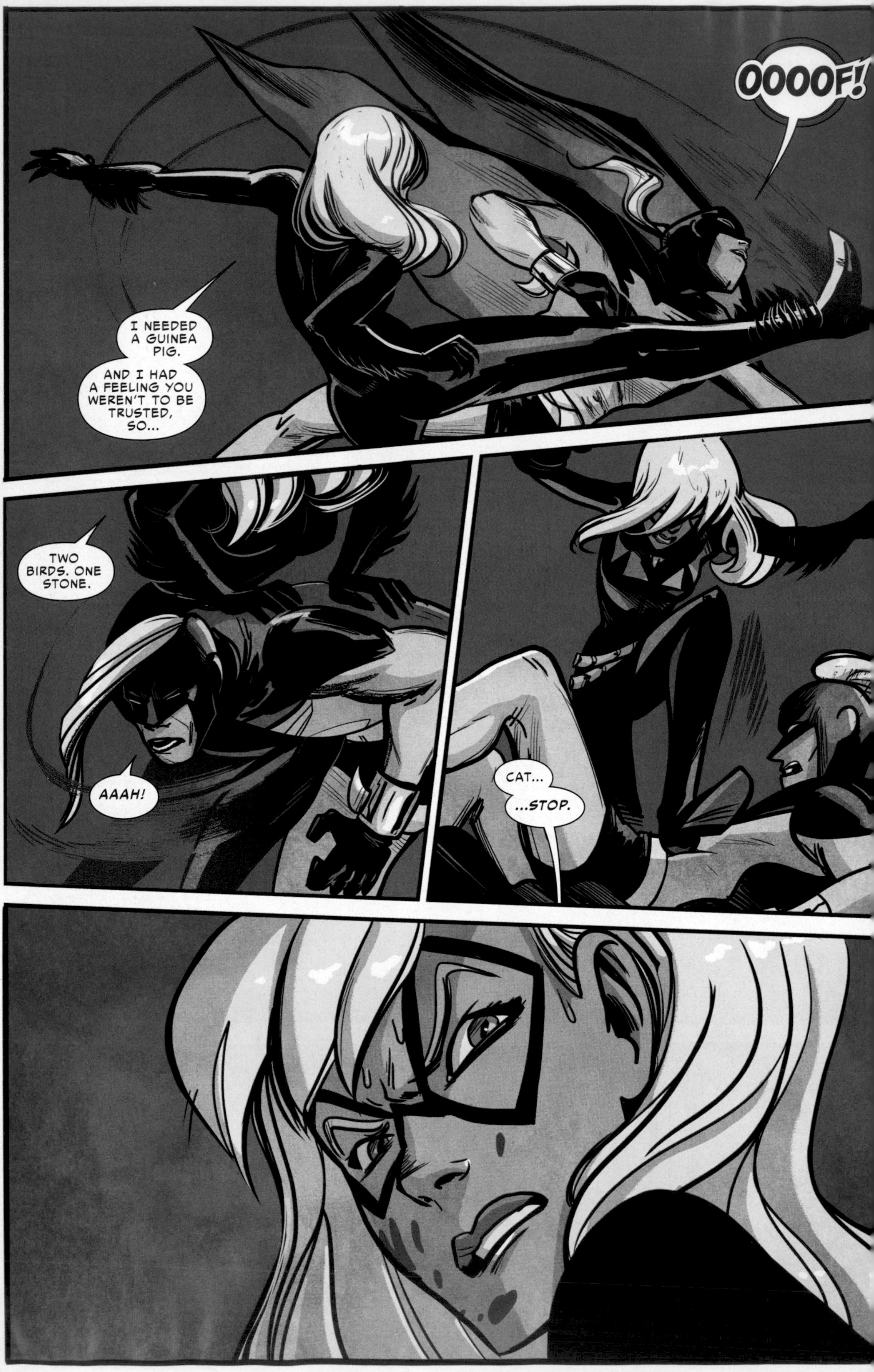
OOOOF!
I NEEDED A GUINEA PIG.
AND I HAD A FEELING YOU WEREN'T TO BE TRUSTED, SO...
TWO BIRDS. ONE STONE.
AAAH!
CAT...
...STOP.

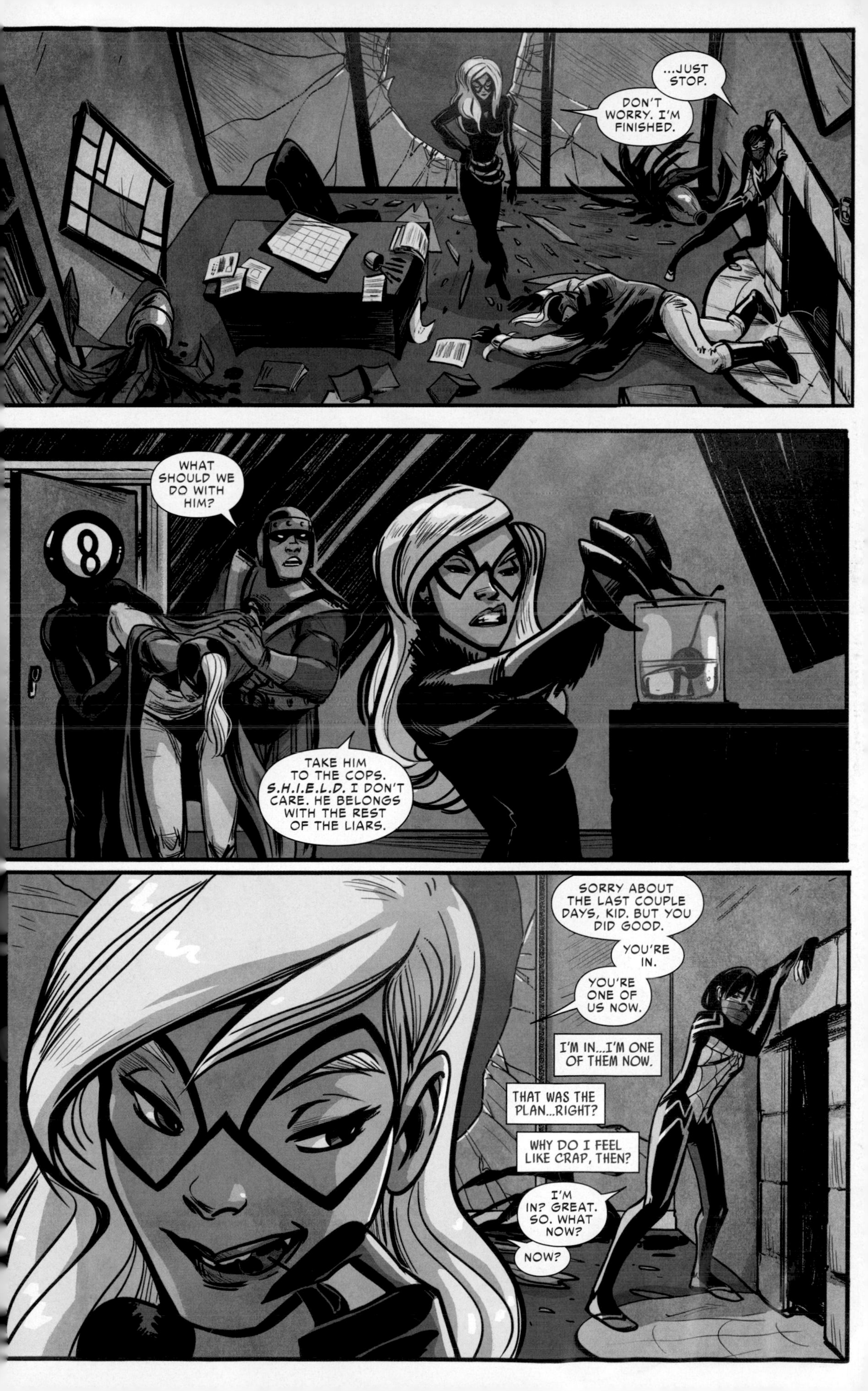
...JUST STOP.
DON'T WORRY. I'M FINISHED.
WHAT SHOULD WE DO WITH HIM?
TAKE HIM TO THE COPS. S.H.I.E.L.D. I DON'T CARE. HE BELONGS WITH THE REST OF THE LIARS.
SORRY ABOUT THE LAST COUPLE DAYS, KID. BUT YOU DID GOOD.
YOU'RE IN.
YOU'RE ONE OF US NOW.
I'M IN...I'M ONE OF THEM NOW.
THAT WAS THE PLAN...RIGHT?
WHY DO I FEEL LIKE CRAP, THEN?
I'M IN? GREAT. SO. WHAT NOW?
NOW?

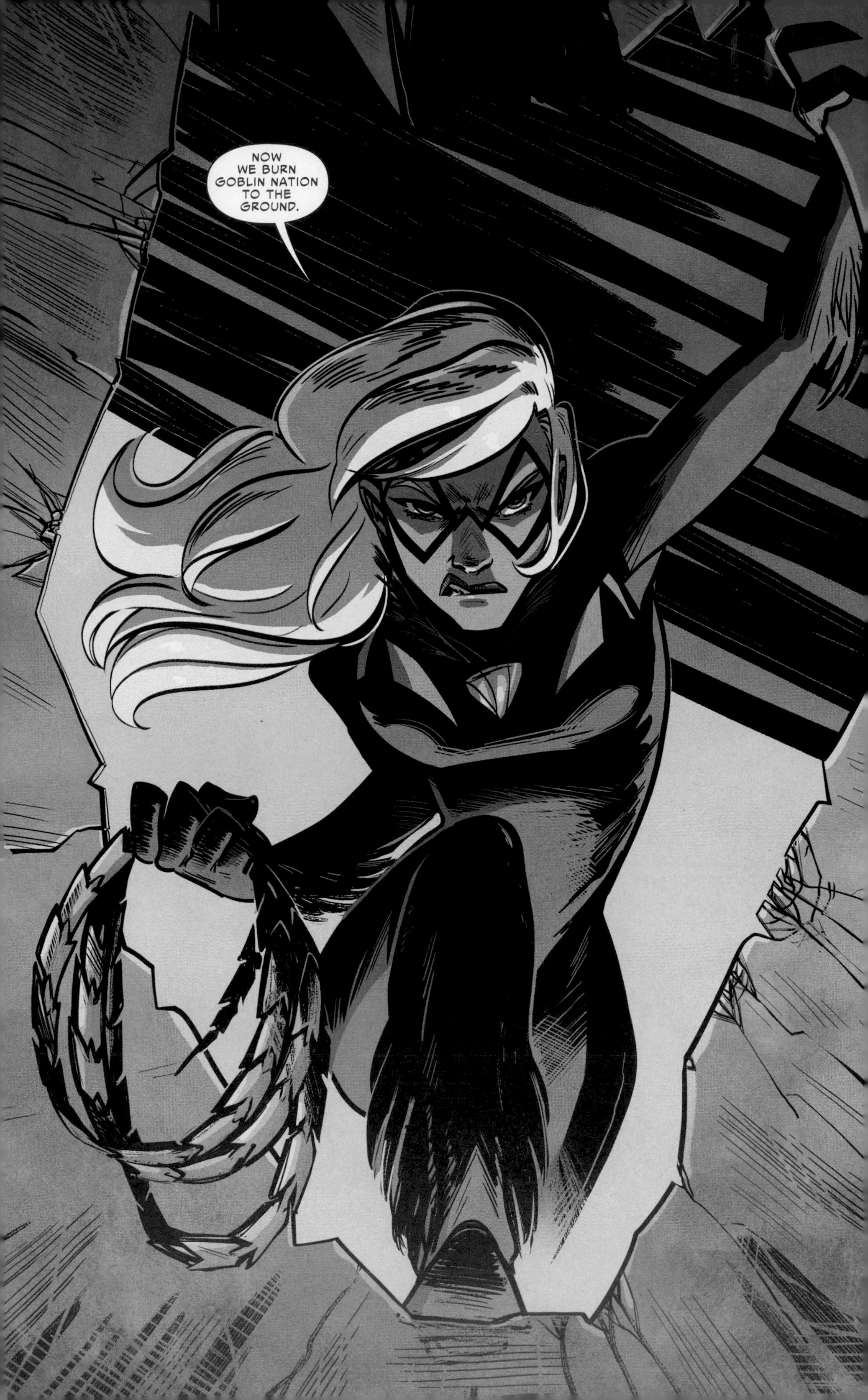
NOW WE BURN GOBLIN NATION TO THE GROUND.

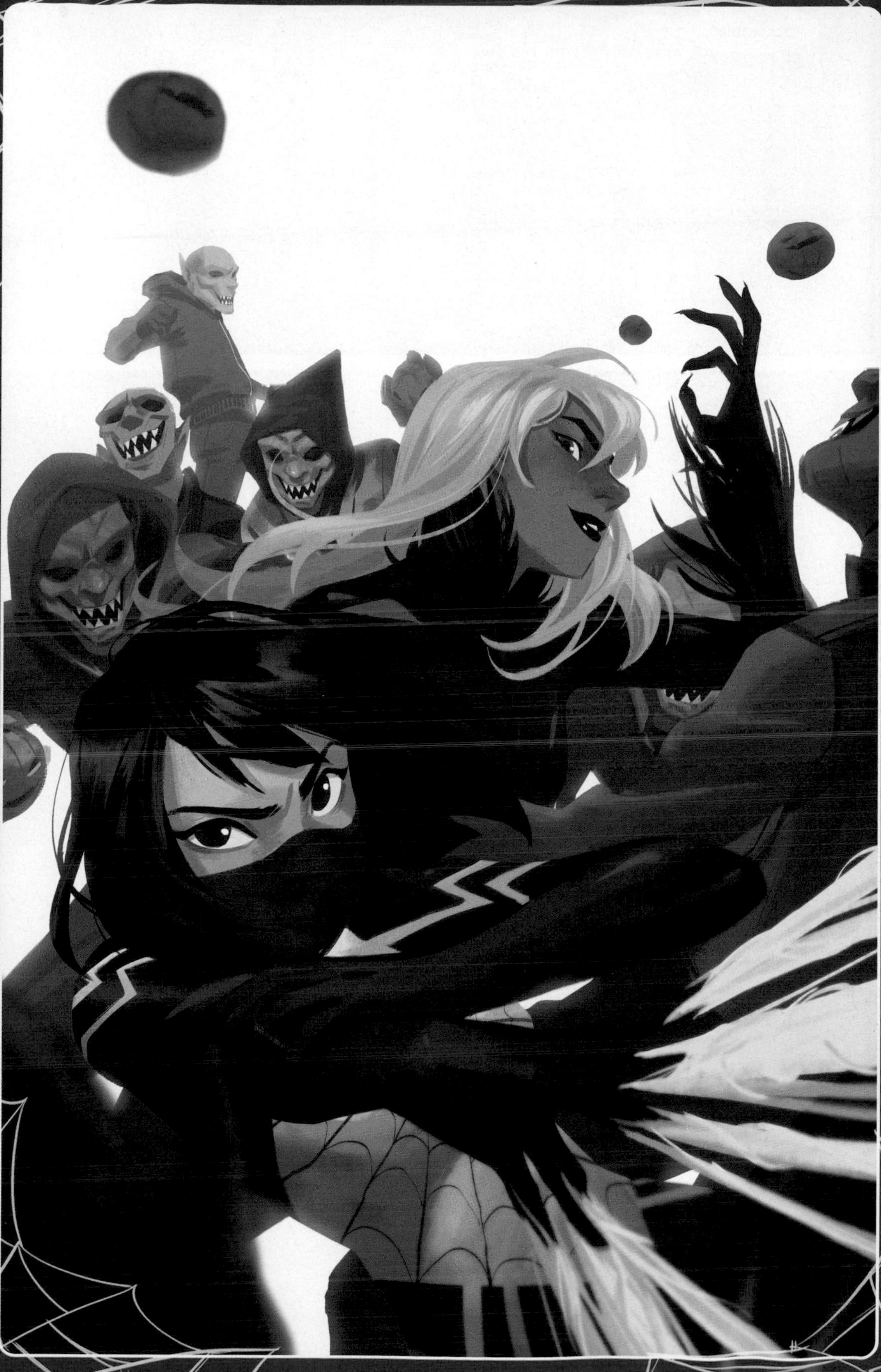

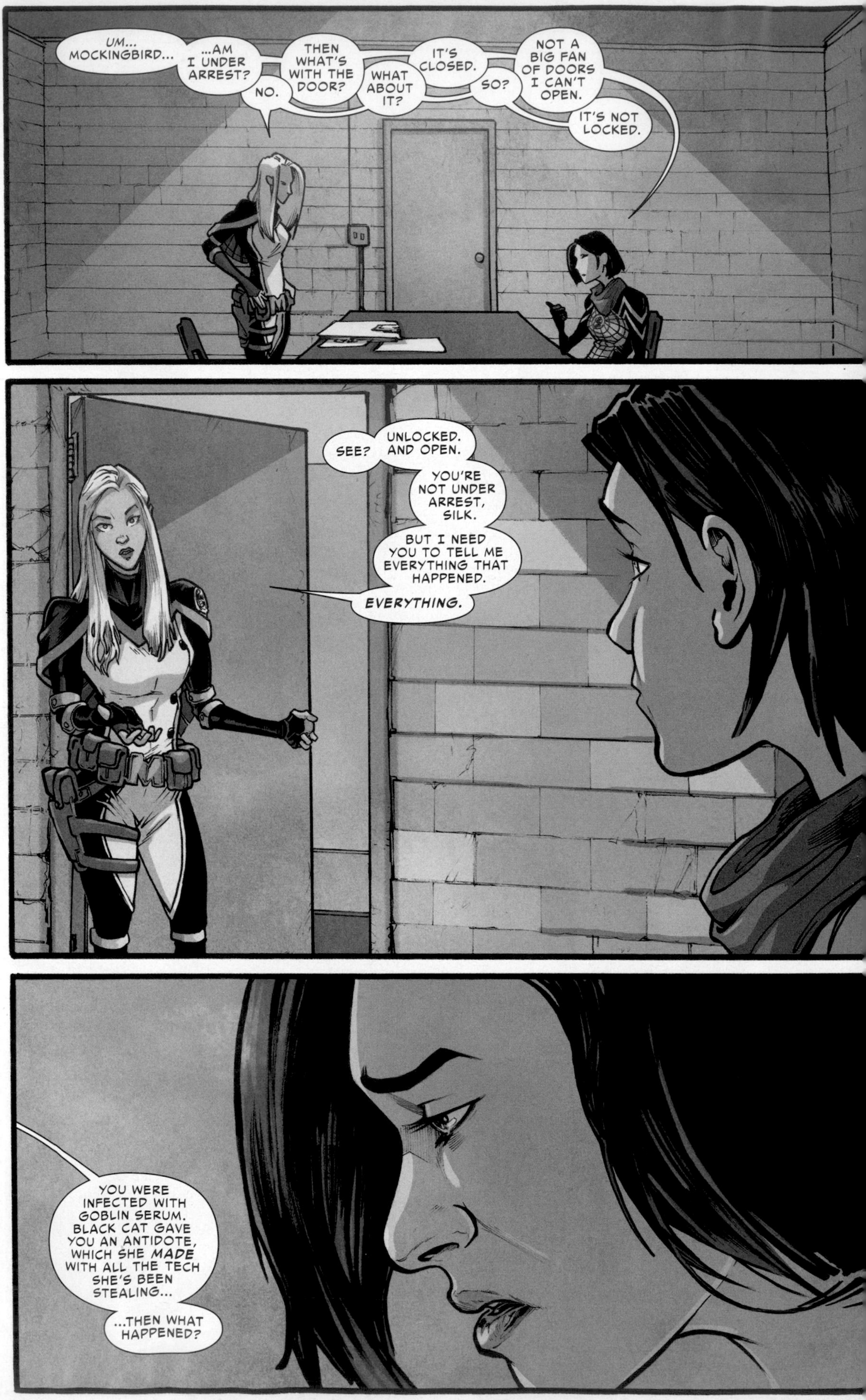
UM... MOCKINGBIRD...
...AM I UNDER ARREST?
NO.
THEN WHAT'S WITH THE DOOR?
WHAT ABOUT IT?
IT'S CLOSED.
SO?
NOT A BIG FAN OF DOORS I CAN'T OPEN.
IT'S NOT LOCKED.
SEE?
UNLOCKED. AND OPEN.
YOU'RE NOT UNDER ARREST, SILK.
BUT I NEED YOU TO TELL ME EVERYTHING THAT HAPPENED.
EVERYTHING.
YOU WERE INFECTED WITH GOBLIN SERUM. BLACK CAT GAVE YOU AN ANTIDOTE, WHICH SHE *MADE* WITH ALL THE TECH SHE'S BEEN STEALING...
...THEN WHAT HAPPENED?

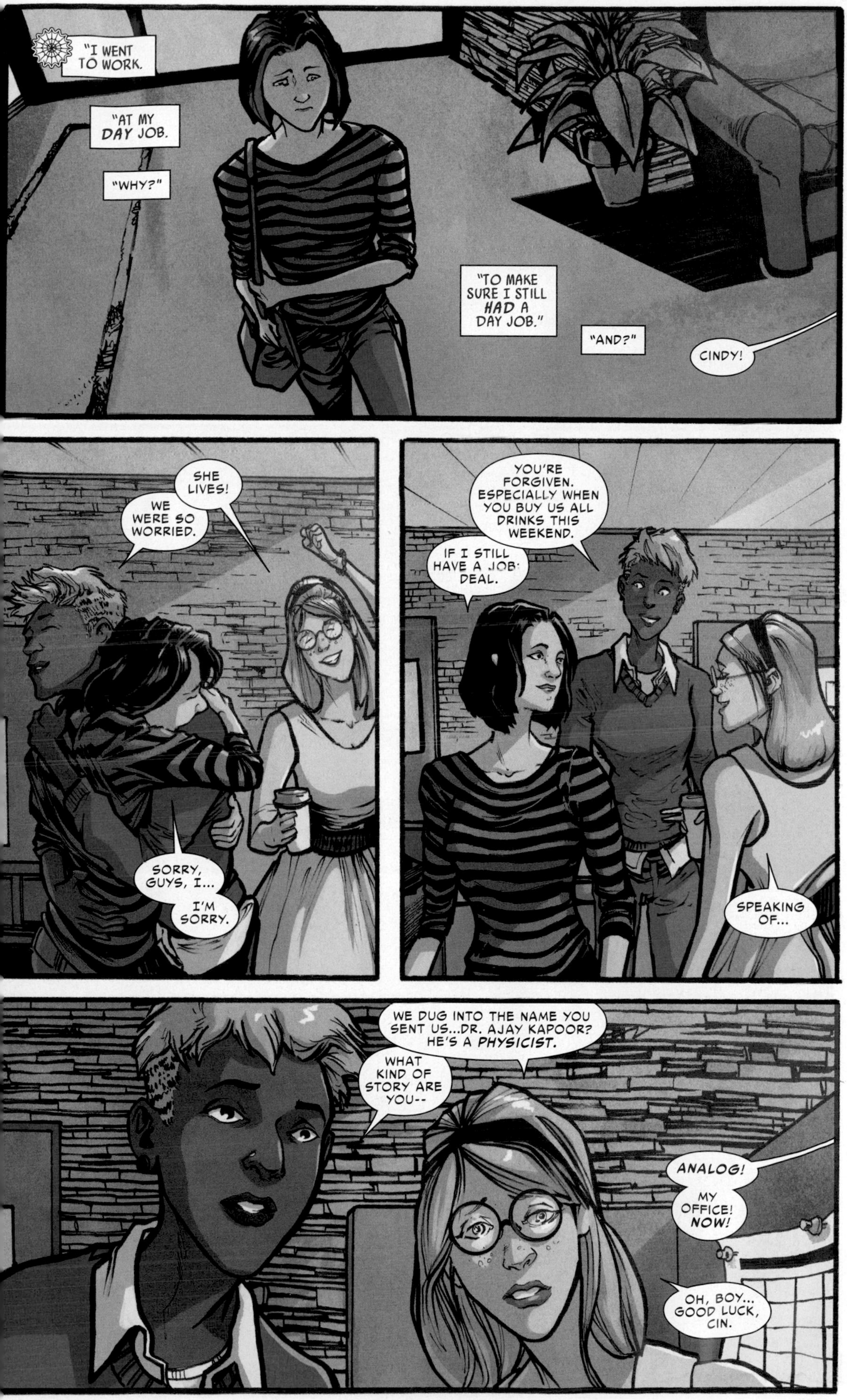
"I WENT TO WORK.
"AT MY DAY JOB.
"WHY?"
"TO MAKE SURE I STILL HAD A DAY JOB."
"AND?"
CINDY!
SHE LIVES!
WE WERE SO WORRIED.
SORRY, GUYS, I...
I'M SORRY.
YOU'RE FORGIVEN. ESPECIALLY WHEN YOU BUY US ALL DRINKS THIS WEEKEND.
IF I STILL HAVE A JOB: DEAL.
SPEAKING OF...
WE DUG INTO THE NAME YOU SENT US...DR. AJAY KAPOOR? HE'S A PHYSICIST.
WHAT KIND OF STORY ARE YOU--
ANALOG!
MY OFFICE! NOW!
OH, BOY... GOOD LUCK, CIN.

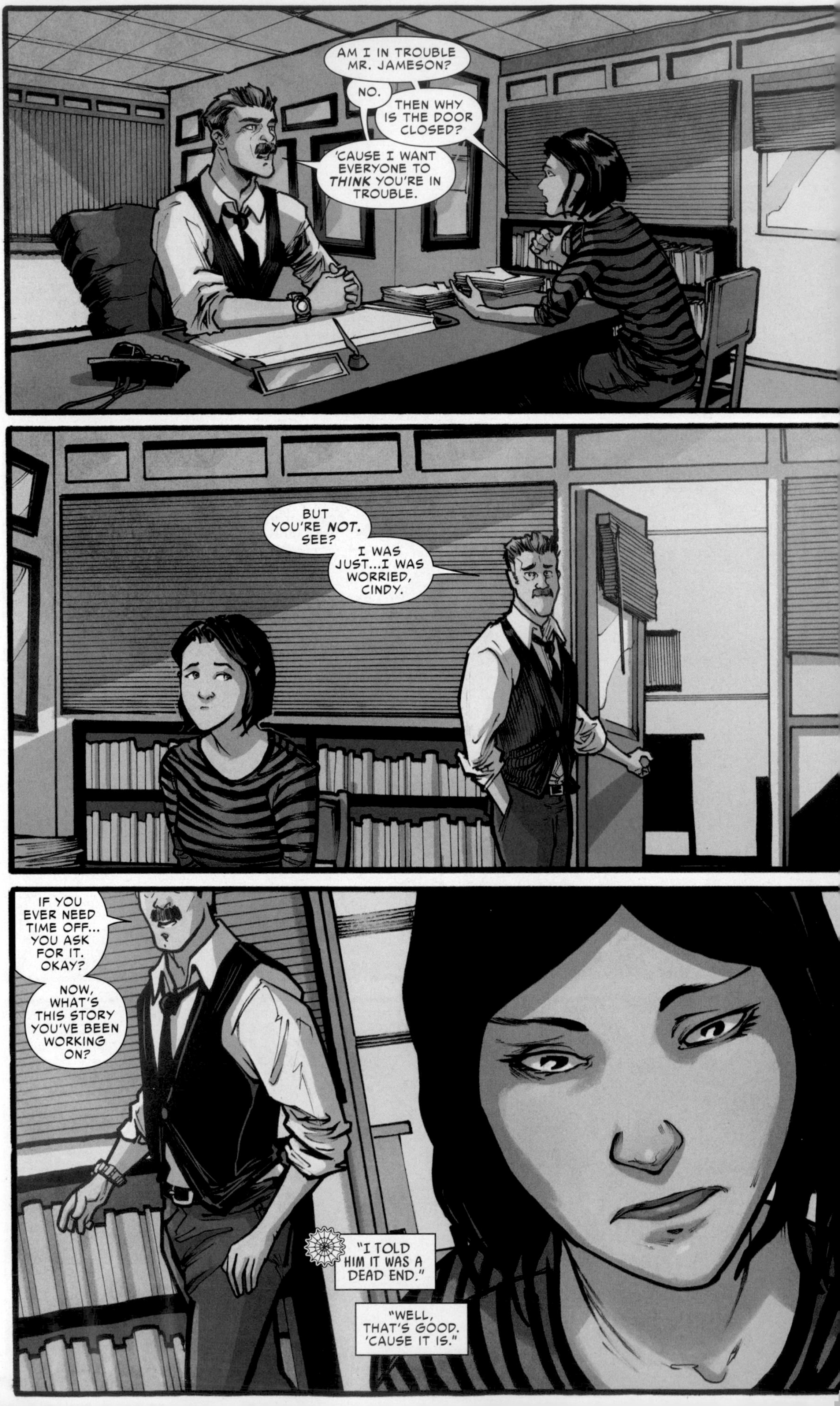
AM I IN TROUBLE MR. JAMESON?
NO.
THEN WHY IS THE DOOR CLOSED?
'CAUSE I WANT EVERYONE TO *THINK* YOU'RE IN TROUBLE.
BUT YOU'RE *NOT*. SEE?
I WAS JUST...I WAS WORRIED, CINDY.
IF YOU EVER NEED TIME OFF... YOU ASK FOR IT. OKAY?
NOW, WHAT'S THIS STORY YOU'VE BEEN WORKING ON?
"I TOLD HIM IT WAS A DEAD END."
"WELL, THAT'S GOOD. 'CAUSE IT IS."

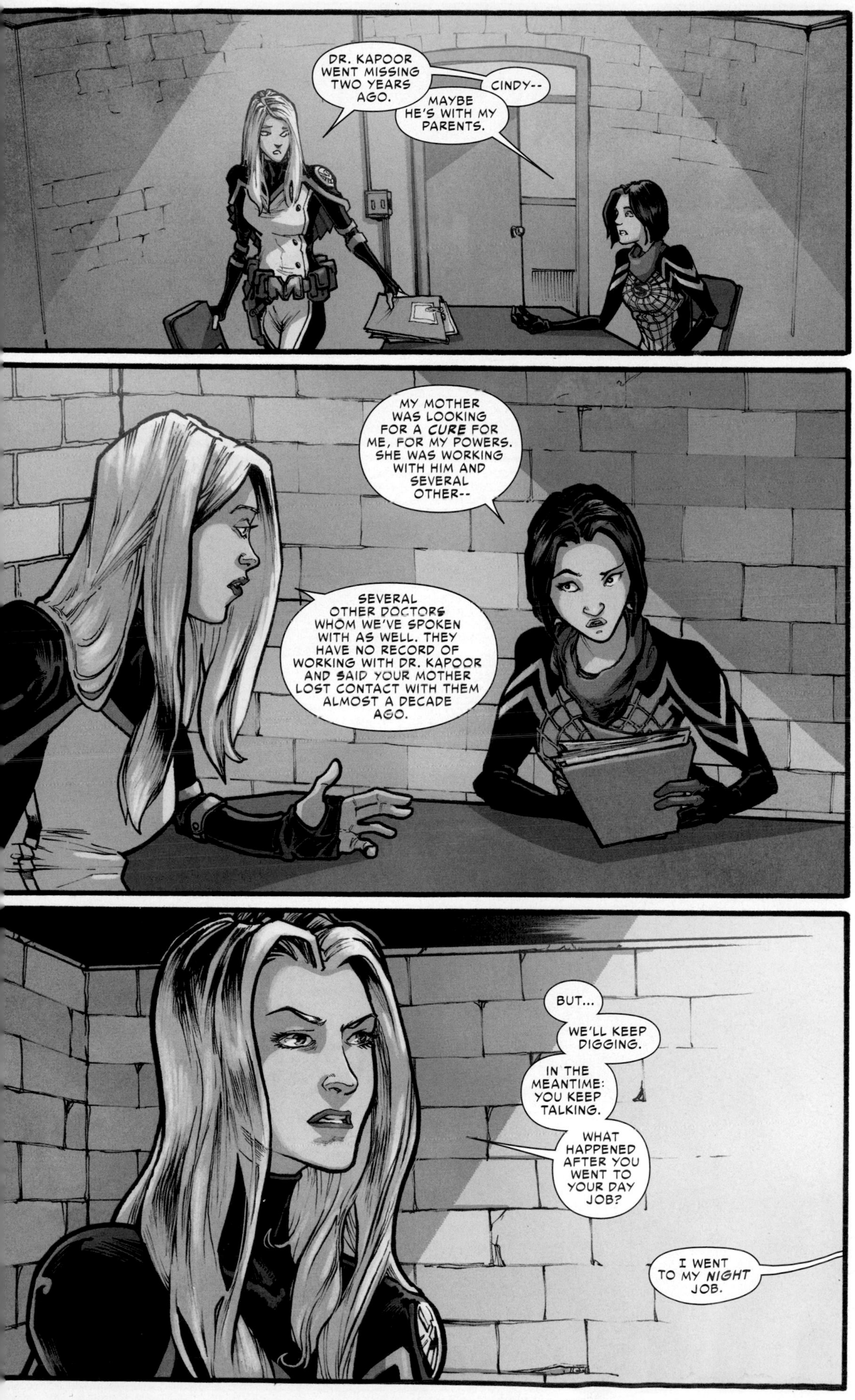
DR. KAPOOR WENT MISSING TWO YEARS AGO.
CINDY--
MAYBE HE'S WITH MY PARENTS.
MY MOTHER WAS LOOKING FOR A CURE FOR ME, FOR MY POWERS. SHE WAS WORKING WITH HIM AND SEVERAL OTHER--
SEVERAL OTHER DOCTORS WHOM WE'VE SPOKEN WITH AS WELL. THEY HAVE NO RECORD OF WORKING WITH DR. KAPOOR AND SAID YOUR MOTHER LOST CONTACT WITH THEM ALMOST A DECADE AGO.
BUT...
WE'LL KEEP DIGGING.
IN THE MEANTIME: YOU KEEP TALKING.
WHAT HAPPENED AFTER YOU WENT TO YOUR DAY JOB?
I WENT TO MY NIGHT JOB.

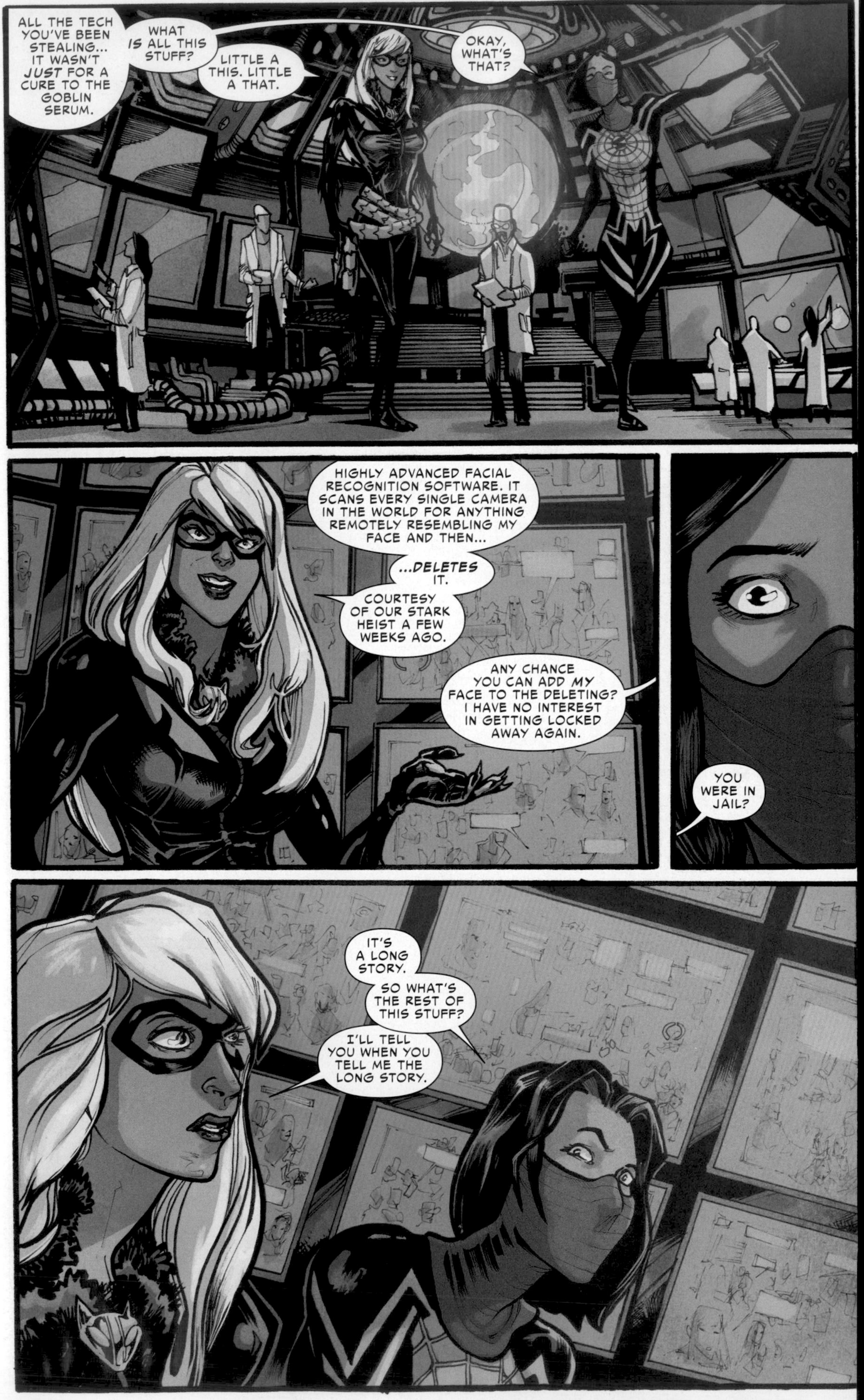
ALL THE TECH YOU'VE BEEN STEALING... IT WASN'T JUST FOR A CURE TO THE GOBLIN SERUM.
WHAT IS ALL THIS STUFF?
LITTLE A THIS. LITTLE A THAT.
OKAY, WHAT'S THAT?
HIGHLY ADVANCED FACIAL RECOGNITION SOFTWARE. IT SCANS EVERY SINGLE CAMERA IN THE WORLD FOR ANYTHING REMOTELY RESEMBLING MY FACE AND THEN...
...DELETES IT.
COURTESY OF OUR STARK HEIST A FEW WEEKS AGO.
ANY CHANCE YOU CAN ADD MY FACE TO THE DELETING? I HAVE NO INTEREST IN GETTING LOCKED AWAY AGAIN.
YOU WERE IN JAIL?
IT'S A LONG STORY.
SO WHAT'S THE REST OF THIS STUFF?
I'LL TELL YOU WHEN YOU TELL ME THE LONG STORY.

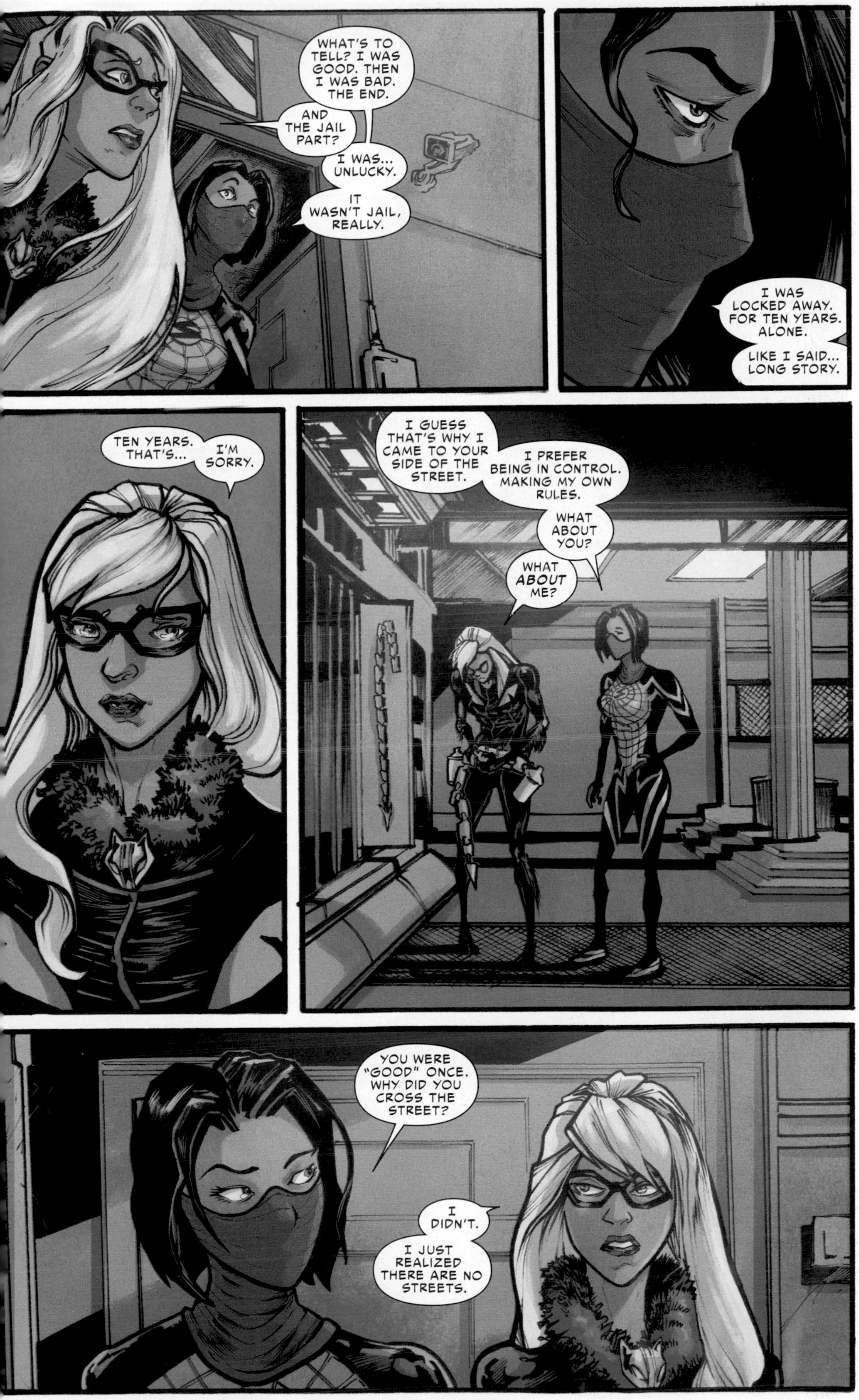
WHAT'S TO TELL? I WAS GOOD. THEN I WAS BAD. THE END.
AND THE JAIL PART?
I WAS... UNLUCKY.
IT WASN'T JAIL, REALLY.
I WAS LOCKED AWAY. FOR TEN YEARS. ALONE.
LIKE I SAID... LONG STORY.
TEN YEARS. THAT'S...
I'M SORRY.
I GUESS THAT'S WHY I CAME TO YOUR SIDE OF THE STREET.
I PREFER BEING IN CONTROL. MAKING MY OWN RULES.
WHAT ABOUT YOU?
WHAT ABOUT ME?
YOU WERE "GOOD" ONCE. WHY DID YOU CROSS THE STREET?
I DIDN'T.
I JUST REALIZED THERE ARE NO STREETS.

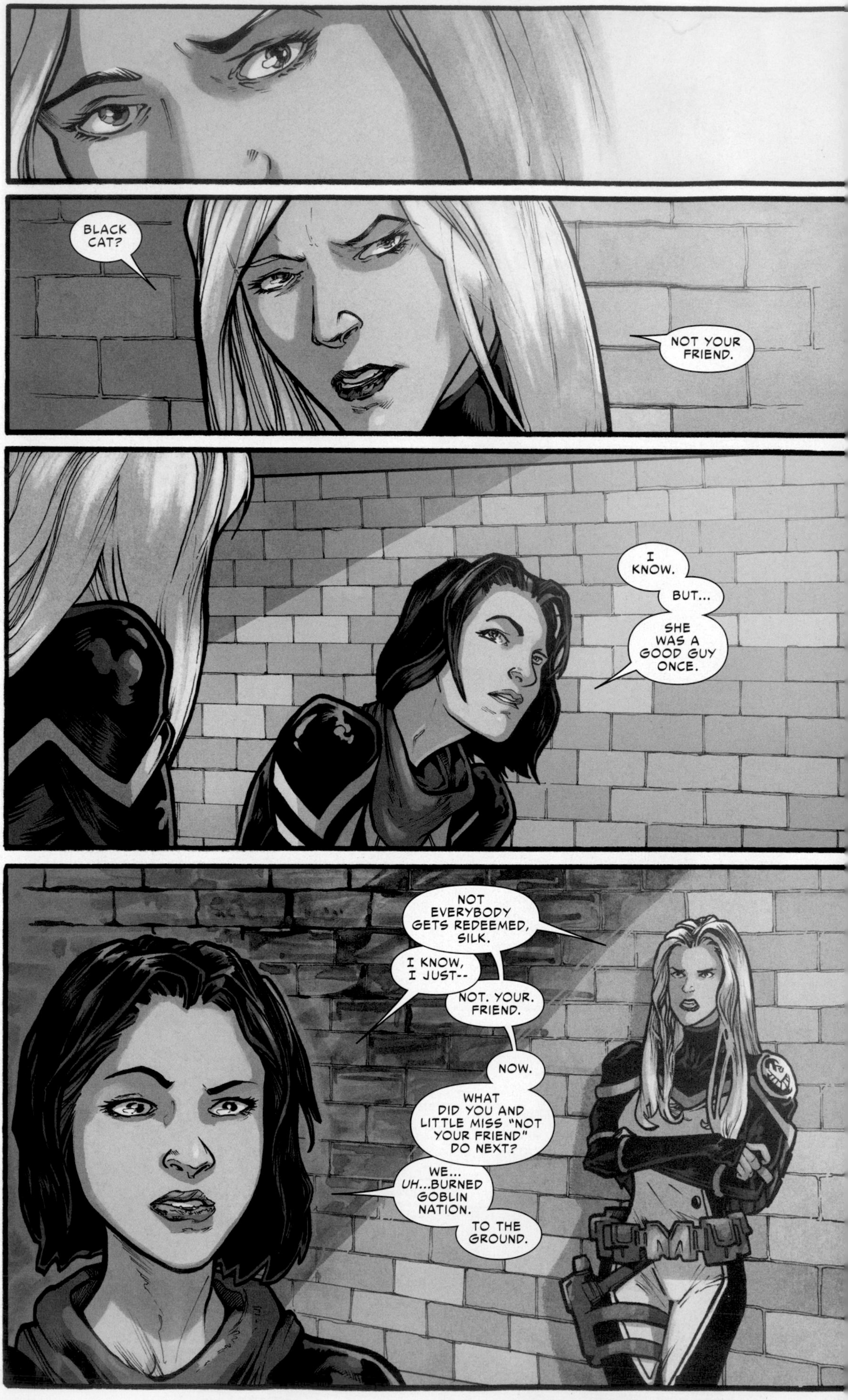
BLACK CAT?
NOT YOUR FRIEND.
I KNOW.
BUT...
SHE WAS A GOOD GUY ONCE.
NOT EVERYBODY GETS REDEEMED, SILK.
I KNOW, I JUST--
NOT. YOUR. FRIEND.
NOW.
WHAT DID YOU AND LITTLE MISS "NOT YOUR FRIEND" DO NEXT?
WE... UH...BURNED GOBLIN NATION.
TO THE GROUND.

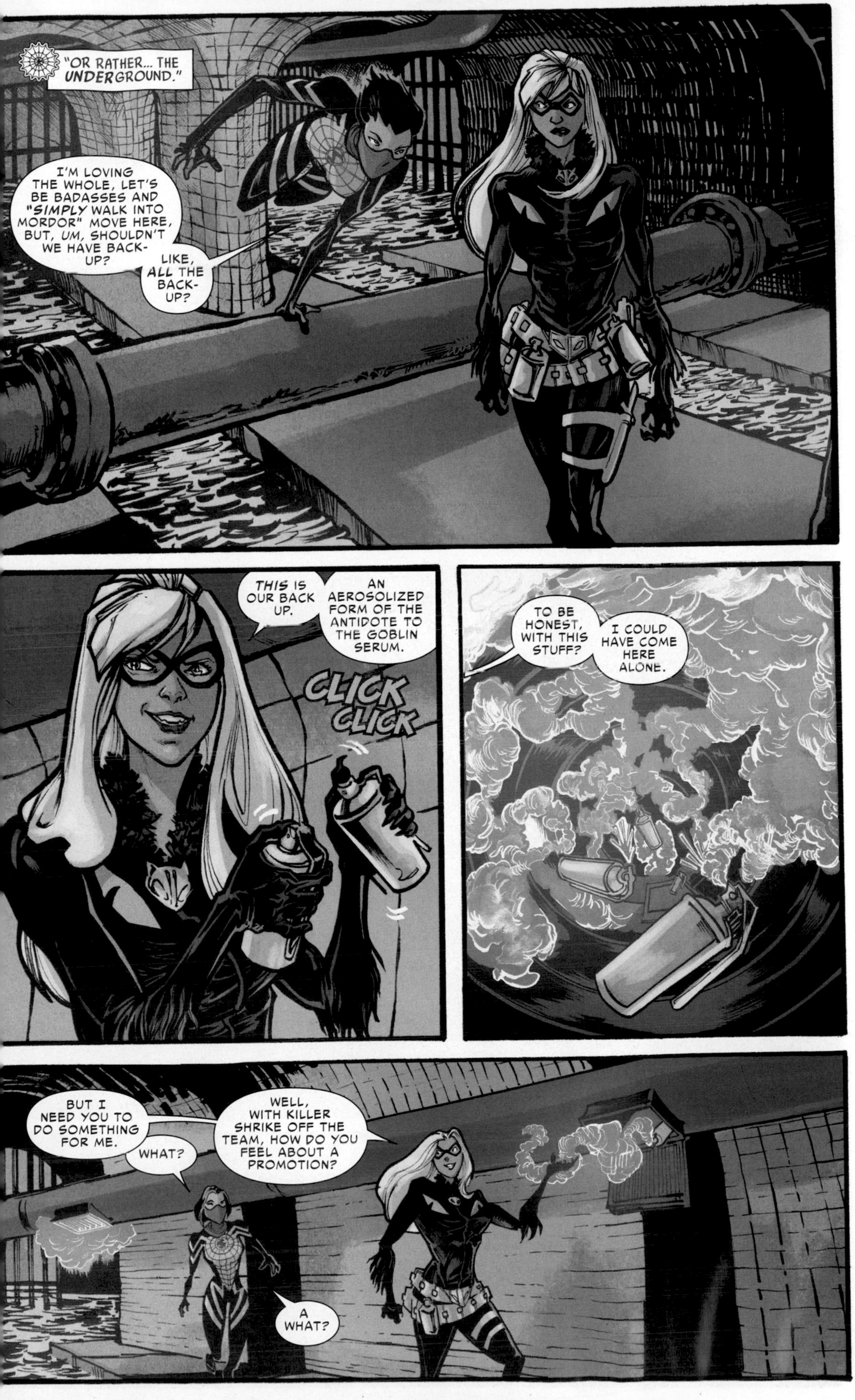

"OR RATHER... THE UNDERGROUND."
I'M LOVING THE WHOLE, LET'S BE BADASSES AND "SIMPLY WALK INTO MORDOR" MOVE HERE, BUT, UM, SHOULDN'T WE HAVE BACK-UP?
LIKE, ALL THE BACK-UP?
THIS IS OUR BACK UP.
AN AEROSOLIZED FORM OF THE ANTIDOTE TO THE GOBLIN SERUM.
CLICK CLICK
TO BE HONEST, WITH THIS STUFF?
I COULD HAVE COME HERE ALONE.
BUT I NEED YOU TO DO SOMETHING FOR ME.
WHAT?
WELL, WITH KILLER SHRIKE OFF THE TEAM, HOW DO YOU FEEL ABOUT A PROMOTION?
A WHAT?

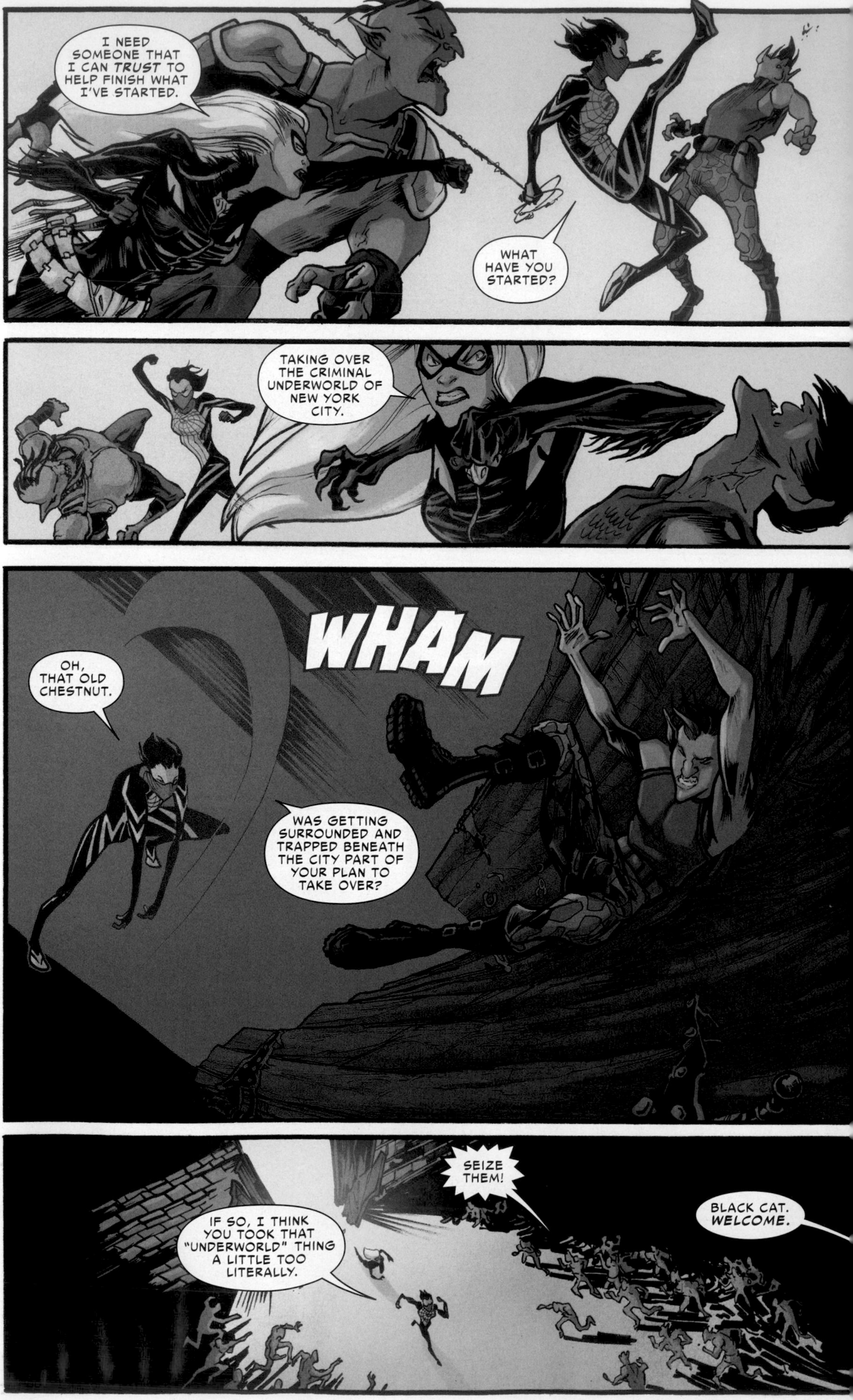
I NEED SOMEONE THAT I CAN *TRUST* TO HELP FINISH WHAT I'VE STARTED.
WHAT HAVE YOU STARTED?
TAKING OVER THE CRIMINAL UNDERWORLD OF NEW YORK CITY.
WHAM
OH, THAT OLD CHESTNUT.
WAS GETTING SURROUNDED AND TRAPPED BENEATH THE CITY PART OF YOUR PLAN TO TAKE OVER?
IF SO, I THINK YOU TOOK THAT "UNDERWORLD" THING A LITTLE TOO LITERALLY.
SEIZE THEM!
BLACK CAT. *WELCOME.*

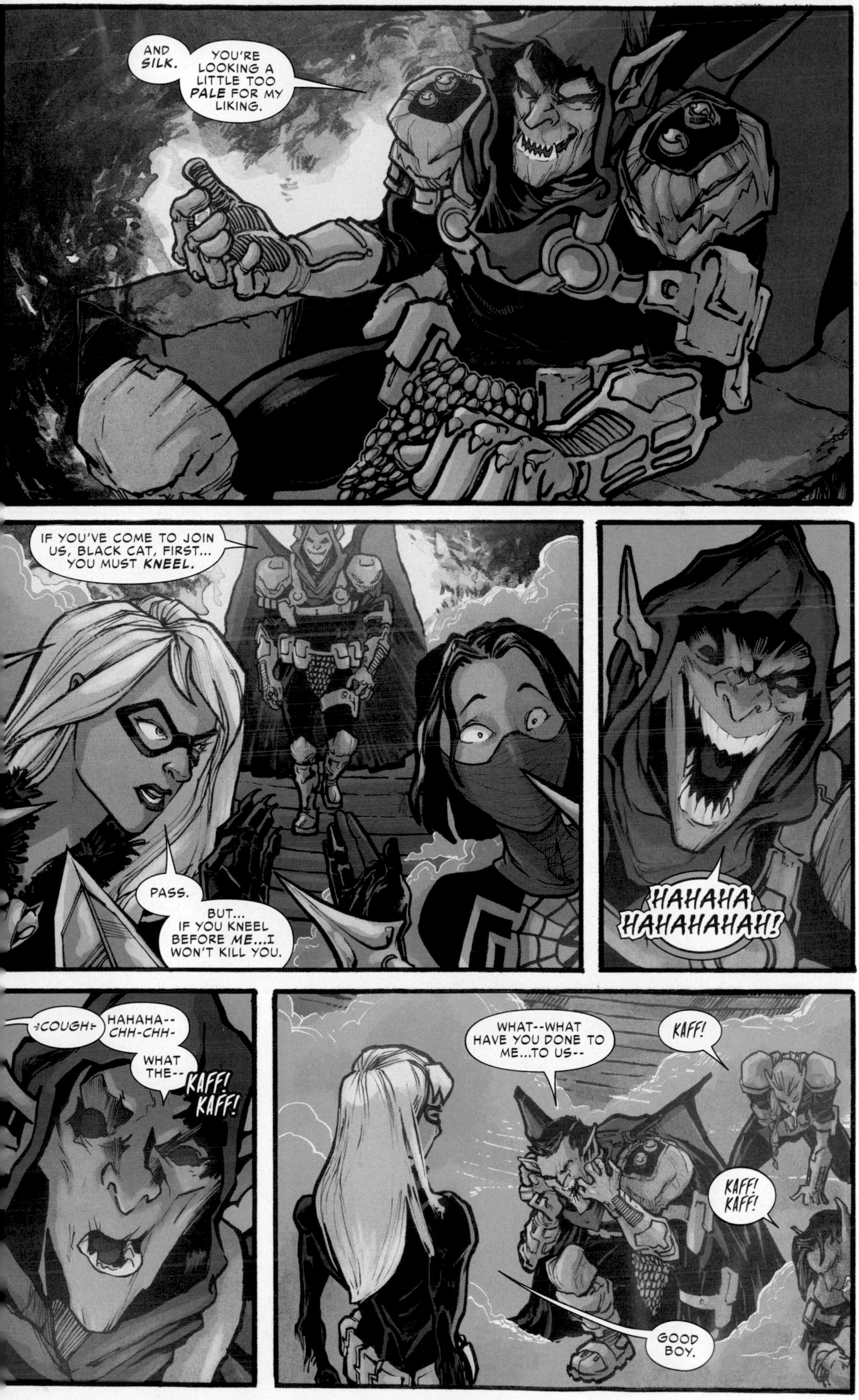
AND SILK.
YOU'RE LOOKING A LITTLE TOO PALE FOR MY LIKING.
IF YOU'VE COME TO JOIN US, BLACK CAT, FIRST... YOU MUST KNEEL.
PASS.
BUT... IF YOU KNEEL BEFORE ME...I WON'T KILL YOU.
HAHAHA HAHAHAHAH!
COUGH
HAHAHA-- CHH-CHH-
WHAT THE--
KAFF! KAFF!
WHAT--WHAT HAVE YOU DONE TO ME...TO US--
KAFF!
KAFF! KAFF!
GOOD BOY.

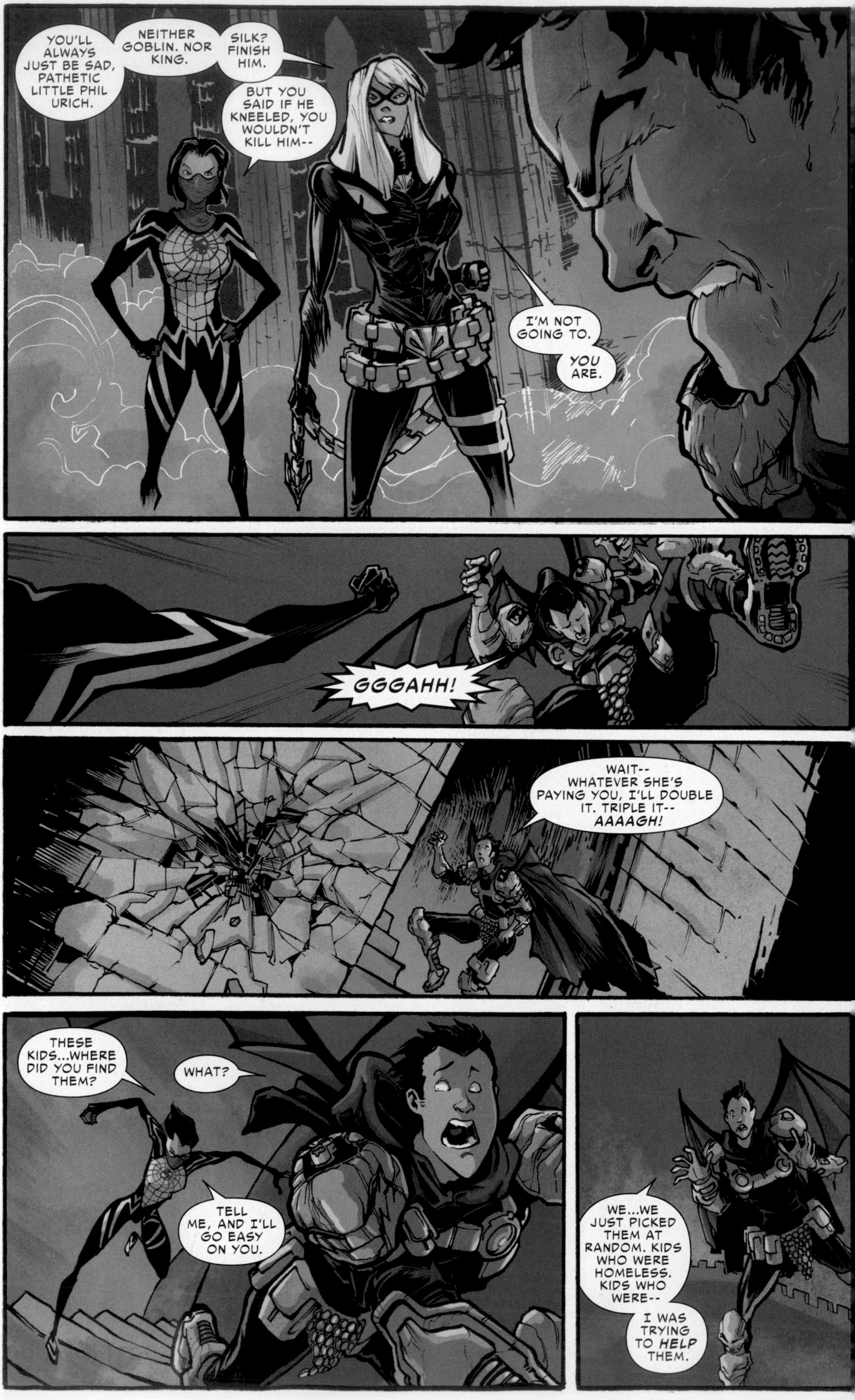

YOU'LL ALWAYS JUST BE SAD, PATHETIC LITTLE PHIL URICH.
NEITHER GOBLIN. NOR KING.
SILK? FINISH HIM.
BUT YOU SAID IF HE KNEELED, YOU WOULDN'T KILL HIM--
I'M NOT GOING TO.
YOU ARE.
GGGAHH!
WAIT-- WHATEVER SHE'S PAYING YOU, I'LL DOUBLE IT. TRIPLE IT-- AAAAGH!
THESE KIDS...WHERE DID YOU FIND THEM?
WHAT?
TELL ME, AND I'LL GO EASY ON YOU.
WE...WE JUST PICKED THEM AT RANDOM. KIDS WHO WERE HOMELESS. KIDS WHO WERE--
I WAS TRYING TO HELP THEM.

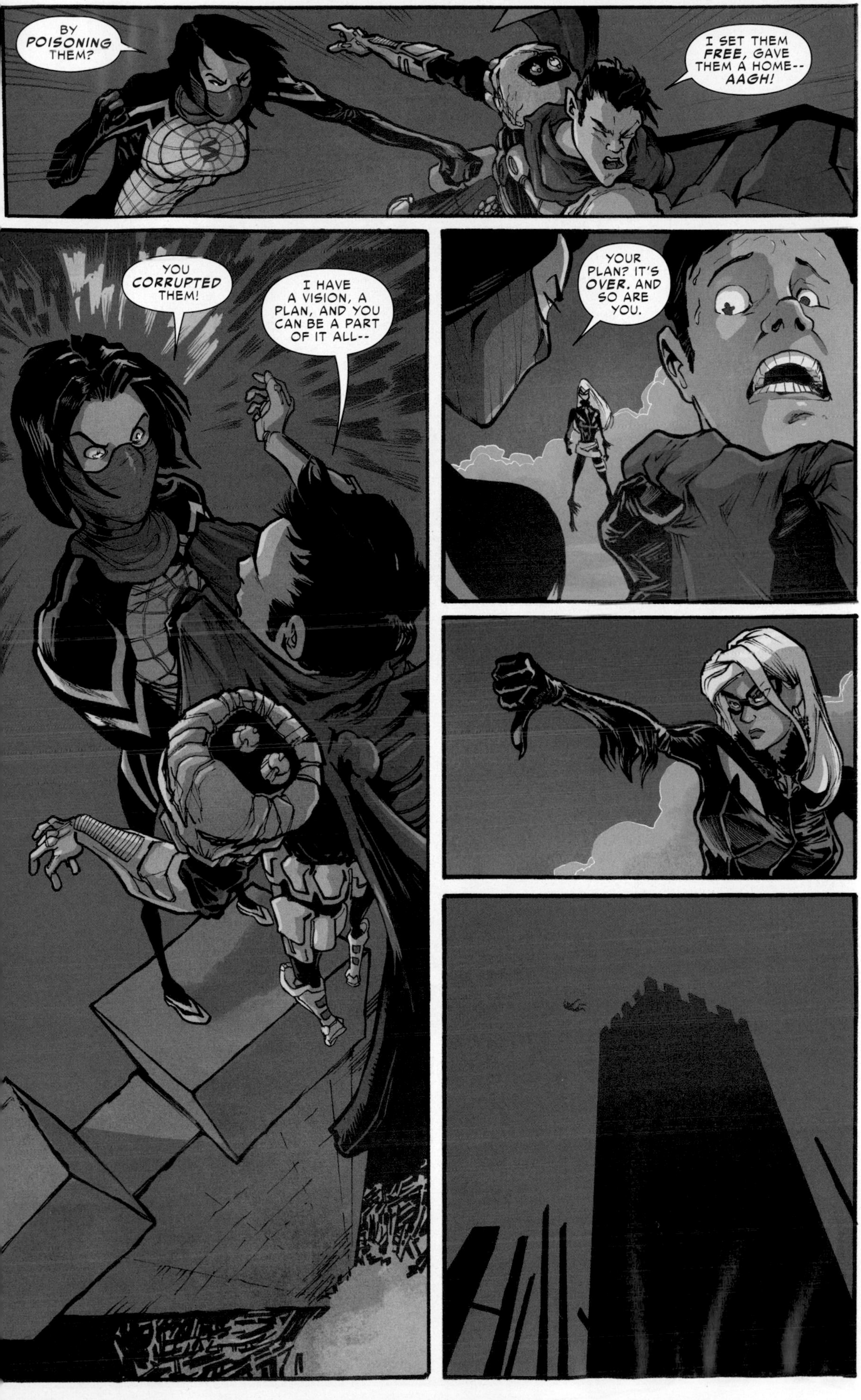

BY POISONING THEM?
I SET THEM FREE, GAVE THEM A HOME-- AAGH!
YOU CORRUPTED THEM!
I HAVE A VISION, A PLAN, AND YOU CAN BE A PART OF IT ALL--
YOUR PLAN? IT'S OVER. AND SO ARE YOU.

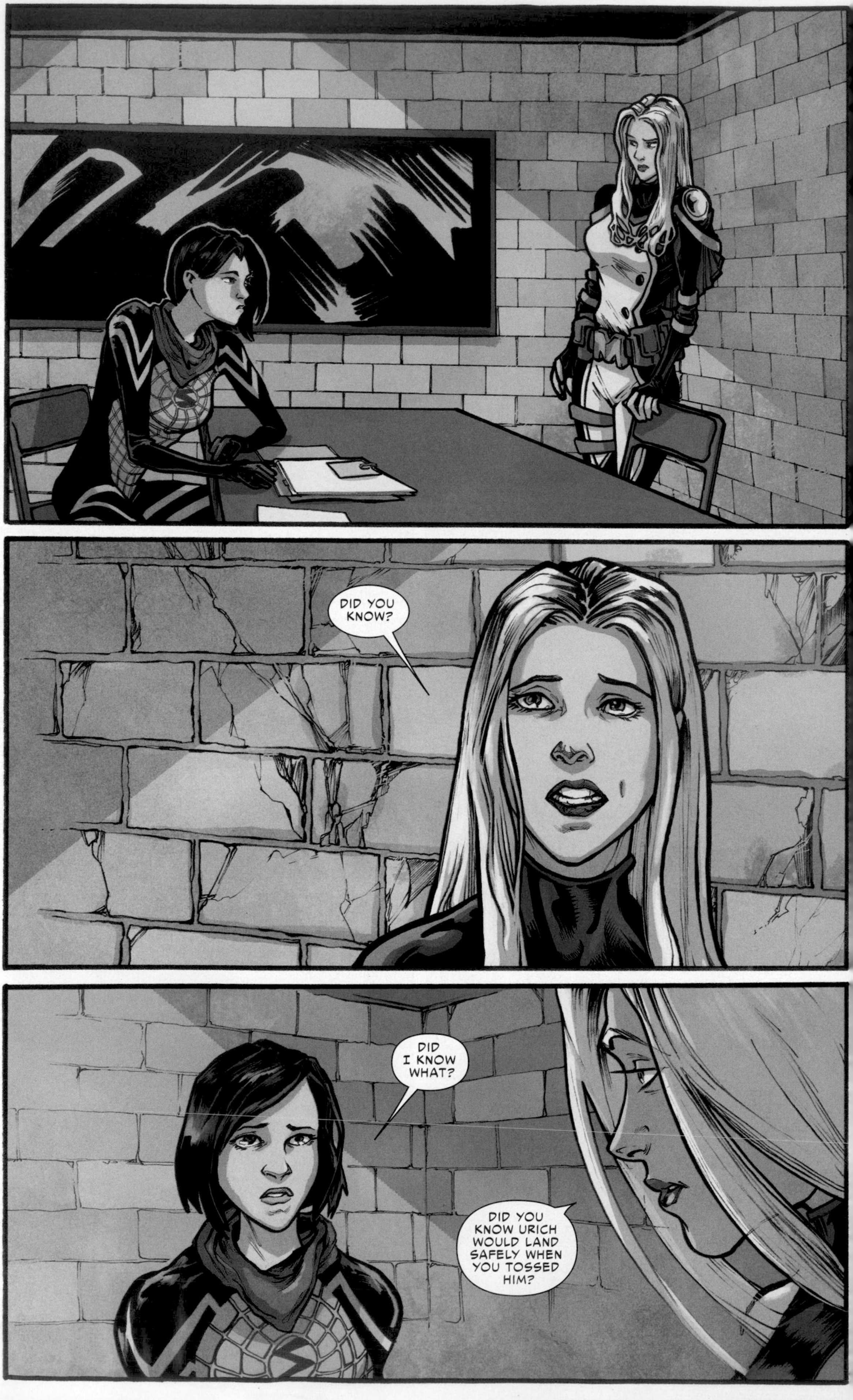
DID YOU KNOW?
DID I KNOW WHAT?
DID YOU KNOW URICH WOULD LAND SAFELY WHEN YOU TOSSED HIM?

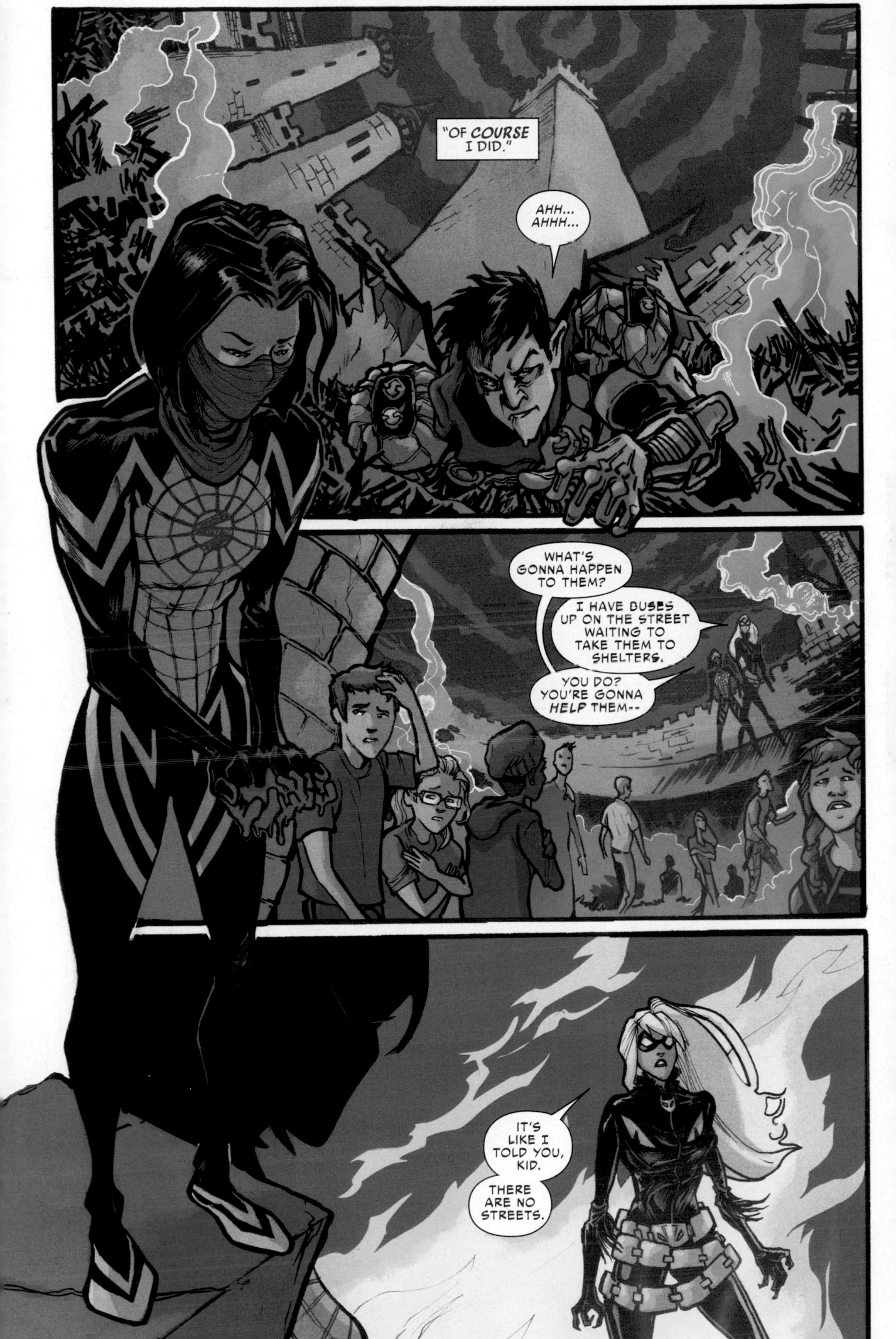
"OF COURSE I DID."
AHH... AHHH...
WHAT'S GONNA HAPPEN TO THEM?
I HAVE BUSES UP ON THE STREET WAITING TO TAKE THEM TO SHELTERS.
YOU DO? YOU'RE GONNA HELP THEM--
IT'S LIKE I TOLD YOU, KID.
THERE ARE NO STREETS.

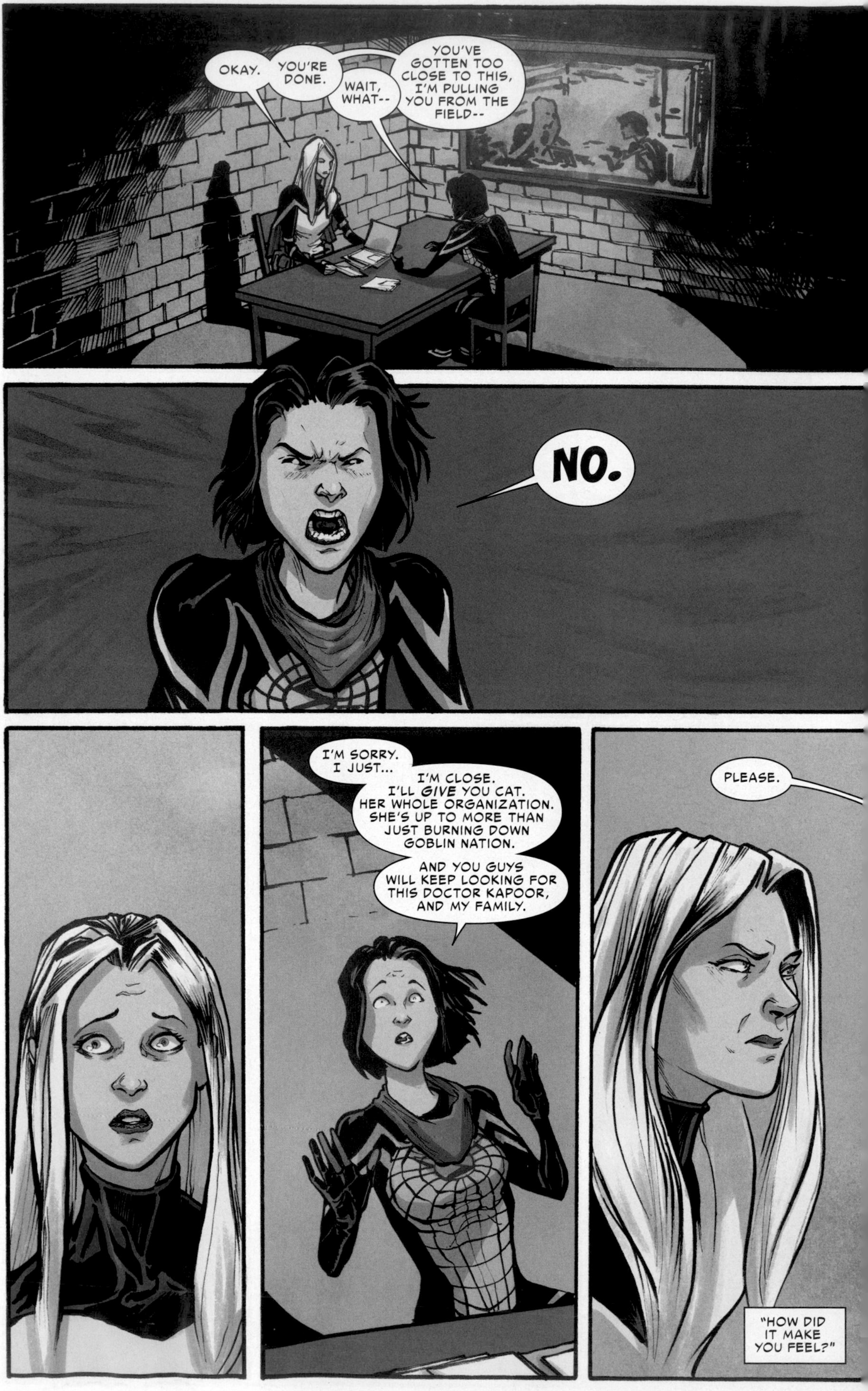
OKAY.
YOU'RE DONE.
WAIT, WHAT--
YOU'VE GOTTEN TOO CLOSE TO THIS, I'M PULLING YOU FROM THE FIELD--
NO.
I'M SORRY. I JUST...
I'M CLOSE. I'LL *GIVE* YOU CAT. HER WHOLE ORGANIZATION. SHE'S UP TO MORE THAN JUST BURNING DOWN GOBLIN NATION.
AND YOU GUYS WILL KEEP LOOKING FOR THIS DOCTOR KAPOOR, AND MY FAMILY.
PLEASE.
"HOW DID IT MAKE YOU FEEL?"

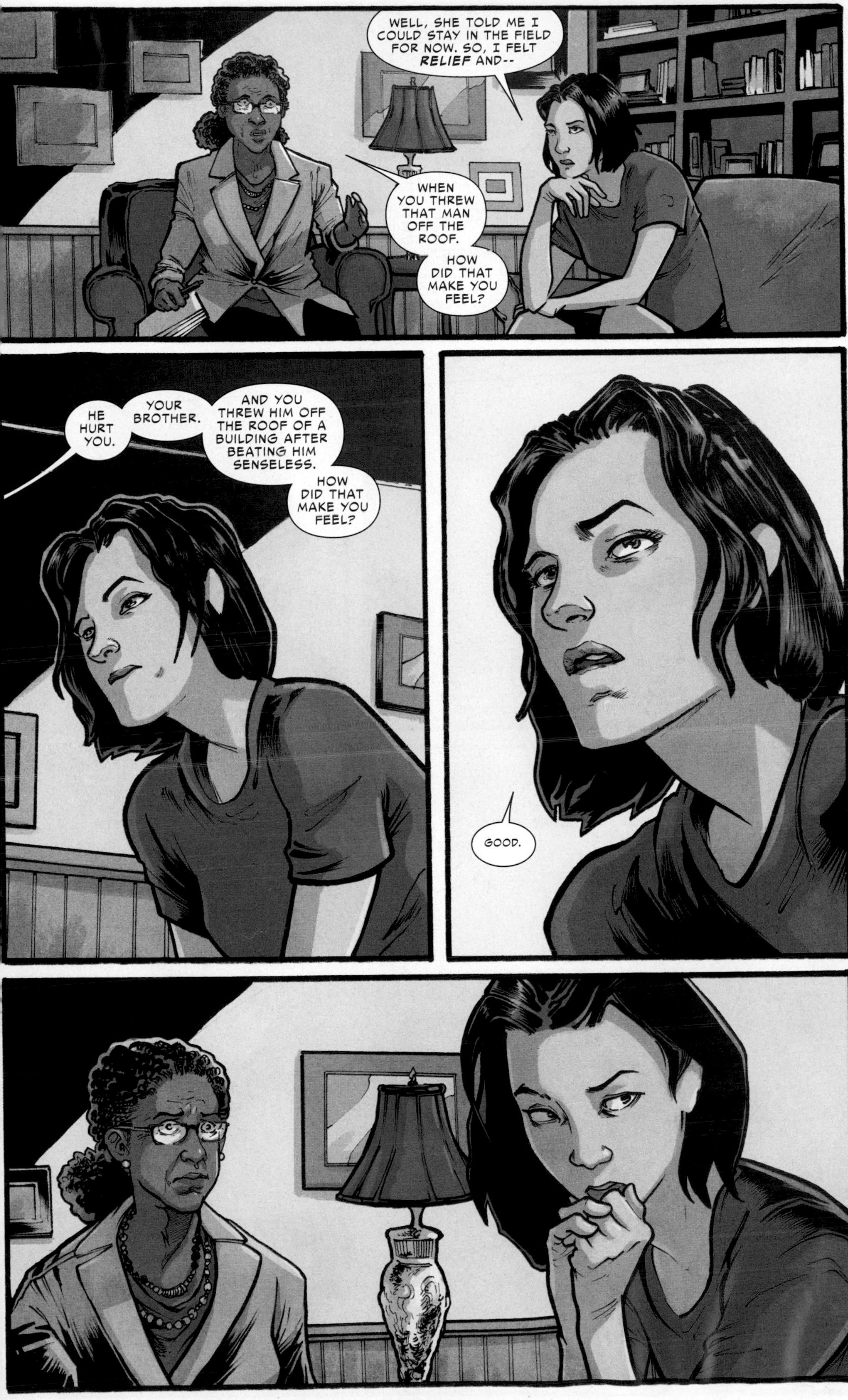
WELL, SHE TOLD ME I COULD STAY IN THE FIELD FOR NOW. SO, I FELT *RELIEF* AND--
WHEN YOU THREW THAT MAN OFF THE ROOF.
HOW DID THAT MAKE YOU FEEL?
HE HURT YOU.
YOUR BROTHER.
AND YOU THREW HIM OFF THE ROOF OF A BUILDING AFTER BEATING HIM SENSELESS.
HOW DID THAT MAKE YOU FEEL?
GOOD.

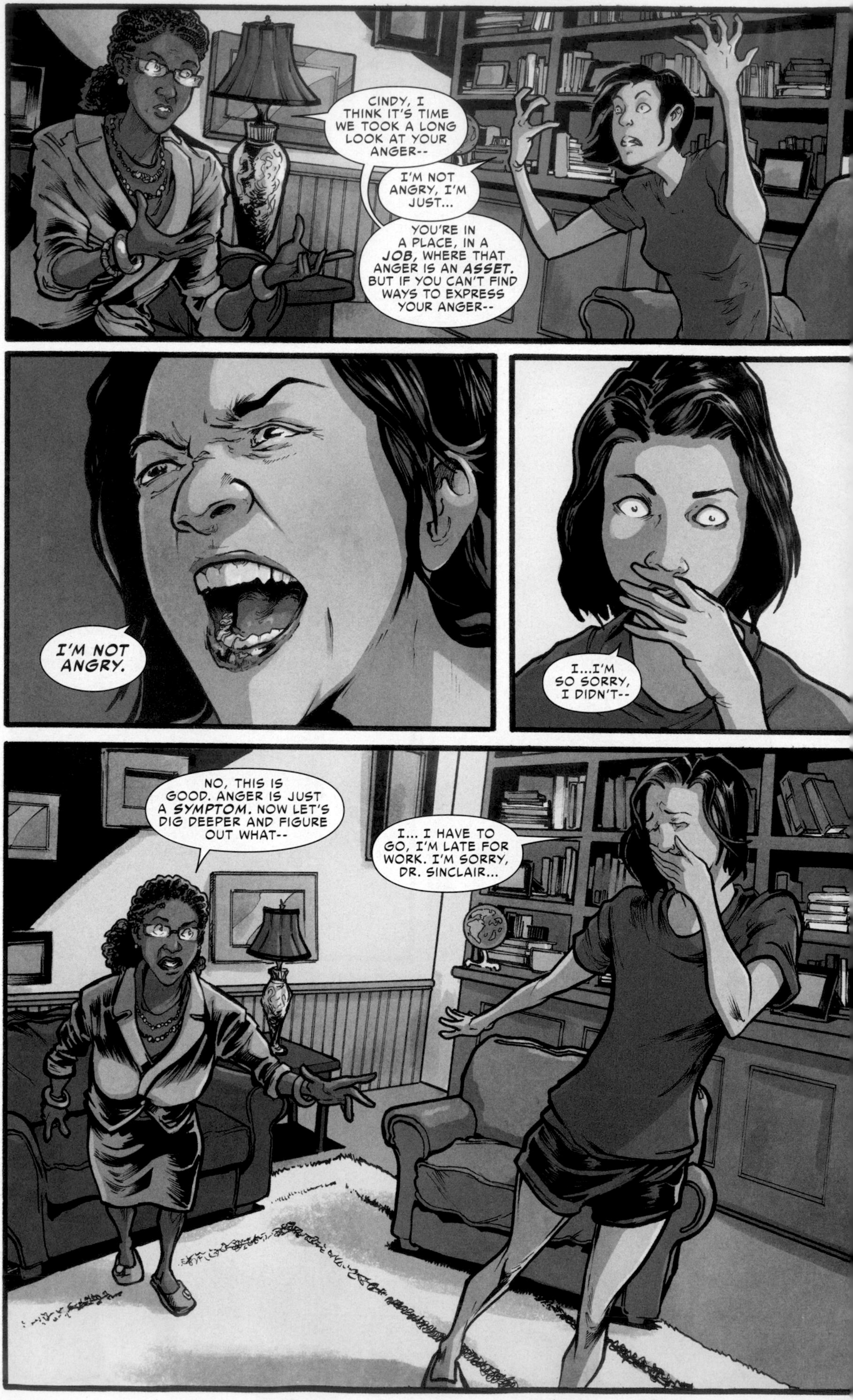
CINDY, I THINK IT'S TIME WE TOOK A LONG LOOK AT YOUR ANGER--
I'M NOT ANGRY, I'M JUST...
YOU'RE IN A PLACE, IN A JOB, WHERE THAT ANGER IS AN ASSET. BUT IF YOU CAN'T FIND WAYS TO EXPRESS YOUR ANGER--
I'M NOT ANGRY.
I...I'M SO SORRY, I DIDN'T--
NO, THIS IS GOOD. ANGER IS JUST A SYMPTOM. NOW LET'S DIG DEEPER AND FIGURE OUT WHAT--
I... I HAVE TO GO, I'M LATE FOR WORK. I'M SORRY, DR. SINCLAIR...

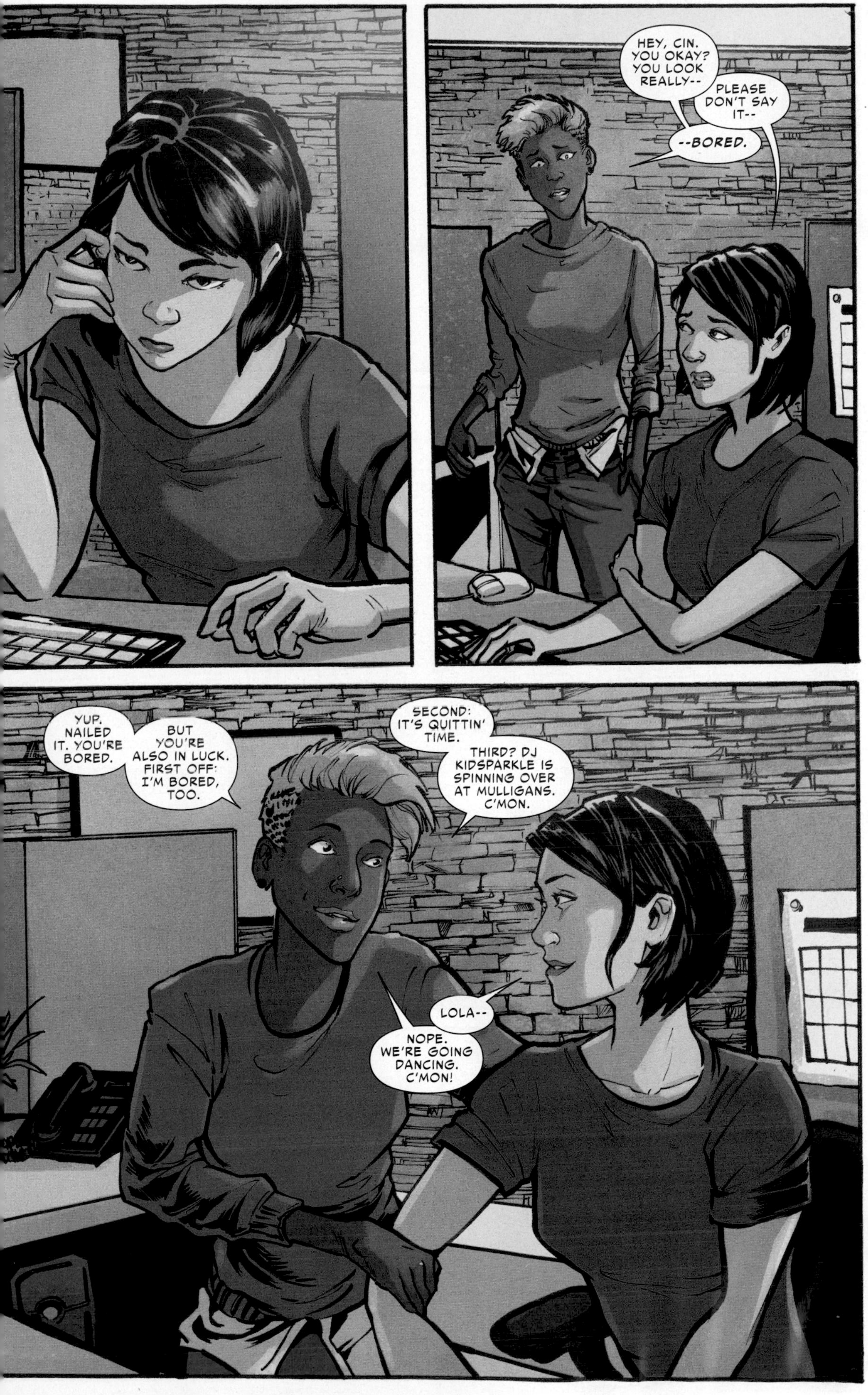
HEY, CIN. YOU OKAY? YOU LOOK REALLY--
PLEASE DON'T SAY IT--
--BORED.
YUP. NAILED IT. YOU'RE BORED.
BUT YOU'RE ALSO IN LUCK. FIRST OFF: I'M BORED, TOO.
SECOND: IT'S QUITTIN' TIME.
THIRD? DJ KIDSPARKLE IS SPINNING OVER AT MULLIGANS. C'MON.
LOLA--
NOPE. WE'RE GOING DANCING. C'MON!

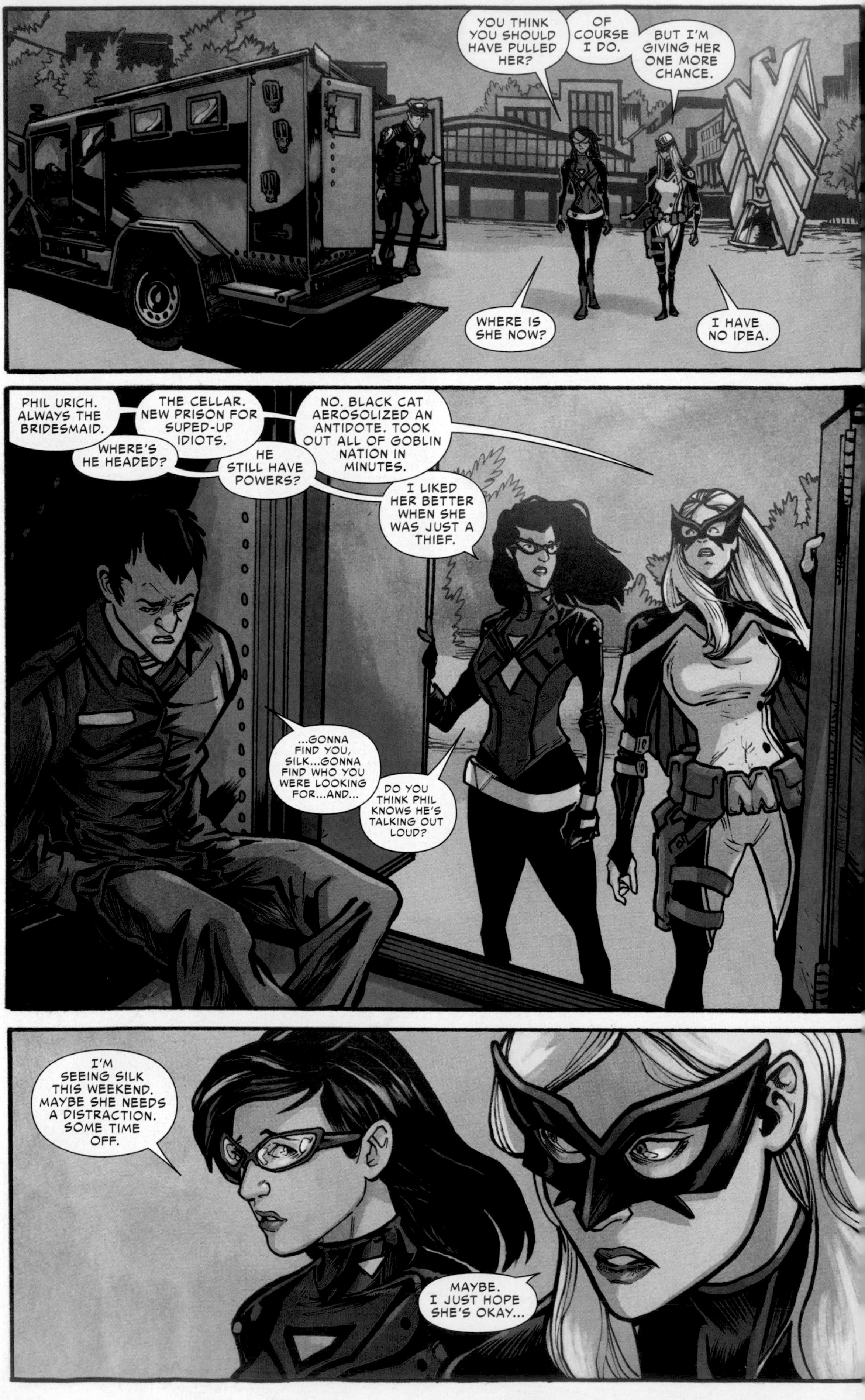
YOU THINK YOU SHOULD HAVE PULLED HER?
OF COURSE I DO.
BUT I'M GIVING HER ONE MORE CHANCE.
WHERE IS SHE NOW?
I HAVE NO IDEA.
PHIL URICH. ALWAYS THE BRIDESMAID.
WHERE'S HE HEADED?
THE CELLAR. NEW PRISON FOR SUPED-UP IDIOTS.
HE STILL HAVE POWERS?
NO. BLACK CAT AEROSOLIZED AN ANTIDOTE. TOOK OUT ALL OF GOBLIN NATION IN MINUTES.
I LIKED HER BETTER WHEN SHE WAS JUST A THIEF.
...GONNA FIND YOU, SILK...GONNA FIND WHO YOU WERE LOOKING FOR...AND...
DO YOU THINK PHIL KNOWS HE'S TALKING OUT LOUD?
I'M SEEING SILK THIS WEEKEND. MAYBE SHE NEEDS A DISTRACTION. SOME TIME OFF.
MAYBE. I JUST HOPE SHE'S OKAY...

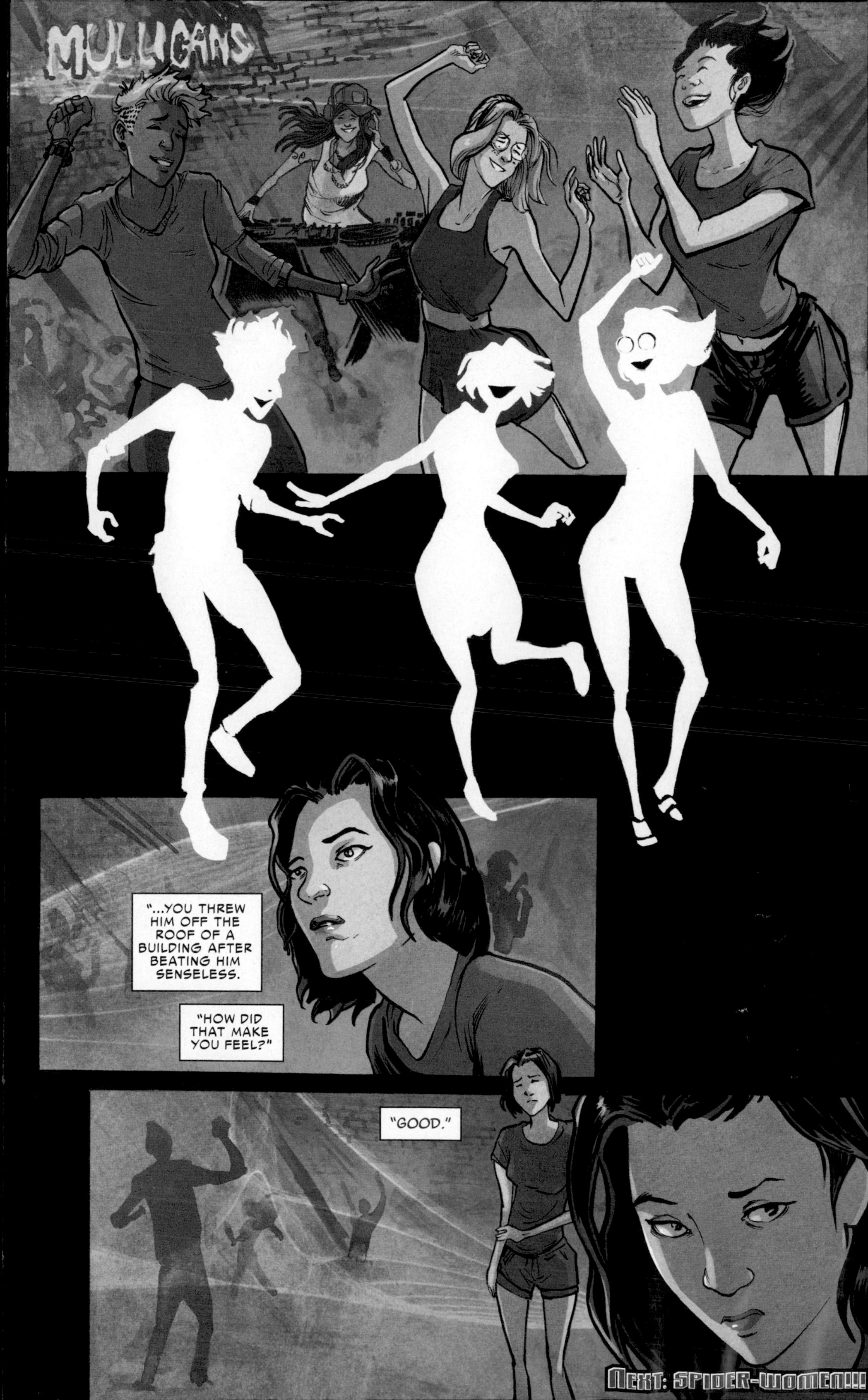
MULLIGANS
"...YOU THREW HIM OFF THE ROOF OF A BUILDING AFTER BEATING HIM SENSELESS.
"HOW DID THAT MAKE YOU FEEL?"
"GOOD."
NEXT: SPIDER-WOMEN!!!

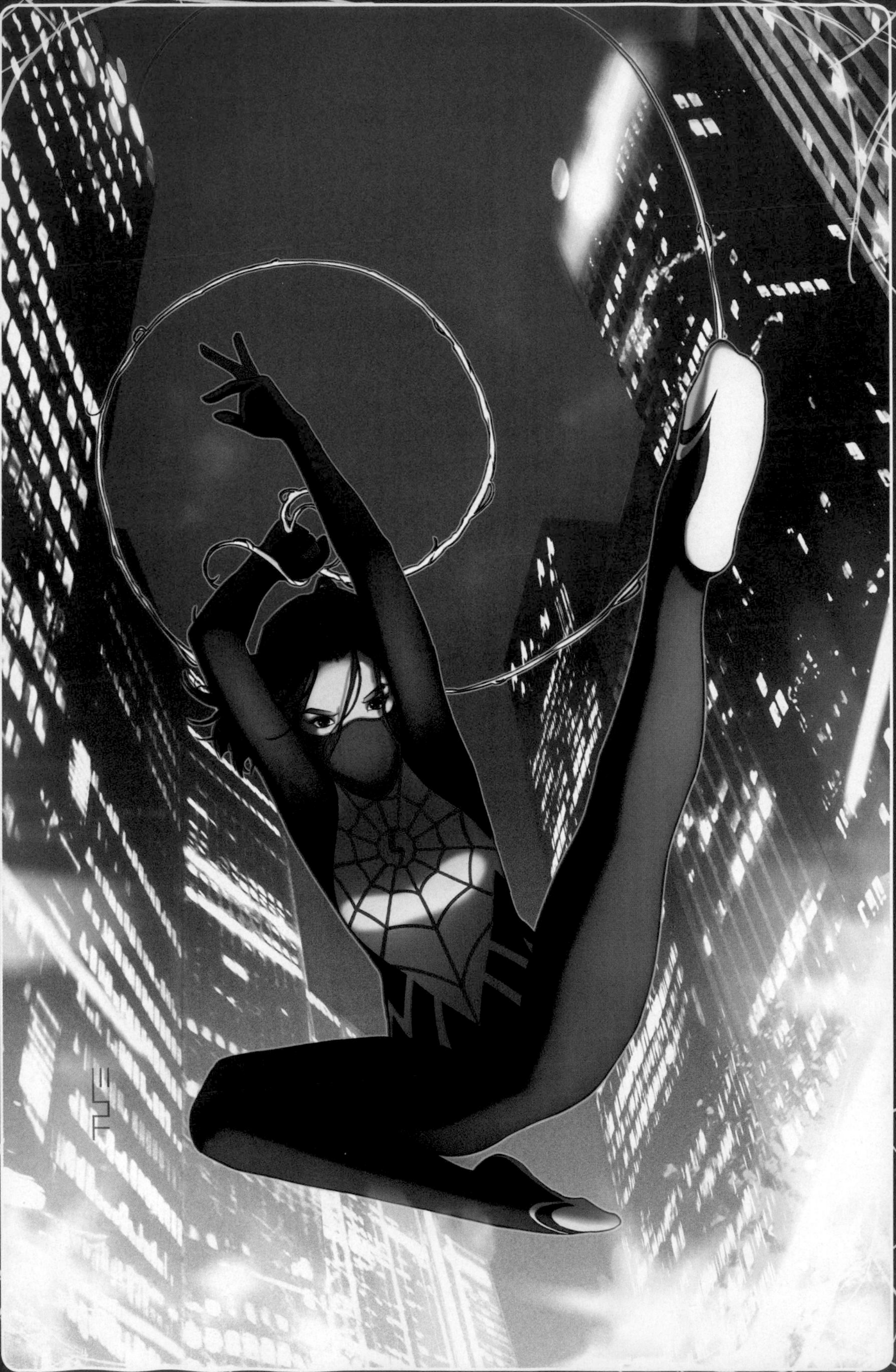

SILK #1 variant by W. Scott Forbes

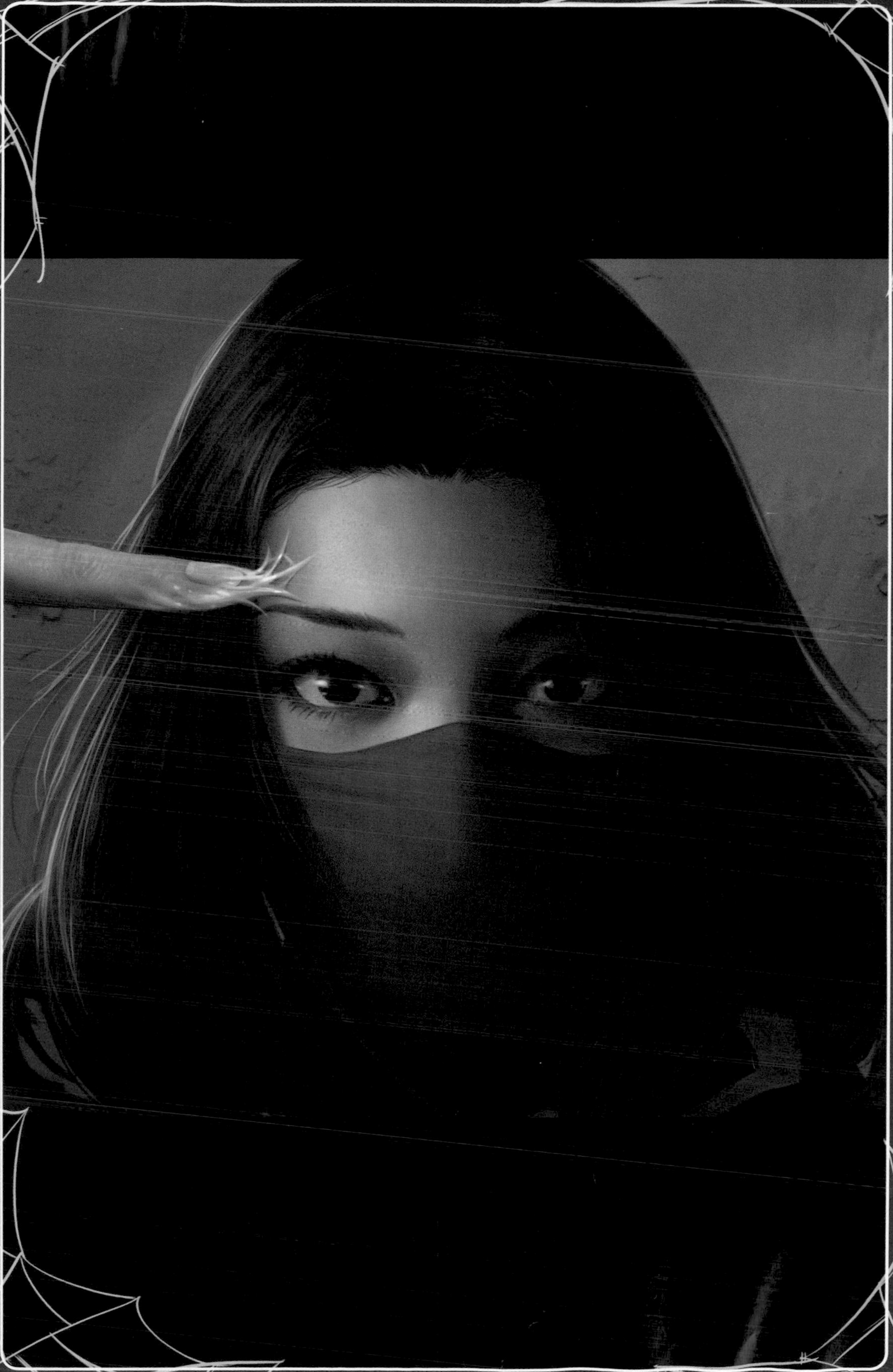

SILK #1 hip-hop variant by **Woo Dae Shim**

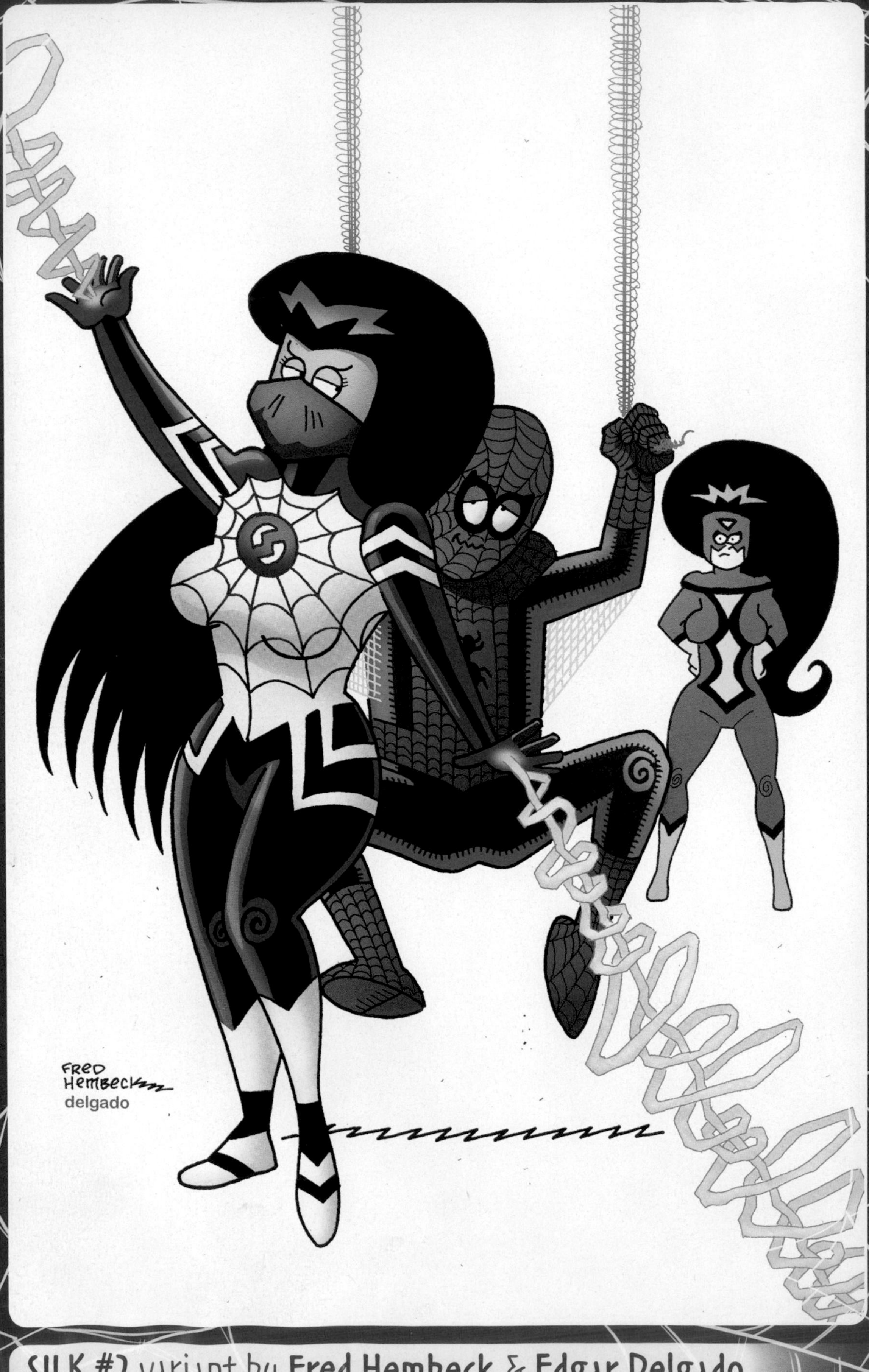
FRED
HEMBECK
delgado

SILK #2 variant by Fred Hembeck & Edgar Delgado

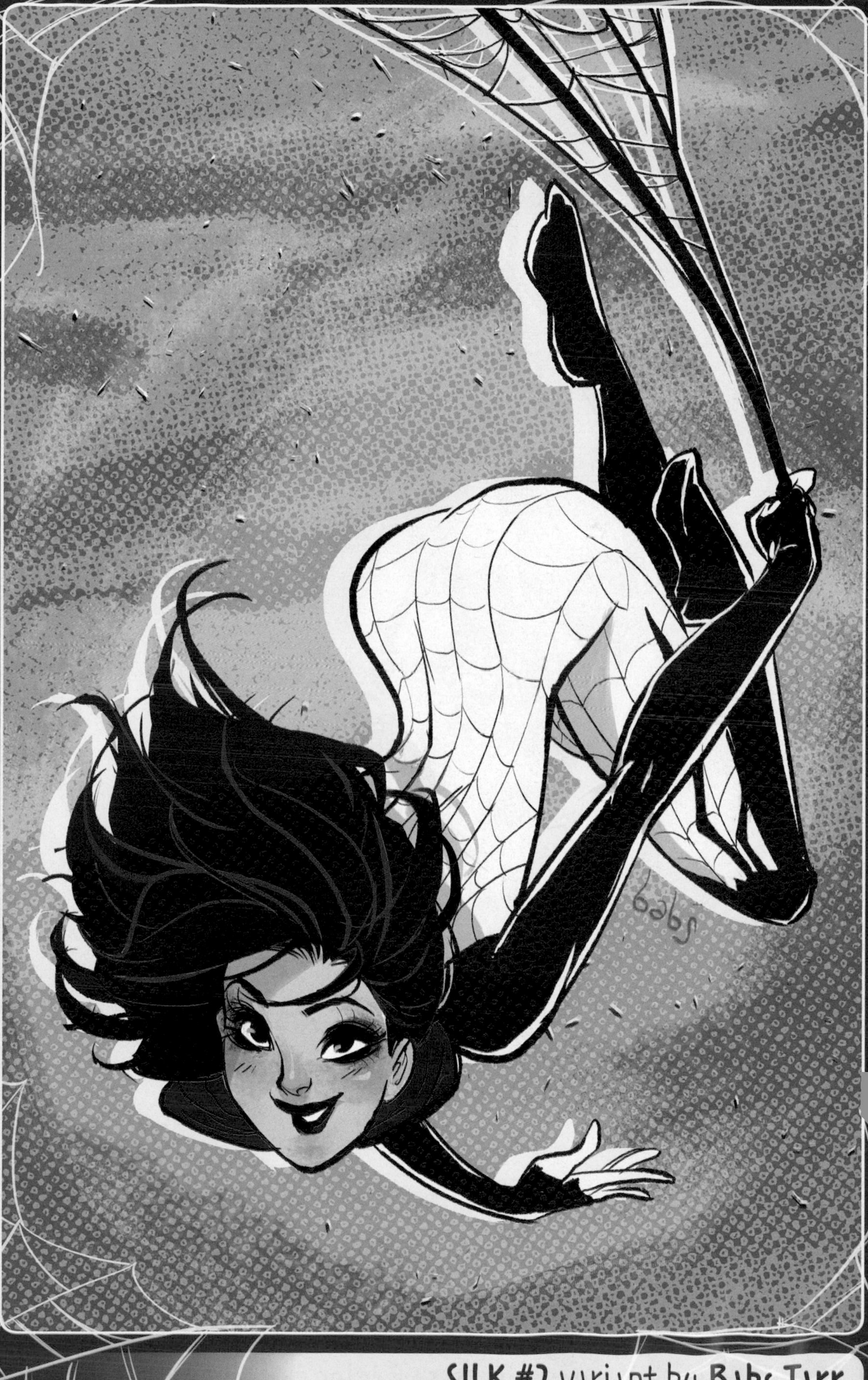
babs

SILK #2 variant by Babs Tarr

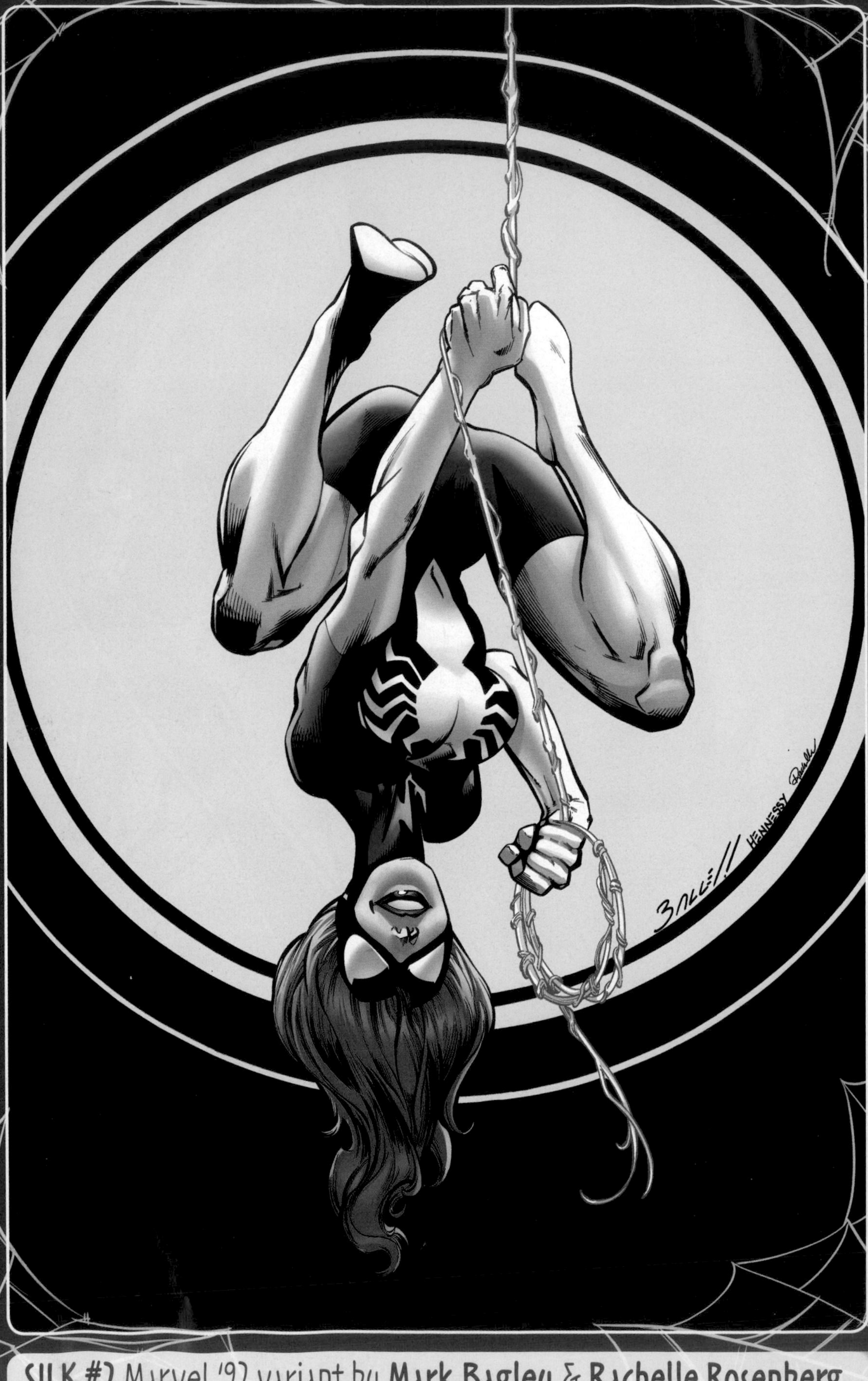
HENNESSY

SILK #2 Marvel '92 variant by **Mark Bagley** & **Rachelle Rosenberg**

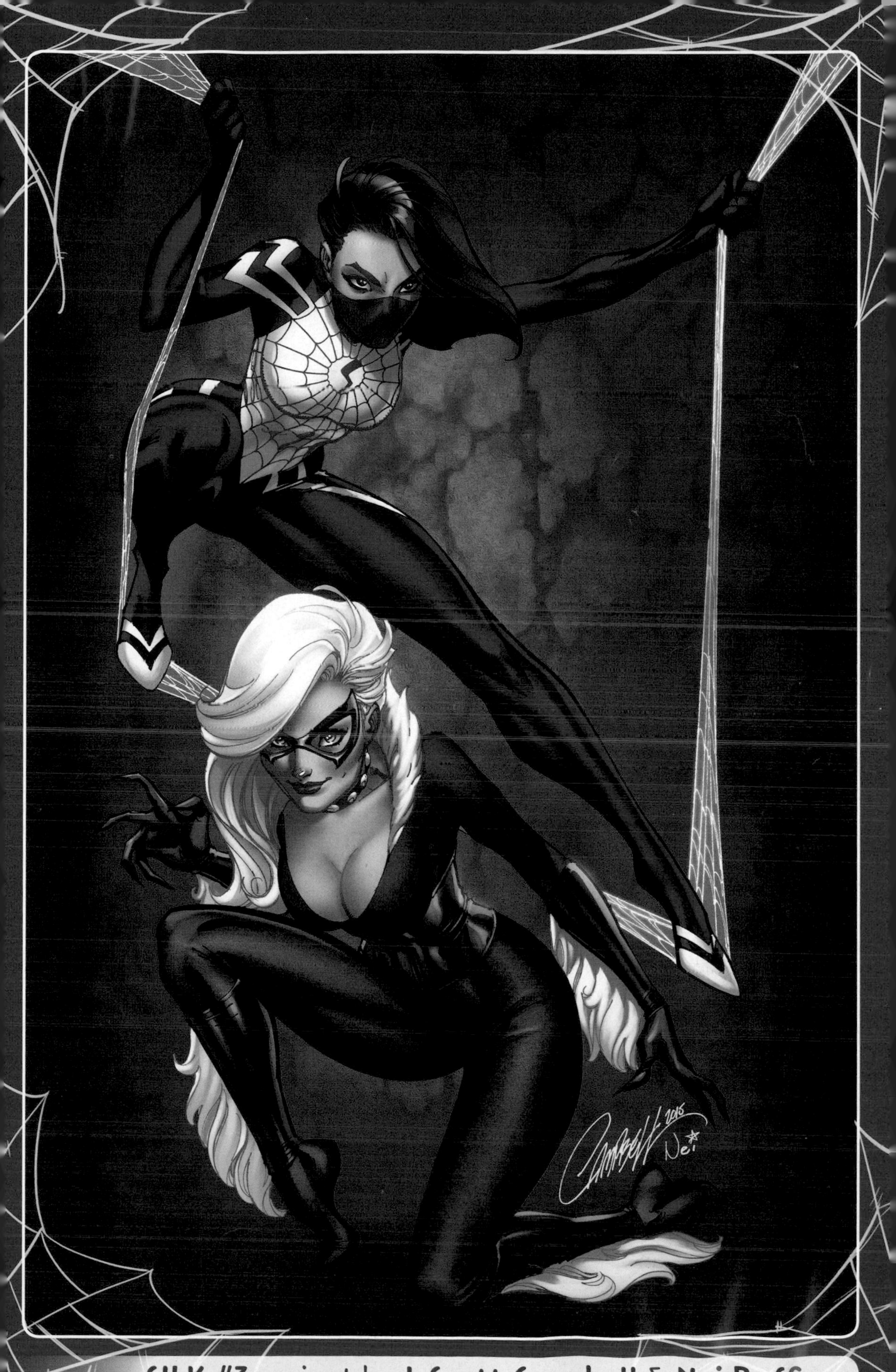

SILK #3 variant by J. Scott Campbell & Nei Ruffino

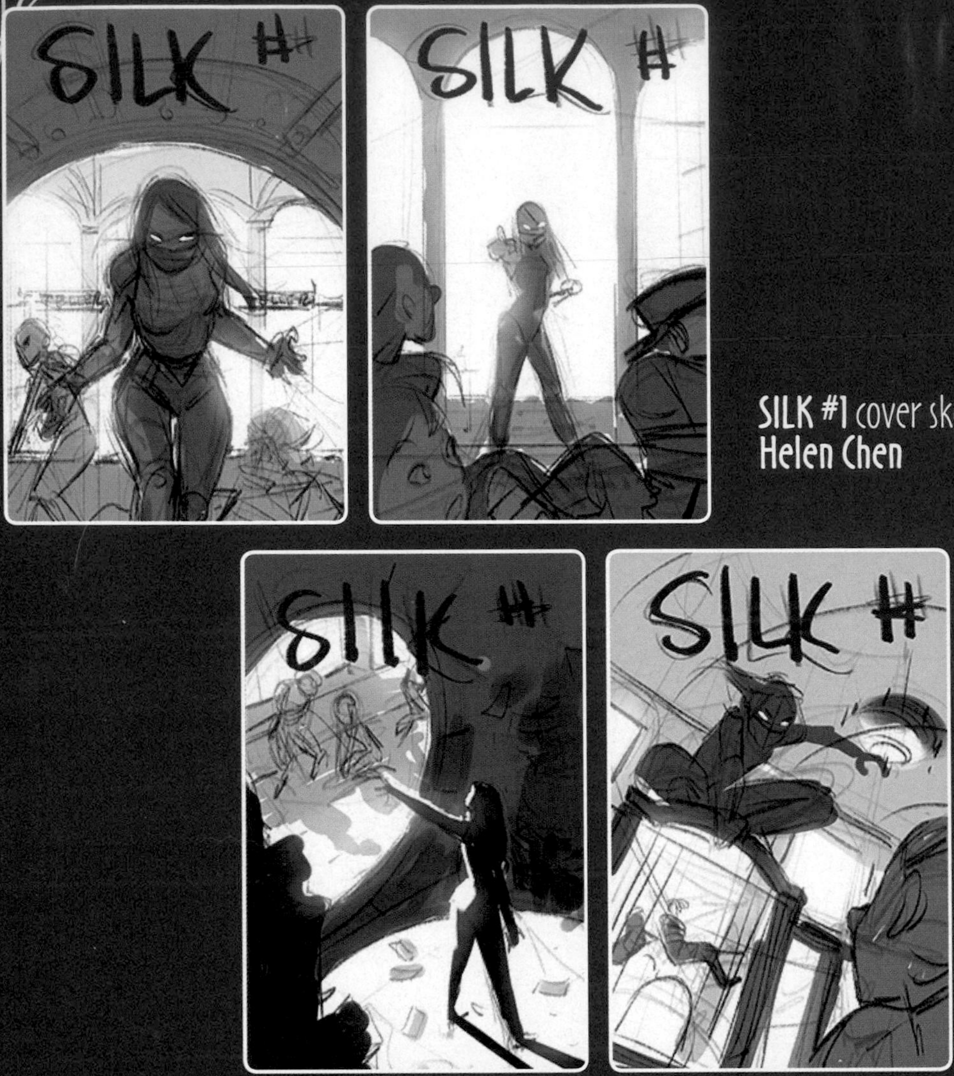
SILK #
SILK #
SILK #
SILK #

SILK #1 cover sketches by
Helen Chen

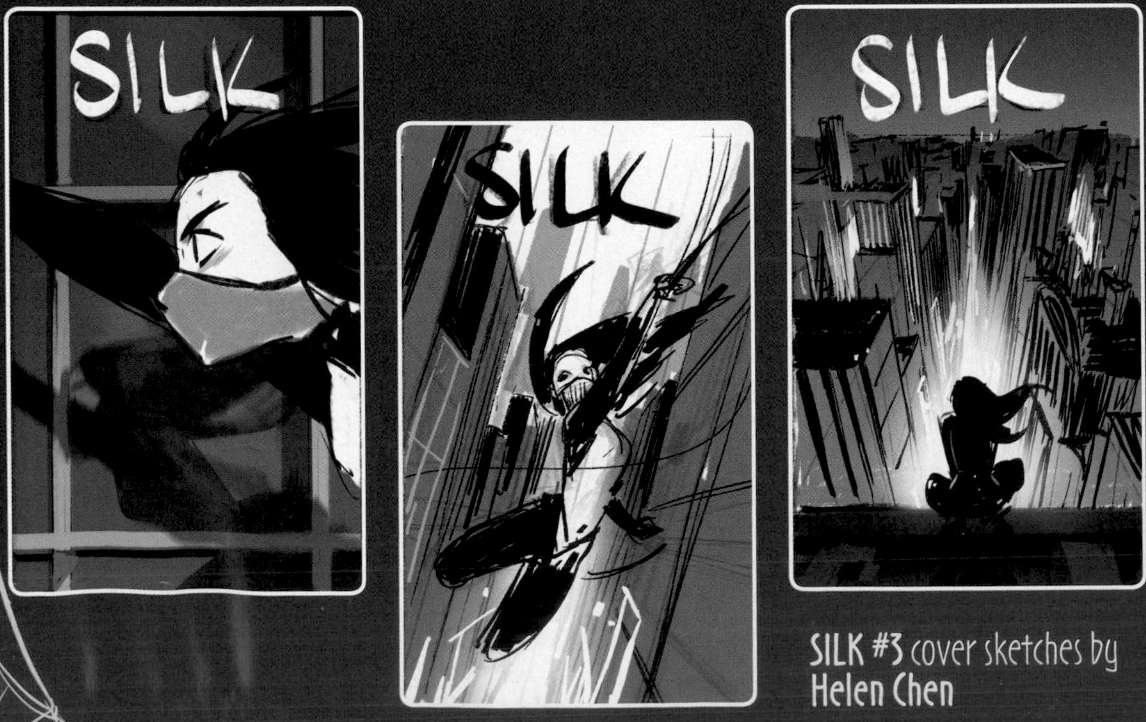
SILK
SILK
SILK

SILK #3 cover sketches by
Helen Chen

SILK
SILK
SILK
SILK

SILK #4 cover sketches by
Helen Chen

SILK
SILK
SILK
SILK

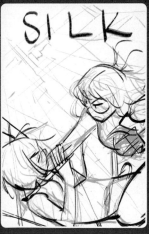

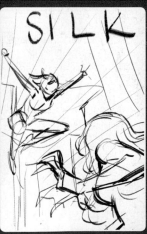

SILK #5 cover sketches by
Helen Chen

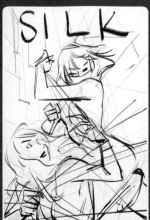

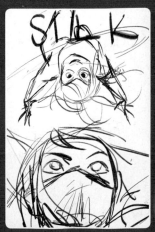

SILK #6 cover sketches by Helen Chen

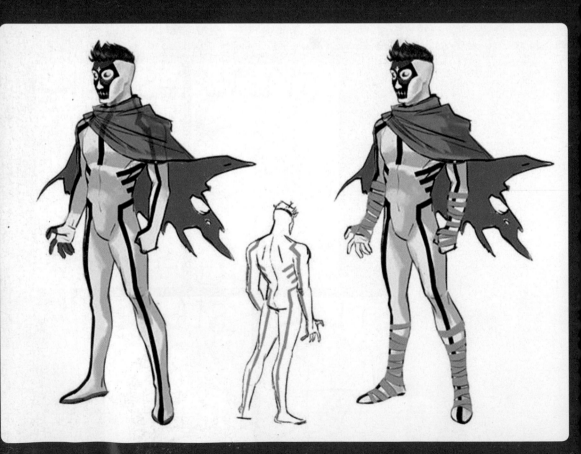

SPECTRO character designs by Helen Chen